The tradition of Irish soldiers in the British Army can be traced back many hundreds of years. Henry V at Agincourt faced a superior French Army with his small band of brothers, which included in their ranks a unit of Irish hoblairs. This force of light cavalry – some 1,500 strong – had left the port of Cork under the command of Thomas Butler, Prior of Kilmainham, and served with the King throughout his campaign in France. By the time of Agincourt, the numbers remaining would have been much less, but contributed to an Irish presence nonetheless.

The inclusion of Irish soldiers in the army continued unabated into the reign of Queen Victoria – and the General Army Return of 1880 notes the following breakdown of soldiers by place of birth: English 69.7 percent, Scottish 8 percent, Irish 20.9 percent and 'Others' as 1.3 percent. The Welsh would appear to be included in the English total. Again, this is by place of birth and does not include men born outside Ireland or on foreign stations of Irish parents – nor can it include those who, for various reasons, lied about their place of birth (a not infrequent occurrence).

This book tells the story of some of the Irish men who served as soldiers in Queen Victoria's Army before, during and after the Zulu War of 1879 – men who fought not necessarily for a Queen or a country, but most often for their regiment; a regiment that had seen numerous fellow Irishmen – and often, preceding family members – serve in its ranks.

This book is not about the Zulu War of 1879 per se; enough has already been written on that account. It is the story of some of those Irishmen who volunteered for service in Queen Victoria's Army and found themselves involved in not only the greatest defeat of the British soldier at the hands of a native enemy, but also some remarkable victories.

In his book *The Road To Kabul, The Second Afghan War, 1878-1881*, Brian Robson writes: 'Above all, it seemed curious to me that, while there are books in profusion on such relatively unimportant campaigns as the Zulu War, there is very little indeed on the very much more important subject of the Second Afghan War'. In this he is correct: on the world stage, the Zulu War contributed little, if anything. However, for those who were there, careers were made and ruined, heroes were found and cowards unearthed.

David Truesdale has been a soldier, milkman and civil servant – thankfully retiring in 1998 to change what was a hobby into a full-time writing career. Since then he has written for film and television and has produced two battlefield guides on behalf of the Royal Irish Fusiliers Museum: *The First Eagle: The 87th Foot at the Battle of Barrosa* and *Regulars By God!: The 89th Foot at the Battle of Lundy's Lane*.

He is the author of *Brotherhood of the Cauldron: Irishmen in the 1st Airborne Division at Arnhem*; *Angels and Heroes: The Story of a Machine Gunner with the Royal Irish Fusiliers August 1914 to April 1915* [with Amanda Moreno] and *Irish Winners of the Victoria Cross* [with Richard Doherty]. With David R. Orr, he has written *The Rifles Are There: The 1st and 2nd Battalion Royal Ulster Rifles in the Second World War* and *A New Battlefield: The Royal Ulster Rifles in Korea*. They are currently in collaboration on a history of the Ulster Volunteer Force and 36th [Ulster] Division in the Great War.

For Dutch publisher Robert Sigmond, he has assisted Peter Gijbels with *Leading The Way To Arnhem: An Illustrated History of the 21st Independent Parachute Company* and Gerrit Pijpers with *Arnhem Their Final Battle: The 11th Parachute Battalion 1943-1944*. With Bob Gerritsen and Martijn Cornelissen, he has written *Arnhem Bridge: Target Mike One, An Illustrated History of the 1st Airlanding Light Regiment RA 1942-1945, North Africa–Italy–Arnhem–Norway*.

His utterly final book on Operation 'Market Garden', *Steel Wall at Arnhem: The History of 4 Parachute Brigade*, will be published by Helion in 2016.

For relaxation, David paints in watercolour and acrylic – following the Kelly School of Innovation – photographs wildlife, listens to good music, pushes model soldiers around a table top, drinks red wine and finds that Tomaso Albinoni [1671-1751] and his 'Oboe Concerto in D Minor, Op9, no2' has been an inspiration during difficult times and dark days.

John Young was born in London in 1956. He has Irish roots on both the maternal and paternal sides of his family. He was educated in Blackheath and North-West London.

A visit to the cinema in 1964 sparked his passion in the Zulu War – a passion which he has maintained throughout his adult life. During that time, he has contributed to a number of works on the Zulu War. His first experience of writing on the subject was in *Soldiers of The Queen: The Journal of the Victorian Military Society*, in which he served as an officer of the society, before being elected as the Chairman of Anglo-Zulu War Research in 1991. The society was relaunched as the Anglo-Zulu War Royal Research Trust – in which John is the only officer of the Trust who is not a member of the Zulu Royal House.

His previous book on the Zulu War was *They Fell Like Stones: The Battles and Casualties of the Zulu War, 1879*, which was published in 1991. As well as this, he has written a number of articles on the Zulu War which have been published in various journals and online.

He is married with two adult sons.

Victoria's Harvest

The Irish Soldier in the Zulu War of 1879

David Truesdale & John Young

A nation reveals itself not only by the men it produces but also by the men it honors, the men it remembers.

JFK

 Helion & Company Limited

Helion & Company Limited
26 Willow Road
Solihull
West Midlands
B91 1UE
England
Tel. 0121 705 3393
Fax 0121 711 4075
Email: info@helion.co.uk
Website: www.helion.co.uk
Twitter: @helionbooks
Visit our blog http://blog.helion.co.uk/

Published by Helion & Company 2016
Designed and typeset by Mach 3 Solutions Ltd (www.mach3solutions.co.uk)
Cover designed by Paul Hewitt, Battlefield Design (www.battlefield-design.co.uk)
Printed by Gutenberg Press Limited, Tarxien, Malta

Text © David Truesdale & John Young 2016
Illustrations © David Truesdale & John Young unless noted otherwise
Maps © Roy McCullough

Front cover: 'The Drums of the 24th' by S. G. Lark, originally published circa 1914,
John Young Collection.

ISBN 978-1-910294-52-9

British Library Cataloguing-in-Publication Data.
A catalogue record for this book is available from the British Library.

For details of other military history titles published by Helion & Company Limited
contact the above address, or visit our website: http://www.helion.co.uk

We always welcome receiving book proposals from prospective authors.

Contents

List of Illustrations

List of Maps

Preface

The *Shorter Oxford English Dictionary on Historical Principles* defines propaganda as 'any association, systematic scheme, or concerted movement for the propagation of a particular doctrine or practice'. In 1964, a Welsh actor named Stanley Baker presented a masterful display of propaganda that has, to this day, not been bettered in the cinema.

An entire generation has grown up thinking that a small band of Welshmen, with superb baritone voices, held an almost overwhelming horde of barbaric savages at bay for a day and a night – the climactic Zulu attack being held off by a rousing chorus of 'Men of Harlech'. As usual, with these things, the truth is somewhat different.

This is the story of some of the men who served as soldiers in Queen Victoria's Army before, during and after the Zulu War of 1879 – men who fought not necessarily for a Queen or a country, but most often for their regiment; a regiment that was their 'family' and one that had seen numerous fellow Irishmen – and often, preceding family members – serve in its ranks. These were the men harvested for service in the British Army, although in most cases, it was a willing harvest.

The Irish Famine lasted approximately from 1841-1850 and saw some 1.3 million people leave their homeland for a life elsewhere. Of the majority, some 70 percent went to America and 28 percent went to Canada, while a mere 2 percent went to Australia. However, these figures do not include those who went to England, Scotland or Wales, as Ireland was, at that time, part of the United Kingdom – and as such, no figures would be recorded.

The General Army Return of 1880 notes the following breakdown of soldiers by place of birth: English 69.7 percent, Scottish 8 percent, Irish 20.9 percent and 'Others' as 1.3 percent. The Welsh would appear to be included in the English total. Again, this is by *place* of birth and does not include men born outside Ireland or on foreign stations of Irish parents – nor can it include those who, for various reasons, lied about their place of birth (a not infrequent occurrence).

The tradition of Irish soldiers in the British Army can be traced back many hundreds of years. Henry V at Agincourt faced a superior French Army with his small band of brothers, which included in their ranks a unit of Irish hoblairs. This force of light cavalry – some 1,500 strong – had left the port of Cork under the command of Thomas Butler, Prior of Kilmainham, and served with the King throughout his

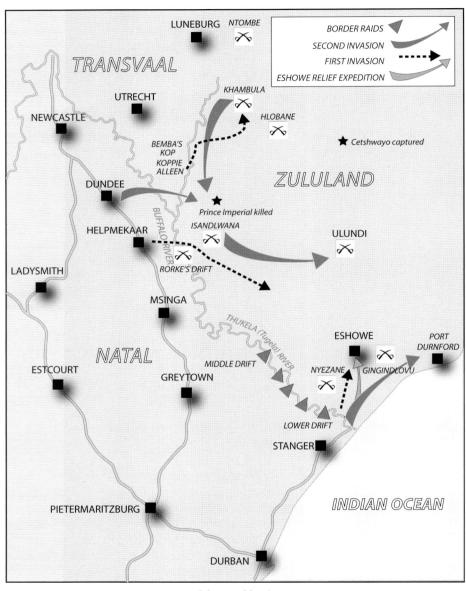

Map 1 – Natal.

campaign in France.[1] By the time of Agincourt, the numbers remaining would have been much less, but contributed to an Irish presence nonetheless.

Officially, the British Army was born with the Restoration of the monarchy in 1660. When Charles II returned from exile, he brought with him several of those regiments that had served him during his time on the Continent. Among these was a regiment of Irish Guards, but this unit was not taken on to the English establishment. Nevertheless, it is evidence of the length of service of Irish soldiers to the Crown.

The senior Irish regiment in the army was the 18th Foot, the Royal Irish Regiment. Raised on 1 April 1684 from independent companies of pike men, they were originally named The Earl of Granard's Regiment. As was the custom, it continued to be named after its succeeding colonels until 1747, when it was numbered the 18th Regiment of Foot – becoming the 18th (Royal Irish) Regiment of Foot in 1751 (a title it carried until 1922).

At the Battle of Waterloo, it has been estimated that the Duke of Wellington (himself an Irishman) commanded up to 40 percent of Irish redcoats in the ranks of the Allied Army[2] – troops that would appear to have been valued according to Henry Addington, 1st Viscount Sidmouth and then Home Secretary, in a letter dated 24 June 1815: 'Troops from that source (Ireland) tilted the scales at Waterloo, and unless a fresh supply can be raised from the same source, Lord Wellington will not be able to lead such an army in the field again'.

Within the rank and file were to be found many sets of brothers – the younger having followed in the footsteps of the elder, who in turn had probably followed in the footsteps of the father. In South Africa there were many Kellys, Byrnes and Murphys, but there were also a great number of men who, for reasons of their own, enlisted under an assumed name. These included several members of the garrison at Rorke's Drift – one of whom would be awarded the Victoria Cross.

This book is not about the Zulu War of 1879 per se; enough has already been written on that account. It is the story of some of those Irishmen who volunteered for service in Queen Victoria's Army and found themselves involved in not only the greatest defeat of the British soldier at the hands of a native enemy, but also some remarkable victories.

1   Bredin, A.E.C., *The Irish Soldier* (Belfast: Century Books, 1987).
2   The National Archives, Kew.

Acknowledgements

David would like to thank Roy McCullough for the maps, his usual superb job. To Heather Crawford Kennedy, for her friendship and support during a time when things were bad – and for managing to get me back on an aircraft. Special thanks to my son Nathan, my fiercest critic and strongest support; Dave Bradley for ammunition and support, William Latimer for the privilege of firing 10 rounds rapid from a Martini-Henry, Dr Kathy Neoh for the usual, Christian Ewen for the copy-editing and Mach 3 Solutions Ltd for the typesetting.

John would like to thank Sir Timothy Ackroyd, Frank Allewell, Alan Critchley, Gwil Colenso, Martin Everett, the late Kenneth Griffith, Peter Harman, Tom Hyde, Alan Baynham Jones, Elizabeth Lydekker, Paul Naish, the late John Radburn, the late David Rattray, His Royal Highness Prince V.A. Shange and Ron Sheeley.

Glossary and Abbreviations

ADC – aide-de-camp (military assistant to a senior officer)
AMD – Army Medical Department
Assegai – an Arabic word meaning 'spear'
CB – Most Honourable Order of the Bath (a knighthood)
Chunam – quicklime, plaster or mortar (a building material in India)
CMR – Cape Mounted Rifles
FLH – Frontier Light Horse
HMS – Her Majesty's Ship
Ikhanda – a military settlement
Impi – a regiment or armed body of men ('*ibutho*' in Zulu)
Indaba – a discussion or conference
Isicoco – a Zulu head ring
JP – Justice of the Peace
Kop, or *kopje* – A hill or peak
Kraal – a contemporary term for a native village (more correctly known as an *umuzi* in Zulu)
Laager – an encampment formed by wagons (usually in a circle)
lb – pounds (imperial weight)
MP – Member of Parliament
Nek – a mountain pass
NMP – Natal Mounted police
NNC – Natal Native Contingent
NNPC – Natal Native Pioneer Corps
oz – ounce (imperial weight)
Picket/Picquet – a guard or series of sentry posts around a camp
Pont – a river ferry operated by a cable running between the banks
Punkah – a type of fan dating back to 500 BC
RA – Royal Artillery
RE – Royal Engineers
Rev – Reverend
RIC – Royal Irish Constabulary
RN: Royal Navy

Schanse (also Schanze) – an earthen field work built for defence

Shrapnel – an artillery shell that explodes – scattering fragments (used in the anti-personnel role)

Sluits – a water channel

Tattie – a screen commonly made from coarse fibres to cover a window

Umuzi – a Zulu village

VC – Victoria Cross

Veldt – the open landscape of South Africa

1

South Africa

When the fighting in the Eastern Cape came to an end in 1821, the regiments went home, but a number of the men remained. For some it was because their enlistment had expired and they were determined to make a new life in South Africa; for others it was desertion, as the unknown of the foreign land was an improvement on returning to life in the ghettos of London, Glasgow, Manchester, Belfast or Dublin.

James Rorke – soldier, trader, hunter and future household name – came to the banks of the Buffalo River in 1849. Rorke was the son of an Irish soldier who had served in an Irish regiment during the fighting in the Eastern Cape. The regiment had contained two brothers and a cousin all named Rorke. One of the brothers had remained in the Cape when the regiment departed. Whether this was due to his enlistment having expired, or through simple desertion, is not known. He married locally and had a son, also named James.

James, in turn, married locally and set up in business as a trader. He bought a farm of 1,000 acres and built his home close to a natural crossing point (or drift) on the Buffalo River – a natural barrier between the British-governed colony of Natal and the independent kingdom of Zululand. The post was also close to a hill known to the natives as 'Shiyane' – meaning 'the eyebrow'. Here he constructed two single-storey stone buildings thatched with straw. One he used as a house; the other as a store for his goods. The Zulu proved to be enthusiastic customers for anything Rorke had on offer, such as trinkets, alcohol, glass beads, cloth and guns. They called the trading post 'kwaJimu' ('Jim's place').

Rorke had previously served as a member of the Army Commissariat during the Seventh Cape Frontier War of 1846. While prospering as a trader, he also became a respected member of the local community – and in the aftermath of a native uprising, he was commissioned as a First Lieutenant in the Buffalo Border Guard. One of the duties of this unit was to prevent the smuggling of arms across the border into Zululand – something Rorke must have found difficult to enforce with any conviction.

In 1875, a Norwegian missionary society – represented by one Karl Titlestad – approached James Rorke with an offer to purchase his home for the establishment of a permanent mission station. From here it was intended that the 'heathen native'

An engraving depicting the original buildings at Rorke's Drift.

might be brought into the Christian fold. Rorke accepted the offer, but within a short time, he was stuck down with illness. James Rorke died on 24 October 1875; he was 48 years old. There was a rumour at the time that he had shot himself while in a rage, but this has never been proved.

He was buried close to his home in the shadow of the Shiyane – overlooking the Buffalo River – and fellow members of the Buffalo Border Guard paid for a finely-built grave with a brass plaque. His widow continued with the sale and the Rorke's Drift trading post passed into the hands of the Norwegian Missionary Society in 1878, but Mrs Rorke did not do well from the sale. Visited some time later by the missionary Titlestad and his wife, he reported that 'Mrs Rorke has not been left too well off', which increases her plight'.

In the wake of the sale, the first resident missionary was a Swede – Otto Witt – who arrived with his wife and daughters.

His first change to the post was to convert the storehouse into a church. He then renamed the hill behind the mission station 'the Oskarberg' in honour of the King of Norway and Sweden. His attempt to convert his neighbouring Zulu to Christianity proved less than successful. Cetshwayo, the Zulu King, was wary of the white missionaries. He much preferred to deal with the European traders – and earthly wealth far outweighed heavenly reward! There was one Zulu with which Witt had a little more success: the local chieftain Sihayo kaXongo. Sihayo was a close favourite of King Cetshwayo, who had not only supported his rise to power, but continued to support him during the bitter war of Zulu succession. He was also a man of progressive thoughts – adopting European clothing and sharing in the Witt's hospitality. He possessed a wide network of trading connections, was rich in wagons, horses, oxen and firearms, and was the husband of two unfaithful wives.

South Africa had, for years, been plagued by tribal wars. For many of the native people, this was a way of life – and none more so than to the Zulu. The Zulu military system was based on universal conscription and the premise that no warrior had proved himself until he had washed his spear in the blood of an enemy. The threat of invasion from the Zulu kingdom was a fear constantly on the minds of the white settlers in Natal, despite the promise from Cetshwayo that he would never cross the Buffalo River into Natal. The word of a black savage was not good enough for the British; their aim was federation under a central government – and Sir Henry Bartle Edward Frere was tasked with achieving this. The annexation of the Zulu people would be undertaken by force – and this force would be applied by a military invasion of Zululand.

One of the sparks to ignite the invasion came in July 1878 when a party of Zulu warriors crossed the Buffalo River in pursuit of Sihayo's two unfaithful wives. The women were taken back across the river, put on trial, summarily found guilty and executed. The government in Natal protested at this, but Cetshwayo's reply was that the women were guilty under Zulu law, were his subjects and had been executed on Zulu land – not in Natal.

The Reverend Otto Witt.

King Cetshwayo kaMpande.

Sir Henry Bartle Edward Frere –
Governor General of the Cape Colony
and Her Majesty's High Commissioner
for Southern Africa.

The spark for war: the murder of
the two errant wives of Sihayo
kaXongo.

Sir Theophilus Shepstone –
Secretary of Native Affairs
of Natal.

Frere, with the assistance of Sir Theophilus Shepstone – Secretary of Native Affairs – used this incident as a reason for the 'ultimatum' delivered to the Zulu delegation on the banks of the Lower Tugela River on 11 December 1878. These demands – seven in all – included the placement of a British Resident in the Zulu capital, Ulundi; a complete reformation of the Zulu justice system; and the disbandment of the Zulu Army. It would only be brought together with the permission of the Great Council of the Zulu nation, which in turn, would seek permission from the British Government.

These were impossible demands on King Cetshwayo – not least the disbandment of the Zulu Army. This was an ultimatum Frere knew would prove unacceptable – and the result would be war and the annexation of Zululand.

Frere – in his guise as Commander-in-Chief, Southern Africa – placed the mantle of responsibility for military success on the shoulders of Lieutenant General (local rank) Sir Frederic Augustus Thesiger. His previous service in the Crimea and in India during the Mutiny had caused little notice; he was considered as a somewhat conservative and rather indecisive officer. While serving on General Sir Robert Napier's staff during the conflict in Abyssinia, he had maintained that the principle of the thin red line remained the best defence against any attacking force. Unfortunately, the Zulu were to prove more resilient to British firepower than the warriors of Abyssinia. On the death of his father on 5 October 1878, Thesiger succeeded to the title Lord Chelmsford.

The *indaba* [discussion or conference] of 11 December 1878 – at which the ultimatum was delivered to the Zulu nation.

Lieutenant General (local rank) Frederic Thesiger, 2nd Baron Lord Chelmsford – General Officer commanding the invasion force.

2

The Plan and the Men

Chelmsford then prepared for the offensive. His forces would consist of five columns; three of these would cross into Zululand at different points on the border and converge on Cetshwayo's capital at Ulundi. It was hoped that this would not only divide the Zulu Army, but with each passing day, it would have the advantage of bringing the divided columns closer together to lend mutual support.

A fourth column would constitute a reserve in Natal; it could come to the aid of the invasion force in Zululand and hopefully deter any Zulu invasion of Natal. The fifth column would protect the border with the Transvaal.

The troops available to Chelmsford varied from seasoned redcoats in the various Imperial battalions to colonial militia and native levies. While Chelmsford had dependable infantry and artillery, he lacked regular cavalry – having to depend on the colonial volunteers to act as his eyes while in Zululand. The British soldier had come some way since Wellington's 'that article' – a remark made by the Duke of Wellington that he would win against Napoleon because of 'that article' (referring a colleague to the sight of a British private soldier he saw in the street).

The infantryman still sported a red coat – a heavy serge tunic worn over a woollen shirt, which was, in turn, tucked into blue trousers. On his feet, he wore high black leather boots shod with iron. On his head, a cork helmet covered in white drill bearing the badge of his particular regiment or corps. It was normally stained to a dark brown using tea or coffee to make it less conspicuous. He also had a fatigue, or off-duty cap. This was a Glengarry, which was made from dark blue cloth and bound along the bottom edge with black silk, with two black ribbons hanging down the back. The crown of the cap was fitted with a small black woollen pom-pom.

His 1871 equipment, which was all leather, consisted of one set of braces and one waist belt with circular locket clasp. These, in turn, supported two pouches – each holding 20 rounds of ammunition – and an expense pouch holding a further 30 rounds. He also had one pair of greatcoat straps, one pair of mess-tin straps and one pair of valise supporting straps to hold the relevant items. The valise held his service kit, while the greatcoat – when supported by the straps – made a package eight inches high by 16 inches wide. In the field, the greatcoat was normally rolled and

Well seasoned material.
A pair of Old Colony bush fighters).

W. Lloyd.

Veteran soldiers of the 1st Battalion, 24th Regiment on campaign, as depicted by Lieutenant William Whitelock Lloyd of Strancally Castle (near Cappoquin, County Waterford).

worn 'banderol' fashion on the left shoulder. The valise was carried on the back and supported by the buttocks, while a water bottle was fitted above it in the small of the back. Photographic evidence shows pouches made from both white and black leather – and even within the same unit, you could find variety.

His equipment had changed considerably, as had his firearm. Gone were the smoothbore muzzle-loading flintlocks of Wellington's day and the percussion muskets of the Crimea and Indian Mutiny. The model 1871 Martini-Henry had replaced them both. This was a single-shot breechloader firing a black powder .45 centre fire Boxer cartridge, which had been named after Colonel Edward Boxer – Superintendent of the Royal Laboratory at Woolwich. The cartridge was of thin rolled brass with a heavy lead slug – the whole thing weighing 480 grams. The rifle was accurate to a range of 1,000 yards – and it was not unknown for battalion targets to be engaged at 600 to 800 yards. Even an average marksman could hit a man-sized target at 300 yards. The soft lead slug was designed as a 'man-stopper' – smashing bone and muscle and leaving vicious wounds. The weapon did, however, have its drawbacks: after the firing of several rounds, the barrel of the weapon became fouled with powder residue – and its already heavy recoil multiplied tenfold. The black powder used in the Boxer cartridge produced a thick cloud of white smoke, which on occasion, could reduce visibility. Nevertheless, fitted with a 22-inch triangular bayonet – known as 'the lunger' – it far outreached the Zulu spear in hand-to-hand fighting. Referred to in many books as the 'assegai', this was an Arabic word – as well as the Berber name for a spear that could be made from the wood of an assegai tree.

The men themselves were, in many cases, extremely literate. The collection of letters written by those who served in the war of 1879 show not only a degree of good grammar, but a capacious understanding of just what was going on. Some of the letters written to family, friends and sweethearts used home-made ink (a mixture of water and gunpowder), while many letters had to be posted without stamps – hopefully without the recipient having to pay excess postage!

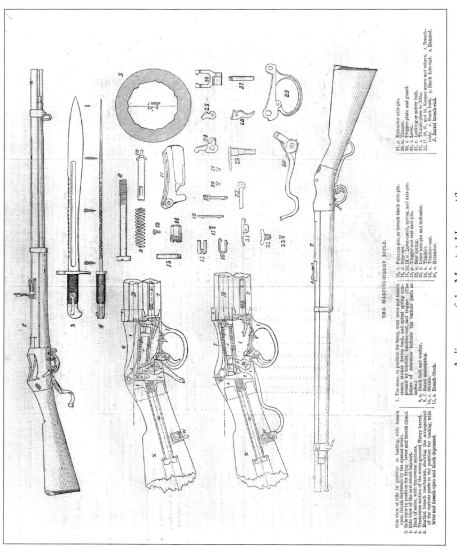

A diagram of the Martini-Henry rifle.

3

The Right Flank, or No.1 Column

Colonel Charles Knight Pearson commanded the right flank column.

This column consisted of two battalions of Imperial infantry: the 99th Regiment and the 2nd Battalion of the 3rd (East Kent) Regiment (Pearson's own regiment). In the ranks of the 99th was to be found Lieutenant George Charles Jefferyes Johnson.

Colonel Charles Knight Pearson
– formerly of the 3rd (East Kent,
The Buffs) Regiment.

Lieutenant George Charles Jefferyes Johnston, 99th Duke of Edinburgh's (Lanarkshire) Regiment.

The son of William Johnson of the town land of Vosterberg in County Cork, George was born on 25 April 1850 at Woodlands House on the outskirts of Cork City. His father, who had been a High Sheriff and a magistrate, was related to Lieutenant Colonel Noble Johnson of the 87th Royal Irish Fusiliers, who was killed in action during the attack on Montevideo, Uruguay on 3 February 1807.

George was educated at Cheltenham College and Northgrove House, Southsea, where he read for the Army Examination – scoring highly. Appointed to the 97th Regiment in February 1872, he was sent to Sandhurst, where he applied himself with great zeal to his studies and obtained a first class certificate. On leaving Sandhurst, he joined the 99th Regiment – having been exchanged to that regiment while studying. There followed a series of home postings: Shorncliffe, Fort George, the Curragh, Templemore and Chatham. During this time, he obtained a first class certificate from the School of Musketry at Hythe. In 1874 he was promoted to Lieutenant and appointed as Instructor of Musketry to the regiment. In December 1878 he embarked for Natal – and on landing in Durban, proceeded with his regiment to the Lower Thukela Drift.

There was also a detachment of Mounted Infantry drawn from the ranks of the 2nd Battalion, 24th Regiment; the 90th Light Infantry; and 99th Regiment – all under the command of Brevet Major Percy Barrow.

Percy Harry Stanley Barrow was the son of Major General Lousada Barrow, CB of the Indian Army – a soldier who had played such a prominent part in the relief of Lucknow during the Indian Mutiny; his memory there commemorated by a statue in that city. Percy – described as 'a short, slight man with a shock of red hair and a mobile, expressive face' – was born in County Louth on 15 October 1858. The

Officers of the 3rd (East Kent) Regiment.

Barrow family had arrived in the county from the West Indies in the early 1700s. Percy was commissioned into the 19th Hussars and was considered to be a superb cavalryman, as well as being one of the youngest men in the British Army to hold a Major's command at this time.

Mounted Infantry had been known in Victoria's Army from 1875 – and like the grenadier and light companies of Napoleonic infantry regiments, they seemed to entice the more adventuresome officers and men. The majority consisted of volunteers drawn from the regular infantry battalions – and they were usually better than average shots. As being a member of a Mounted Infantry unit signified an increased chance of seeing action, there was never a shortage of volunteers. In the field, a high degree of organisation, innovation and initiative was demanded from the officers – and many a future general began his career in the ranks of the Mounted Infantry. During the 1879 campaign, the men were armed with the standard Martini-Henry

Percy Barrow, 19th Hussars. His father had gained undying fame during the Indian Mutiny – a feat Percy would emulate on the African continent.

HMS *Active's* landing brigade December 1878, with cannon and Gatling gun.

rifle and bayonet. On earlier occasions, they had been equipped with carbines – and on one occasion, swords had been issued. Regimental tunics were worn with breeches and canvas gaiters; the helmet was occasionally replaced with a slouch hat.

The column had the support of some 200 men of the Naval Brigade courtesy of HMS *Tenedos* and HMS *Active*: two Royal Navy corvettes.

Many of these men were veterans of the fighting in past battles and campaigns. The brigade brought with them two 7-pounder field guns and a Gatling gun; the coming campaign was to be the baptism of fire for the Gatling gun in British service. Invented by an American – Dr Richard Gatling – this was a multi-barrelled rifle calibre weapon with a rapid rate of fire. While not a true machine gun – being powered by an external hand crank – it was, on occasion, extremely effective against the mass targets presented by a native enemy. The gun did not take well to the Boxer cartridge, as after a bout of prolonged firing, the barrels became very hot and the extractors of the gun tore the base from the thin rolled brass cartridge – causing a jam.

Other mounted troops consisted of colonial volunteers serving in units with names ranging from the rather banal (Durban, Alexandra, Stanger, Victoria) to the exotic (Isipingo Mounted Rifles).

The Natal Native Pioneer Corps – under Captain G.K.E. Beddoes – was one of the better native units to serve in Chelmsford's army. Colonel Anthony Durnford, who would play a major role in the forthcoming campaign, had raised this force from among the best of the best of the Natal Native Contingent – and had even managed to uniform them in red tunics and white trousers. As well as his pick or shovel, each man was issued with a firearm.

The force was completed by the 2,256 men of the 2nd Regiment, Natal Native Contingent, which was organised into two battalions under Major Shapland Graves of the 2nd Battalion, 3rd (East Kent) Regiment.

Warriors of the Natal Native Contingent armed with spears.

Supplies for the column were carried on 3,400 pack animals and 384 ox wagons – accompanied by 620 civilian conductors, drivers and voorloopers.

A wagon convoy crossing a drift.

The column also had a detachment of Royal Engineers attached; these would be required for the many obstacles between the border and Ulundi. They were commanded by Captain Warren Richard Colvin Wynne, who was the eldest surviving son of Captain John Wynne, Royal Horse Artillery, of Wynnestay, County Dublin by his marriage with Anne – the daughter of Admiral Sir Samuel Warren, KCB. Wynne had been born at Collon House, County Louth and was later educated at the Royal Naval School, New Cross, where he excelled in many subjects – including prizes for Classics and Mathematics. He passed out of the two-and-a half-year course at the Royal Military Academy, Woolwich fourth on the list of successful candidates. As a result of this, he was gazetted to a free commission as a Lieutenant in the Royal Engineers on 25 June 1862. His first Foreign Service post was on Gibraltar, where he remained for the next five years. Wynne then returned to England and first married in 1872 to Eleanor – the daughter of J.B. Turbett Esq of Dublin; she tragically died in 1873. In 1876 he married Lucy – the daughter of Captain Alfred Parish, Royal Naval Reserve. This was a happy and contented marriage and they had three sons. In December 1878 – on 24 hours' notice – Wynne was appointed to the command of the 2nd (Field) Company, Royal Engineers (then at Shorncliffe) and received orders to proceed to Natal in view of the expected invasion of Zululand.

Despite the lavish interest in the Zulu War shown by the cinema, television and a plethora of books over the last number of years, it must be remembered that to the government and people of Britain, this was a minor skirmish in current world affairs. It was much more important to keep the forces of the Tsar of Russia from gaining the upper hand in the great game for possession of Afghanistan, but this opinion would change somewhat in the months following the debacle at Isandlwana.

4

The Centre, or No.3 Column

The centre column was under the nominal command of Colonel Richard Glyn, 1st/24th Regiment.

Colonel Richard Thomas Glyn,
24th (2nd Warwickshire)
Regiment.

Officers of the 1st Battalion, 24th Regiment.

The 24th Foot (2nd Warwickshire Regiment) had originally been formed for service in Ireland in 1689 when Colonel Sir Edward Dering raised a regiment of Foot to serve in the army of William of Orange in his war against King James. The regiment was destined not to fight in Ireland and first saw action at the siege of Namur in 1695. During Marlborough's campaign in Flanders, the regiment served under no fewer than three separate colonels: initially John Churchill himself, followed by Brigadier Tatton and a Colonel Primrose. For a time, the regiment was known as 'Howard's Greens' after a colonel and the colour of their facings.

The regiment fought with distinction at de Scheelenberg, Blenheim, Ramillies, Oudenarde, Malplaquet and many other engagements. When regiments ceased to be named after their colonels, the regiment became the 24th Regiment of Foot.

It served in the Seven Years' War, the American War of Independence, the Revolutionary and Napoleonic Wars, the Sikh War and the Indian Mutiny. During the Sikh War, the 24th had been part of a force under the command of General Gough during the Battle of Chillianwallah, where the battalion suffered over 50 percent casualties and lost their colours, although these had not been captured by the enemy. Chillianwallah was a battle so fierce that all subsequent disasters were measured against it. After the Charge of the Light Brigade, Lord Lucan remarked: "This is a most serious matter," to which General Airey replied: "These sorts of things will happen in war. It is nothing to Chillianwallah."

Two of the officers who died at Chillianwallah were Captains Lee and Travers – both from County Cork. Captain Robert William Travers was killed while leading the Grenadier Company, and there is a memorial tablet in St Fin Barre's Cathedral in Cork City.[1] A second battalion was formed in 1858, with an initial draft of men from

1   In this cathedral, there is also a memorial window to Lieutenant Melvill, 1st/24th Regiment.

The Countess of Kimberley presenting the 24th Regiment's colours at the Curragh, June 1866.

the Royal Irish Constabulary brought in to act as non-commissioned officers.[2] The battalion served in the Indian Ocean theatre and in India itself. It was sent to South Africa in 1878 – joining the 1st Battalion, which had been there since 1875.

The column consisted of the 1st and 2nd Battalions of the 24th less three companies of the 1st Battalion, who remained at Helpmekaar, and 'B' Company of the 2nd Battalion (detailed to guard the stores held at Rorke's Drift). Irish influence with the 24th ranged from officer to enlisted man – and research has revealed the numbers to somewhat more than a smattering of saints and scholars.

Attached to the column was Major Cornelius Francis Clery, who acted as a senior staff officer to Colonel Glyn. Clery was born at 2 Sidney Place, Cork and had been educated at Clongowes Wood College, County Kildare.

He was a Staff College graduate and a former Professor of Tactics at Sandhurst. While on half pay from the

Cornelius Francis Clery – photographed in 1890.

2   *Irish Times*, 12 February 1879.

32nd (Cornwall) Light Infantry, he had travelled to South Africa in the expectation of securing a plum staff position and was subsequently attached to the command of Colonel Henry Evelyn Wood VC CB.

Wood had originally enlisted in the Royal Navy and had served as a midshipman on board HMS *Queen*. In 1854 he had served as part of a naval landing brigade on the Crimea Peninsula – taking part in the Battle of Inkerman and the siege of Sevastopol. During the assault against the Grand Redoubt on 18 June 1855, Wood was severely wounded – and it was a surgeon's decision that the only treatment was amputation. However, Wood managed to convince the surgeon not to carry out the operation. He was evacuated to a hospital at Tarabya (then known by its Greek name of 'Therapia') – located on the European shoreline of the Bosphorus. After a period of recuperation, Wood returned to England and elected to join the army. He was commissioned into the 13th Light Dragoons as a Coronet on 7 September 1855 and immediately applied to return to the Crimea – his request being granted in December 1855.

On 22 January the following year, the troopship on which he was travelling docked at the post of Scutari, where Wood quickly came down with typhoid. For several months, his life hung in the balance – during which time the war in the Crimea came to an end with the signing of the Treaty of Paris on 30 March 1856. Once again

Colonel Henry Evelyn Wood
VC CB.

returning to England, Wood – now a lieutenant – contemplated leaving the army and enlisting in the French Foreign Legion. However, this proposed change in career was not to be due to events in India in 1857. Here the *sepoys* of The Honourable East India Company revolted at Meerut – and soon troops were again being shipped abroad. Wood exchanged regiments – being assigned to the 17th Lancers – and would earn a Victoria Cross during what became known as the 'Indian Mutiny'.

Nominally serving with the 17th Lancers as a Lieutenant, he had raised an irregular cavalry regiment and was awarded his Victoria Cross for a fearsome, outnumbered attack against bandits in the rescue of a kidnapped merchant. Despite being plagued by ill health throughout his life – sometimes in the most spectacular fashion, including once being trodden on by a giraffe – he was regarded as one of the most professional soldiers of his day.

The friendship between Wood and Clery went back many years – and in temperament and character, they were well matched. Nevertheless, at the last moment he was transferred to Glyn's column. Brevet Lieutenant Colonel John North Crealock, Chelmsford's military secretary, had this to say of Clery: "…do not expect anything (of him). He is a purely regimental officer with no ideas beyond it." If this view of Crealock's is correct, one wonders why he was appointed to the command in the first place.

In the 1st Battalion, 24th (2nd Warwickshire) Regiment, there was Lieutenant Nevill Josiah Aylmer Coghill – staff officer and ADC. He was the eldest son of Sir John Jocelyn Coghill, Bart of Castletownsend, Drumcondra, County Dublin and Katherine Frances – the daughter of Lord Plunket.

The Coghill family was considered to be well-to-do, with over 6,000 acres of land in County Cork, a town house in Bray (south of Dublin) and another in London. They were also a family with a strong military tradition. Nevill's uncle, Colonel Kendal Coghill, CB, commanded the 19th Hussars.

Coghill was born on 25 January 1852 – one of four other children (three sisters and a brother). He had been educated with his brother at Haileybury College, Hertfordshire from 1862 to their leaving at Christmas 1869. In July 1870 Nevill sat the entrance examination for an army appointment. He was an intelligent youth with keen outdoor pursuits – having climbed in the Austrian Tyrol. He was appointed as an officer in the County of Dublin City Militia as of 13 May 1871 – and two years later, gained

Lieutenant Nevill Josiah Aylmer Coghill, 1st Battalion, 24th (2nd Warwickshire) Regiment.

a commission as an Ensign in the 24th Regiment on 26 February 1873. He was posted to the 1st Battalion – then at their depot at Warley, near Birmingham. He attended the Royal Military College, Sandhurst for a two-month course prior to sailing to Gibraltar on 22 May 1874. When the battalion left for service in the Cape, he did not accompany them, but returned to the new depot now situated at Brecon in Wales.

Coghill again attended Sandhurst and passed an examination in the course of instruction in June 1875. The following August, he was promoted to Lieutenant. In January 1876 he sailed from Southampton aboard the SS *European* to join his battalion in South Africa. He was appointed as aide-de-camp to General Sir Arthur Cunyngham. As well as accompanying the general on various tours of the colonies, he continued to act as his ADC during the Ngqika and Gcaleka campaign. He had returned to England for a short time with Cunyngham when General Thesiger (later Lord Chelmsford) replaced Cunyngham in South Africa.

On the onset of the Zulu War, Coghill returned to the Cape and was soon appointed as ADC to Sir Bartle Frere. He then requested leave of absence to rejoin his regiment and was subsequently appointed as an extra ADC to Colonel Glyn.

Officers of the 1st Battalion, 24th Regiment together with the officers and staffs of Sir Henry Bartle Edward Frere and Lieutenant General Sir Arthur Cunyngham in 1877.

James Patrick Daly was born in Galway in 1855. He was educated at St Mary's College, Oscott in Birmingham and at The Rev E. Barney's School at Gosport. On completing his education, he served for two years with the Galway Militia before being gazetted as a Lieutenant in the 1st Battalion of the 24th Regiment as of 1 June 1872.[3]

He joined the 24th in Gibraltar and within a short time, had embarked for service in the Cape. Lieutenant Daly served with the battalion throughout the 1877 Cape Frontier campaign – being engaged in several arduous duties. In November 1878 he accompanied the battalion to Natal to take part in the invasion.

Lieutenant James Patrick Daly, 1st Battalion, 24th (2nd Warwickshire) Regiment.

Born in 1854, Lieutenant George Frederick John Hodson was the son of Sir George Hodson, Bart of Holybrooke, Bray, County Wicklow. Another former pupil of Haileybury, he was gazetted as a Sub-Lieutenant in the 1st Battalion on 28 February 1874. He joined the regiment at Aldershot and embarked for Gibraltar the following May – and six months later, proceeded to the Cape of Good Hope.[4]

Shortly after his arrival in South Africa, Hodson was appointed as aide-de-camp to Sir Bartle Frere. During the Ngqika and Gcaleka campaign of 1877, he was also promoted to Lieutenant and had served as orderly officer to Colonel Richard Glynn. This was a campaign that saw his name mentioned in official despatches on more than one occasion.

With the completion of this campaign, he returned to his post with Frere and remained there until summoned to Natal for its part in the forthcoming invasion. Hodson was present with the centre column during its action against Sihayo's stronghold in the Bashee Valley on 13 January 1879 – and then proceeded on to Isandlwana.

Francis Freeman White was born on 5 February 1829 – the second son of Benjamin Finch White Esq of Kings County, Ireland. Despite what many think today, this county was named in honour of Philip II of Spain – husband of Mary Tudor; it is

3   *London Gazette.*
4   There is a memorial to Lieutenant Hodson in Delgany Protestant Church, County Wicklow and a commemoration tablet at Hailebury College.

Lieutenant George Frederick John Hodson, 1st Battalion, 24th (2nd Warwickshire) Regiment.

today County Offaly. Francis was schooled by The Rev H. Tyrrel, curate of Shinrone (then a small village), which in Irish means 'the seat of the seal'.[5]

He had originally served with the 73rd Regiment prior to transferring his Ensigncy to the 24th in 1850. White purchased a Lieutenancy on 5 May 1854 and was appointed Paymaster on 11 July 1856. Promotion to Honorary Captain and then Major followed at regular intervals.

He served in the Indian Mutiny and was present at Jhelum on 7 July 1857 when the regiment found itself heavily engaged with the 14th Bengal Native Infantry, who had mutinied. At the end of a hard day of bitter fighting, the 24th had lost a total of 36 men killed in action and later dying of wounds.[6] White survived the action unscathed and returned to England in 1859, where he remained until again going abroad with the regiment – this time to Malta and Gibraltar.

In 1874, at the age of 45, he married Agnes – the daughter of Captain Tracy, Royal Artillery. Shortly after the wedding, he embarked for the Cape – serving with the regiment throughout the Ngqika and Gcaleka campaign of the 9th Cape Frontier War.

5   US President Barack Obama's earliest known relative, Joseph Kearney (who would be the President's seventh great-grandfather), was from Shinrone, where the Kearney family lived for four generations. (Source: Trinity College, Dublin)
6   Tavener, I.T., *Casualty Roll for the Indian Mutiny* (London: 1883).

Paymaster Honorary Major Francis Freeman White, 1st Battalion, 24th (2nd Warwickshire) Regiment – seasoned veteran of the Indian Mutiny.

Among the regimental staff were to be found George Chambers. He had attested at Cork in July 1864 – aged 18 years and six months. Within three years he had been promoted to Corporal – and 10 years later, he was a Sergeant Instructor of Musketry. Prior to leaving for South Africa, he had made an allowance from his pay of 15/6d per week to Miss J. Kedward of Brecon. However, it is also known that he had married Elizabeth – daughter of Isaac Lewis of Brecon – in January 1877. The Regimental Museum holds a coal-port mug that was given to George and his bride as a wedding present.

John Reardon had enlisted at the Curragh in 1844 at the tender age of 14 years. He served in the 24th as a drummer and corporal before being promoted to Lance Sergeant in September 1878. His younger brother, Timothy, also enlisted in the 24th – and following his brother's footsteps, he joined at Cork in June 1874 (again at 14 years of age). Both brothers would be with the battalion at Isandlwana in January 1879.

The officer commanding the battalion also had an Irish connection: Henry Burmester Pulleine, from Spennithorne in Yorkshire, was a 41-year-old career officer. He had been educated at Marlborough College and Sandhurst. In 1866, while still a captain, he had married Frances Catherine – daughter of Frederick Bell, JP of Fermoy, County Cork.

The 2nd Battalion was no less represented within the rank and file, with probably the most famous being Private William Griffith VC from County Roscommon, who served in 'G' Company. Griffith had worked as a collier prior to his enlistment. He

Brevet Lieutenant Colonel Henry
Burmester Pulleine, 24th (2nd
Warwickshire) Regiment.

Brevet Lieutenant Colonel Henry
Burmester Pulleine, 1st Battalion,
24th (2nd Warwickshire) Regiment,
with his wife Frances Catherine
(née Bell).

had been awarded his Victoria Cross in 1867 – one of the few occasions this prestigious medal was awarded for other than wartime activities. In April 1867 the SS *Assam Valley* called at the island of Little Andaman in the Bay of Bengal. Leaving the first mate on board, the captain and seven crewmen put ashore for reasons unknown. After some 48 hours, there was no sign of the captain or crew, and the first mate was left with no alternative but to sail on for Port Akyab, where he reported the incident.

As a result of this, HMS *Sylvia* was dispatched to investigate. Arriving at the island, it was found that the surrounding coral reef made it impossible to get close in to shore; the *Sylvia* was forced to return to base. Some time later, another vessel – the *Kwang Tung* – arrived at the island and managed to land a shore party. Almost immediately after landing, the party came rushing back to the ship, with two members having suffered arrow wounds. By now the matter was in the hands of the Chief Commissioner of British Burma, and he decided to send a properly-equipped expedition to ascertain just what had happened to the captain and crew of the *Assam Valley*.

On 7 May 1867 the SS *Arracan* dropped anchor approximately one-and-a-half miles from the shore of Little Andaman. On board was a detachment of soldiers from the 2nd Battalion, the 24th Regiment. The medical officer accompanying the detachment was Assistant Surgeon Campbell Mellis Douglas MD – a Canadian. Born in Quebec in 1840, he had followed his father into the medical profession and attended the University of Edinburgh, Scotland – graduating in 1861. Three years later, he joined the British Army.

The actual landing part was loaded into two cutters – each commanded by a lieutenant. Supplies for the parties were loaded into a gig, commanded by Douglas – a renowned sailor. Four volunteers from the 2nd/24th assisted him: Privates Cooper, Bell, Murphy and Griffith. As well as carrying supplies for the landing part, the gig was also to act as a standby ambulance.

The trip from ship to shore was uneventful, but it was decided not to unload the stores and the gig was kept some distance from the beach. As the men formed up on the sand, they came under immediate attack from a band of natives; several well-delivered volleys drove these off. The shore party then made their way for approximately one-and-a-half miles, where they found the boat from the *Assam Valley* smashed beyond repair – and a short distance further on, the bodies of the eight missing men.

As the men began to bury the bodies, the weather began to worsen and soon a major storm was blowing. At the coral reef, waves 20 feet high were breaking and the cutters and gig were forced to row further out to sea to avoid being swamped. The natives saw this and launched an attack aimed at cutting the soldiers off from their means of escape. The shore party then began to fight for their lives – their fire keeping the natives at bay, but only just.

Out to sea, both Douglas and Lieutenant Glasford (in command of one of the cutters) spotted the danger. While not in direct contact, both men decided to make an effort to close with the beach and attempt a rescue. As both boats closed with the shore, a huge wave overturned the cutter and swamped the gig. Douglas ordered the four volunteers to row back out to sea – and all then frantically began bailing out the water. When they had reached sufficient buoyancy, Douglas ordered them to make for the overturned cutter. As they neared the cutter, Douglas dived into the storm-tossed waters and successfully rescued Mr Dunn – the coxswain of the SS *Arracan*. As Dunn was hauled aboard the gig, Douglas set off towards Lieutenant Glasford. He was struck by a strong wave and was dashed against a rock – almost drowning. Pulled aboard the gig, he immediately dived into the water again to make a second attempt to reach the stricken lieutenant. As he closed with Glasford, another huge wave swept in and the luckless officer was swept some 75 yards away in an instant – drowning before Douglas could reach him.

Once Douglas was back aboard the gig, it rowed back to the other cutter and transferred five rescued men to it. Meanwhile, back at the overturned cutter, the remaining crewmen were attempting to lash together food kegs and ammunition boxes into a raft in order to float themselves ashore.

Douglas and his intrepid crew then made their fourth trip towards the hostile shore. On the beach, the men of the 24th had just fired off their last cartridges and were engaged in a bloody hand-to-hand struggle. Douglas yelled for the men to wade into the water and out towards the gig. As they obeyed and started to wade out from the beach, the natives followed them – and many men suffered serious back wounds. Lieutenant William Much – the officer in command of the shore party – had struggled onto the raft, but was then washed away by a strong wave. Douglas again entered the boiling sea and brought his safely to the gig – a vessel that could only remain buoyant by the constant bailing of those aboard.

At the end of the day, 17 members of Her Majesty's 24th Regiment of Foot were saved from what would have been certain death. All five men who formed the crew of the gig were awarded the Victoria Cross.

Douglas returned to Canada and retired as Surgeon Lieutenant Colonel in the early 1880s. Settling on a farm near Lakefield, Ontario he became quite famous as an explorer of the inland waterways. He was also the inventor of a collapsible boat, in which he crossed the English Channel. In his later years, Douglas again visited England and settled in the town of Wells, Somerset. It was here that he died in 1909. A Royal Canadian Air Force building in Saskatoon was named in his honour.

Private James Cooper returned to his home in Birmingham and worked as a jeweller. He died on 9 August 1899 and is buried in Warstone Lane Cemetery, Warstone, Hockley, Birmingham. At the time of writing, the grave has no headstone.

The three remaining soldiers were Irish. Private David Bell came from County Down; he lived in England after his military service and died in 1920. Thomas Murphy – a Dublin man – went to America after his service and died in 1900. Private William Griffith VC would continue to serve with the 24th until January 1879.

Also in 'G' Company was Private Robert Buckley – another who had attested at Cork, which was one of the foremost recruiting areas in Ireland during Victoria's reign. Elsewhere in the ranks was to be found Private John Kelly from Drung in County Cavan, and Private Thomas Kennedy from Clonmel – both of whom served in 'A' Company.

Major John Dartnell –
commander of the Natal
Mounted Police.

Nevertheless, it must be remembered that this was a British regiment – and irrespective of the nationality, politics, religion or birth of the majority of the men in the ranks, their loyalty was directed to the regiment before anything else.

Accompanying the column was a force of No.1 Squadron Mounted Infantry – mostly men from the ranks of the 24th, 2nd/3rd, 1st/13th and 80th Regiment, along with Major John Dartnell's Natal Mounted Police.

John George Dartnell – a member of a Limerick family – had joined the 86th Foot (Royal County Down Regiment) as an Ensign on 11 March 1856. He had served in the Indian Mutiny as a lieutenant and had been recommended for a Victoria Cross for his actions during the attack on Jhansi on 3 April 1858. During the onslaught, the storming ladders had been placed against the city walls and the assault party had charged into the enemy-held city, with Lieutenant Dartnell in the van. During the fierce fighting on the city wall, Dartnell was constantly on the forefront of the action and received four separate sword cuts – losing three fingers on his left hand. On one occasion, he owed his life to the quick reactions of Lieutenant Fowler who, firing his pistol, killed a *sepoy* that was attempting to shoot Dartnell in the back as he grappled with another mutineer.

In the aftermath of the battle, it was discovered that a large amount of money and precious stones had been seized. It was understood that this was to be considered as a prize, but for some reason, Dartnell refused £250 as his share of the booty. He was much aggrieved some 11 years later, when in 1869 the government allotted him the princely sum of £26 as his correct share. Despite a much-deserved recommendation for a Victoria Cross, he failed to receive this either!

On 24 May 1859 he was appointed as a Captain in the 16th (Bedfordshire) Regiment. He sold his commission as a Major in 1869 to try his hand at farming in Natal. This proved unsuccessful and he was about to return home when he was invited by Sir Benjamin Pine, Governor of Natal, to spend two weeks in King William's Town to observe the Frontier Armed and Mounted Police in action. As a result of this, he returned to Pietermaritzburg and in turn, formed the Natal Mounted Police – the first member of which, Edward Babington of County Londonderry, was enrolled on 12 March 1874.

Dartnell's command for the crossing into Zululand consisted of 120 men: 46 members of the Natal Mounted Police (under Inspector Mansel), 27 Natal Carbineers (under Theophilus 'Offy' Shepstone), 20 Newcastle Mounted Rifles and 16 members of the Buffalo Border Guard.

Artillery support for the column came from 'N' Battery, 5th Brigade, of the Royal Artillery. It consisted of six guns under the command of Lieutenant Colonel Arthur Harness.

The guns were 7-pounder rifled muzzle-loaders originally designed to fit a mountain carriage (possibly for use on the North West Frontier). The narrow gauge of the wheels proved unsatisfactory for travelling on the veldt and the guns were fitted to Kaffrarian carriages – a modified version of that normally used for 9-pounder guns.

Second-in-command to Harness was Brevet Major Stuart Smith. Smith was the second son of The Rev Stuart Smith of Ballintemple, County Cavan – and his wife, Henrietta (née Graham) of Lisburn, County Antrim. He had been born in Dumlion

Two 7-pounder rifled muzzle-loading cannon of 'N' Battery, 5th Brigade, Royal Artillery.

Lieutenant Colonel Arthur Harness – 'N' Battery, 5th Brigade, Royal Artillery.

Brevet Major Stuart Smith – 'N' Battery, 5th Brigade, Royal Artillery.

Cottage, Ballintemple on 6 October 1844 and was later educated at Dr Stacpoole's School, Kingstown, County Dublin.

The 3rd Regiment, Natal Native Contingent was commanded by Rupert de la Tour Lonsdale – an ex-Imperial officer who had held a commission in the 74th Regiment.[7]

A complement of Natal Native Pioneers completed the infantry arm of the column. Within the regiment, the 1st Battalion was led by Commandant George 'Maori' Hamilton Browne. Hamilton Browne was the son of Montague Browne (of the 24th

Commandant Rupert Lonsdale, 3rd Regiment, Natal Native Contingent.

7   Later the 2nd Battalion, Highland Light Infantry.

Major George Hamilton Browne,
1st Battalion, 3rd Regiment, Natal
Native Contingent.

Regiment) of Cumber House, Claudy, County Londonderry and Miss Margaret
Elizabeth Stack from Omagh, County Tyrone.[8] He was described as being in his early-
thirties and having picked up the nickname 'Maori' while serving in New Zealand.

Hamilton Browne had failed to get into either Sandhurst or Woolwich and became
one of those men who travelled the world in search of different wars in which they
would hopefully find an outlet for their skills.

His alleged career in this manner would last for more than 30 years. His first stint
in uniform was as a driver in the Royal Horse Artillery – a position he left through
purchase. After several months' service with the Papal Zouaves in Italy (cut short by
the death of an opponent in a duel), he moved on to New Zealand – arriving in 1866.
Many Irishmen served with the Papal forces – one of the most famous being Captain
Myles Walter Keogh, who would go on to serve with distinction in the American
Civil War and who was later to be killed with General Custer at the Battle of the
Little Bighorn in 1876. Irishmen also served with the forces of Garibaldi – and one
of these was Dr Joseph Nelson of Wellington Place, Belfast. Dr Nelson was one of
the most distinguished medical men to serve in the ranks of the 'thousand red shirts'.

8   There is some doubt that Miss Stack was his mother, as at the time of the wedding,
     George was already 10 years old!

The war against the Maori – the indigenous people of New Zealand – was now in its sixth year and had devolved from open warfare into vicious bush fighting in some of the most appallingly difficult terrain in the world. It would eventually become known as 'the fire in the fern', as when resistance was beaten down in one place, it would flare up elsewhere. Most of the Imperial battalions had gone home and local militia and irregulars now represented the forces of the Crown. Hamilton Browne enlisted in one such unit, the Forest Rangers, commanded by Major Otto von Tempsky. The Rangers had already seen three years' campaigning against the Maori, and Hamilton Browne became an enthusiastic and willing pupil. In 1867 he obtained a commission in the New Zealand Mounted Defence Force before transferring to the Armed Constabulary. He again transferred (this time as a Captain) to the Field Force – a corps of 1,000 men under Colonel George Whitmore[9] – which was engaged in a campaign against Te Kooti (one of the outstanding guerrilla leaders of the Maori Wars).

With the cessation of the war in New Zealand, Hamilton Browne sailed to Australia in 1870. Here he was engaged in hunting down bushrangers – and it was in the course of one such expedition that he received a severe gunshot wound to the chest. While recovering from this, he decided to move on and was next heard from fighting the Sioux in America. Returning to Ireland, he visited the family home in County Londonderry, but the wound suffered in Australia still caused him a degree of discomfort – the prevailing wet weather not helping – and on his doctor's orders, he sailed for South Africa in 1877. Landing in Cape Town, he made his way to East London, where he discovered that the 1st Battalion of the 24th Regiment was headquartered in King William's Town. Here he paid a visit to the officer's mess and met up with some colleagues he had known in the past.

The Ninth Cape Frontier War (formerly known as the Ninth Kaffir War) was in progress – and the building of a local railway was being held up as a consequence. Here, Major Pulleine of the 1st Battalion was in the process of forming an irregular infantry unit comprising of navvies brought out from Britain to work on the now-delayed railway. He offered Hamilton Browne the command of a company which was to be called 'Pulleine's Rangers'. The offer was accepted – and while Hamilton Browne found the men suitable out in the field, their behaviour in any form of civilised community left a lot to be desired. The Rangers were known in some quarters (and with a degree of irony) as 'Pulleine's Lambs'. They saw little action before the end of the hostilities in 1878 – and once again, Hamilton Browne was unemployed. He made his way to Durban and on the outbreak of the Zulu War, was offered a commission as a Commandant in the 1st Battalion of the 3rd Regiment, Natal Native Contingent.

Within the 1st Battalion were three companies of Zulu – men who had been forced to leave their homeland after a quarrel with a senior Zulu regiment and who had no qualms about returning to fight their former comrades. One of the sergeants in the

9   Later General Sir George Whitmore.

Men of the Natal Native Contingent.

battalion was Hamilton Browne's former Irish servant, while the battalion's intelligence officer was Lieutenant Henry Charles Harford of the 99th Regiment – a fluent Zulu speaker.

Hamilton Browne has been criticised by some writers with regard to his attitude towards native troops. In *The Washing of the Spears* – published in 1965 – Donald R. Morris castigates him for his use of the word 'niggers' when referring to his men, even in official correspondence. While this word today is deemed to be unacceptable, in 1879, things were different and its use was widespread among both officers and enlisted men.

5

The Left Flank, or No.4 Column

Lieutenant Colonel Henry Evelyn Wood VC commanded the left flank column. It crossed into Zululand with orders from Chelmsford to attempt to tie down those Zulu in the north of the country, but how Wood was to achieve this was his own business. This order – practically *carte blanche* – appealed to the independent-minded Wood. Wood's brother-in-law was the Irish nationalist MP Charles Stewart Parnell, through Parnell's marriage to Kitty O'Shea – a divorcee and Wood's sister. Parnell was one of the most outspoken opponents of the Zulu War.

In order to carry out this task, his column consisted of two Imperial battalions – the first being the 90th (Perthshire) Light Infantry under the command of Brevet Colonel Robert Montresor Rogers VC. Rogers, who was born in Dublin in 1834, had been awarded the Victoria Cross while serving with the 44th Regiment in the China War. On 21 August 1860 the 44th (East Essex) and the 67th (South Hampshire) Regiments attacked the Taku Forts on the banks of the River Peiho. Crossing mud flats and swamps swept by Chinese gunfire and artillery, the two battalions began scaling the walls of the forts. As the men climbed the storming ladders, the Chinese defenders succeeded in pushing many of them away. In a desperate alternative to this, officers stuck their swords into the mud walls to make the climbing easier. Four Irishmen were awarded the Victoria Cross that day – of which

Colonel Henry Evelyn Wood VC.

Officers of the 90th (Perthshire Volunteers) Light Infantry at Dover in 1874.

Rogers was one. The others were Lieutenant Nathaniel Burslem from Limerick, Private Thomas Lane from Cork and Hospital Apprentice Andrew Fitzgibbon, who was born in India to Irish parents.

Robert Henry Hackett from County Tipperary would serve with distinction with the 90th Regiment at Khambula; again, he was from a military family. His elder brother, Lieutenant Thomas Bernard Hackett, had served with the 23rd Royal Welch Fusiliers during the Indian Mutiny. On 8 November 1857 he had led a rescue party through the narrow streets of the Secundra Bagh and recovered a wounded fellow officer from near certain death. The officer had been lying in the open – exposed to enemy fire – and Hackett and his men arrived just in time to save him. Later the same day, the lieutenant climbed onto the roof of a bungalow his men were defending and cut away the thatch to prevent it being set alight by the mutineers.

The 1st Battalion of the 13th (Prince Albert's Own Somersetshire) Light Infantry was commanded by Lieutenant P.E.V. Gilbert. Among the officers could be found Majors David Persse and William Knox Leet. Persse was the fifth son of Burton Persse of Myode, County Galway, where the family had resided since the 1670s. By the 1870s, the family owned almost 20,000 acres in Galway and Roscommon.[1] Knox Leet had been born in Dalkey, County Dublin in November 1833. Prior to service in South Africa, he had seen action during the Indian Mutiny.

---

1   Burke, Sir Bernard, *The Landed Gentry of Ireland* (London: 1958).

Major William Knox Leet, 1st Battalion, 13th Regiment (Prince Albert's Own Somersetshire), Light Infantry.

Brevet Lieutenant Colonel Redvers Buller, 60th King's Royal Rifle Corps.

Within the other ranks was Sergeant Major George Headley, who would survive the war to return to his home in Birr, County Offaly and die of old age, and Private John Hayes from Belfast, County Antrim, who would be killed at Khambula. During this campaign, the 13th was composed of at least 30 percent Irishmen – something it had in common with many other regiments of the British Army. Artillery support came from two 7-pounder guns and two rocket tubes commanded by Major E. Tremlett, Royal Artillery.

The cavalry was command by Brevet Lieutenant Colonel Redvers Buller – an officer from the 60th King's Royal Rifle Corps.

This consisted of the Frontier Light Horse, the Transvaal Rangers, the Kaffrarian Vanguard, Weatherley's Border Horse and the Burger Force – in total, just fewer than 700 men. The Frontier Light Horse had been raised in 1877 by Lieutenant General Sir Arthur Cunyngham – known (along with other units) as the 'Five Bob Irregulars' due to being paid five shillings a day without deductions. They were initially recruited in King William's Town – and under the command of Lieutenant Carrington, had performed well in the Ngqika and Gcaleka campaign. The following year, they were in action against the Ngqika – and in April of that year, Carrington left to take up another post. Command fell to Redvers Buller – and as a leader of irregular cavalry, he was second to none. Buller was a superb horseman, an excellent shot and could make use of (and read) ground like a local. His second-in-command was Captain Robert Johnston Barton – seconded from the Coldstream Guards.

Lieutenant and Captain Robert Johnson
Barton, 1st Battalion, Coldstream Guards.

Captain Henry Cecil Dudgeon D'Arcy,
Frontier Light Horse.

Barton was the son of Thomas Joseph Barton of Glendalough, County Wicklow.
Among the Frontier Light Horse was Cecil D'Arcy – the son of an Irish soldier from
County Westmeath and another destined to win a Victoria Cross in the coming
campaign. D'Arcy was born in Wanganui, New Zealand – a garrison town – on 11
August 1850.

His maternal grandfather was Lieutenant Richard Buck of Bideford, who had
served aboard HMS *Superb* with Nelson in the Mediterranean. His paternal grandfather was Captain Edward D'Arcy, who had served with the 43rd (Monmouthshire
Light Infantry) Regiment in the Iberian Peninsula under Wellington. D'Arcy accompanied the 43rd when it was sent to America, where it formed part of the force that
attacked New Orleans in the final battle of the War of 1812. This was a battle that saw
Irish commander pitted against Irish commander. General Andrew Jackson, whose
family had come from Boneybefore, Carrickfergus, County Antrim, commanded the
American forces, while General Sir Edward Pakenham from County Westmeath
commanded the British. During the action, the 43rd lost all their officers save
D'Arcy, although the battle cost him both his legs. He transferred to the 60th Veteran
Battalion (Invalids) and was sent home to Dublin, where he spent the remainder of
his days. Edward's child, Major Oliver Barker D'Arcy, was the only son to marry and

have children – of which he had nine! Henry Cecil Dudgeon D'Arcy was the seventh child.[2]

Another Irishman in the ranks of the Light Horse was Sergeant Edmund O'Toole – described as a 'rip-roaring Irishman, a great fighter, a good man to have with one in a tight corner'.[3] O'Toole and D'Arcy had known each other since boyhood – and O'Toole's future was tied up with D'Arcy's, which would last throughout the war and beyond.

The remainder of the column was made up from some 500 disaffected amaSwazi, who were organised into two battalions of Wood's Irregulars and commanded by a Colonial officer called Thomas Lorraine White. White was assisted by Major William Knox Leet –seconded from the 13th Foot. Knox Leet had seen previous service in the Indian Mutiny, where he had been mentioned in despatches on two occasions.

2   A sister – Annie Rosalie Eva D'Arcy – trained as a nurse and served during the Boer War of 1899-1902. She was highly respected and there is a memorial plaque to her memory at the hospital at Umtata.
3   Quoted in D'Arcy, Patricia, *What Happened To A V.C.* (Dundalk: 1970).

6

Durnford's, or No.2 Column

Chelmsford had prudently elected to leave a reserve force on the Natal border; this was commanded by Brevet Colonel Anthony William Durnford. The column would not only act as a defence against any Zulu incursion across the border, but also supply reinforcements for Chelmsford if this became necessary.

Durnford had been born in Manor Hamilton, County Leitrim on 24 May 1830 to a military family which had, traditionally, sent generations of its sons into the army. He was the eldest son of General E.W. Durnford – Colonel Commandant of the Royal Engineers.

Brevet Colonel Anthony William Durnford, Royal Engineers, commanding No.2 Column.

By his sixteenth birthday, Durnford had received an education in both Ireland and Germany before entering the Royal Military Academy at Woolwich. He received his commission as a Second Lieutenant in the Royal Engineers on 27 June 1848. He spent his first few years in England and Scotland, and in 1851 was posted to Ceylon and the Fort at Trincomalee. Durnford was appointed Assistant Commissioner of Roads and Civil Engineer for Ceylon – and over the next five years, he worked diligently at all tasks asked of him. Nevertheless, he was prone to acting without any regard to the consequences, and was both a heavy (and not very good) gambler.

Lieutenant Durnford married at a time when to do so was considered inadvisable. The old military maxim: 'Captains may marry, Majors should marry, Colonels must marry' held true, and his betrothal to Frances Catherine – the daughter of Lieutenant Colonel Tranchell – resulted in misery.

The Durnfords left Ceylon in 1856 and during the ensuing 10 years, moved to various postings including Malta, England and Gibraltar. Two out of their three children died and Durnford's gambling gradually became worse. As a result of this, his wife had an affair, but the subsequent scandal was carefully hushed up. Divorce was out of the question – even the aggrieved party in such a situation was unable to hold a commission – and Durnford left England to seek positions elsewhere. He left

Mrs Anthony Durnford (Frances) with her only surviving child, Frances, circa 1862.
(Courtesy of Elizabeth Lydekker)

for China in 1865 – sailing in company with Lieutenant Colonel Charles 'Chinese' Gordon. During the voyage out, Durnford suffered a nervous breakdown and disembarked at Trincomalee, where Gordon nursed him back to health. He returned to England, where he spent the following five years before a posting to Ireland for a year. Here he became involved in a railway accident, which nearly cost him his life.

Durnford left Ireland in 1871 and sailed for Cape Town. He was 41 years old – a Captain – and had seen no active service. Within a year of arriving, he had been promoted to Major and was as happy as he was ever going to be. The Durnford family name was connected to Natal from many years previously; Port Durnford was named after a relation. Durnford enjoyed the country and got on well with both the Colonial population and the Africans. Most of all, he enjoyed the company of one Frances ('Nell') Colenso – the daughter of Bishop Colenso.

Towards the end of 1873, there arose differences between the Colonial Government and Langalibalele – the chief of the AmaHlubi tribe. The chief decided he would take his people out of Natal by way of the Drakensberg Mountains. The Colonial powers were not prepared to allow this to happen and set about ways and means of securing the passes leading out of the country.

As usual, military might was seen as the most appropriate solution – and command of the force was given to Lieutenant Colonel Milles of the 75th Regiment. It consisted of two companies of his own battalion – a contingent of Colonial volunteers and approximately 8,000 Natal African levies – serving under Zulu-speaking Colonials. Durnford was appointed Chief of Staff.

The column made its way to Langalibalele's tribal reserve, where it was ascertained that the chief was to attempt his escape via Bushman's River Pass. Milles' plan was

Anthony Durnford with officers of the 75th (Stirlingshire) Regiment, Pietermaritzburg, circa 1873. (Private collection)

that two flanking columns would advance up through the high veldt and through the passes adjacent to Bushman's River Pass – converging at the entrance of the Pass and blocking the exit, which would force back the escapees and where the main force waited below. The first of the flanking columns consisted of 500 Natal Kaffirs, while Durnford commanded the second. This was a much smaller force, which consisted of 25 mounted baTlokwa and 55 European volunteers. Only 17 of the natives were armed with firearms – an assortment of muzzle-loading flintlock and percussion muskets; the remainder carried spears. The Europeans were drawn from the Richmond Mounted Rifles and the Karkloof Troop of the Natal Carabineers – and they were described as being smartly uniformed and all armed with the Terry breech-loading carbine.

Durnford's column departed on the evening of 2 November – and from the outset, things did not go well. Durnford had ordered each man to carry rations for three days and 40 rounds of ammunition per carbine. Instead of carrying these on their person, as regular troops would have done, the European volunteers loaded theirs onto packhorses. During the first night's camp, the packhorses wandered off into the darkness and neither the horses nor the men sent to find them turned up until after the campaign was over. The following morning, Durnford was able to persuade the baTlokwa to share their breakfast with the volunteers and soon they were away towards their destination: Giant's Castle Pass.

The route led upwards through some very rough and broken terrain – and the horses had to be carefully led along narrow ledges strewn with fallen stones (and frequently close to sheer drops). Exhaustion claimed a number of the volunteers – and the party was reduced in strength when these men dropped out. As the column traversed a particularly difficult part of the trail, Durnford's horse – Chieftain – stumbled and lost its footing; mount and rider disappeared over the edge of a cliff. While the horse survived the fall virtually unscathed, Durnford was not so fortunate. In the descent, he had severely cut his head, broken two ribs and, in a collision with a tree limb, had snagged his armpit and dislocated his left shoulder. To many men, this would have spelt the end of the operation, but not Durnford. He was a professional soldier and had been for 25 years. This was his first independent command in which there was a chance of action – and he was not about to let the opportunity slip by. Utilising what first aid was readily available, Durnford remounted and pressed on towards the rendezvous point. They arrived at dawn to find the amaHlubi beginning to make their way out through the Pass. Initially, it looked as if negotiation would do the trick – and persuading the tribe to return all it would take was a firm show of strength. It was not to be. The volunteers – tired, hungry and without proper leadership – refused to stand. In the ensuing melee as the volunteers fell back, several men were killed and Durnford received a spear wound to his right side and the elbow of his already-injured arm. Using his revolver to good effect, he managed to shoot his way to safety. For the remainder of his life, he would keep the withered arm tucked into the front of his service tunic. The entire operation was a disaster and Durnford was held to blame by the Colonial authorities – and there were those who would seek to blame him in the future for Isandlwana. However, Durnford's military reputation did not suffer as a result of Bushman's River Pass and he was promoted to Lieutenant Colonel – a local rank – in December 1873.

Early in 1875, Sir Benjamin Pine – the Lieutenant Governor of Natal – was replaced by Major General Sir Garnet Wolseley (that 'Very model of a Modern Major General', as he would later be personified by Gilbert and Sullivan).

Wolseley was in Natal to ring the changes and hasten the implementation of the confederation plans. His attitudes and bigotry would soon irritate Bishop Colenso – and this, in turn, would have an effect on Durnford because of his affinity with the bishop and his alleged liaison with the bishop's daughter, Frances. Wolseley personally reprimanded him for siding with the liberal cleric and added in a veiled threat that unless Durnford conformed, he would place his position of Acting Colonial Engineer in jeopardy. Wolseley's machinations were coupled with a media-inspired feeling of resentment still held against Durnford over the Bushman's River Pass affair. Neither did little to enhance his career, or his prospects.

In September 1875 Wolseley was replaced by Sir Henry Bulwer as Lieutenant Governor of Natal, but the die was already cast for Durnford to be ousted. On 10 October 1875 he was officially relieved of his civil appointment by Captain Albert Henry Hime of the Royal Engineers. Hime came from Kilcool, County Wicklow and would be appointed to the position of Prime Minister of the Colony of Natal in 1899 on the eve of the Second Anglo-Boer War. Durnford was acutely embarrassed at being relieved by a junior officer of his own corps – especially by one who had only been a Captain for 18 months.

The then Major General
Sir Garnet Joseph
Wolseley.

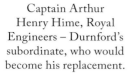

Captain Arthur
Henry Hime, Royal
Engineers – Durnford's
subordinate, who would
become his replacement.

In 1877, there came the British annexation of the Transvaal – and in February 1878, a boundary commission was formed to unravel the complexities of the claims and counter-claims of the Transvaal/Zulu dispute. Durnford was selected to serve as a member of the commission, together with John Wesley Shepstone – the Acting Secretary for Native Affairs – and the Natal Attorney-General Michael Gallwey (a graduate of Trinity College, Dublin). With his wealth of experience in South Africa and his special relationship with native troops, his appointment to the command of the reserve column came as no surprise.

Durnford's force consisted entirely of native troops – albeit troops better trained than the other native regiments. He took care to have the pick of European officers for his command, including Captain William Barton – a fellow Irishman and a veteran of Indian fighting in South America. Many of the officers had a good knowledge of Zulu – something that was necessary if native troops were to gain any trust in their commanders. It was considered that Durnford might command all native troops in the coming campaign, but there were objections from more senior officers. Durnford was, at this time, still a Lieutenant Colonel and instead he was appointed to the command of the 1st Regiment, Natal Native Contingent.

The regiment consisted of three battalions – each of 1,000 men. Initially, Durnford had wanted to equip the men in red tunics and white canvas trousers not only to impress the enemy, but also to identify them to other British troops. With the usual lack of interest on behalf of the authorities, the uniform was relegated to a band of red cloth wrapped around the head or arm. Only one man in 10 was issued with a firearm, with the Martini-Henry being interspersed with the Snider rifle and old percussion Enfield muskets – each supplied with only five rounds per weapon. The re-supply of ammunition and replacement parts must have been a quartermaster's nightmare. Nevertheless, by the beginning of January, the regiment was competent at drill and had gained an element trust in their officers.

As mentioned previously, Durnford also raised a unit of the Natal Native Pioneers. These were the best of the bunch and consisted of 270 men organised into three companies. Durnford had managed to fully uniform them and they carried rifles, as well as their pick and shovels. His mounted arm consisted of various groups of native horsemen – the best of which was the Edendale Contingent (named after the mission station near Pietermaritzburg). The men came fully equipped, uniformed and well mounted – and Durnford had each trooper issued with a carbine and full complement of ammunition.

7

The Fifth Column

Colonel Hugh Rowlands VC – formerly of the 34th (Cumberlandshire) Regiment of Foot – commanded the fifth column. He had earned his Victoria Cross while serving as a 26-year-old Captain in the 41st Foot (The Welsh Regiment) during the Battle of Inkerman in the Crimean War; he was the first Welshman to be awarded the Victoria Cross.

Rowlands was to advance from the Northern Transvaal with a total force of 1,565 all ranks, which included the 80th (Staffordshire) Regiment. It was to be based at Luneberg in the Transvaal, with orders to observe both the Zulu and those dissident factions residing in the Transvaal. It would play only a small part in the coming campaign until part of it was combined with Wood's column. The stage was now set for what many consider one of the most unjust wars of Queen Victoria's reign.

Colonel Hugh Rowlands VC commanding No.5 Column.

8

The Campaign Begins

In the traditional telling of the campaign of 1879, it has been usual to follow the exploits of the centre column in the first instance and then deal with the two flanking columns later. It is our intention to follow the war in the form of a diary, with each day's events laid out in as close to chronological order as possible. The prominence given to the defeat of the centre column at Isandlwana – and the subsequent defence of Rorke's Drift – has frequently overshadowed the role of the other columns. As a result of this, many other actions are given nothing more than a general mention in most books.

Evelyn Wood was the first to cross into Zululand on 10 January – one day before the expiry of the ultimatum to Cetshwayo. Glyn, with the centre column, followed him on 11 January, while Pearson crossed at the Lower Drift of the Tugela the following day.

Wood's No.4 Column made their crossing into Zululand at the headwaters of the Blood River and moved south-east towards Ulundi. Between the date of crossing the Blood River and 20 January, Wood's force saw no major actions against the Zulu, although the Frontier Light Horse constantly patrolled far and wide – occasionally fighting small bitter skirmishes and capturing cattle. Captured cattle not only benefited the column with a supply of fresh meat, but also put an amount of money in the pocket of the officers and other ranks. At the completion of a campaign, men were paid 'cattle money' (basically it means payment for cattle captured). The Commissariat Department was responsible for all rations – and the money for the purchase of rations came from the commanding officer. If soldiers captured/confiscated or whatever any local cattle, they would then be sold to the Commissariat; this was cheaper than buying on the open market and the soldier (or soldiers) would get a bounty. The colonel would do the selling and then each man down the line got a share depending on rank (i.e. company commander, sergeant major, sergeant, then the men who attended the cattle). This was common practice in the British Army up until the 1930s.

Chelmsford attached his headquarters to No.3 Column – therefore relieving Colonel Glyn of any real command. They had mustered at Helpmekaar in December and waited vainly for a reply from the Zulu King. When it became obvious that no

The ponts at Rorke's Drift.

reply would be forthcoming, the column moved up to Rorke's Drift in readiness to cross into enemy country.

Things at the mission station had altered considerably over the past few weeks – and Rorke's Drift proved to be an ideal position for an advanced supply depot to support the invasion. A requisition order had been served on The Rev Witt, and his house and church had undergone changes. The church now bulged with food and ammunition, while his former home served as a makeshift hospital. Witt had sent his wife and family to stay with friends at Msinga, while he lived in a tent close to the mission station to keep an eye on his property.

Ponts had been assembled at the Buffalo River and were prepared to carry across men and wagons. A civilian ferryman named Daniells supervised the ponts – ensuring they were not overloaded and that adequate sources were available to pull them back and forward.

The Rev Witt had himself made several improvements since he had taken up residence. Rorke's original rough cattle *kraal* had been replaced with a strong enclosure surrounded by a breast-high stone wall. To the north of the house, Witt had constructed another wall approximately six feet high and 60 yards long – the purpose of which has never been clear. It is the opinion of a serving officer of Engineers that this wall may have been an uncompleted compound, or simply a structure on which to grow vines or vegetables. This was a land where wood was in short supply and

Nestling beneath the Shiyane Mountain, the trading post founded by James Rorke.

constantly vulnerable to attack by termites – and the availability of local rock and cheap labour would have made this entirely possible.

A quarter of a mile away, the Buffalo River ran flat and smooth, although there were rocky, turbulent waters stretching both up and downstream from Rorke's Drift. Dawn at the drift was overcast, with a light rain falling, as Glyn's force began crossing the Buffalo River at 4.30am on Saturday, 11 January. Colonel Harness' artillery battery had cantered into position and was deployed on the southern bank. Its six guns – organised in three sections of two guns each – were fully manned and their brass muzzles pointed into Zululand. The cavalry led the way across, followed by the Natal Native Contingent. The men of the 24th crossed in the flat-bottomed ponts one company at a time. Men and wagons crossed without any serious mishap and began to prepare for the long, slow journey north-east towards Ulundi.

The heavy wagons – pulled by up to 16 oxen – were loaded with their various burdens, with each one bearing its distinguishing flag. Ammunition wagons flew red, supply wagons, blue; those of the staff were red and white, while the Royal Artillery flew red and blue. Those wagons belonging to the 24th Regiment carried a green flag – replicating the colour of the regiment's tunic cuffs – while the ambulances bore the traditional Red Cross (known at this time as the Geneva Cross). By that evening, the entire column had crossed and established a camp on the north bank.

When one of the ponts broke down, a small party of Royal Engineers was requested. This consisted of one officer and five other ranks of the 5th (Field) Company, RE. They had disembarked at Durban on 5 January and arrived at Rorke's Drift two weeks later. The officer commanding was Lieutenant John Rouse Merriott Chard. Chard came from Devon, was 32 years old and had seen previous service, but no action, in Bermuda. He was still waiting on his first promotion after 11 years' service.

The ponts at Rorke's Drift.

Lieutenant John Rouse
Merriott Chard, 5th
Company, Royal Engineers.

kwaSokhexe Sihayo's *umuzi*.

In order to ensure his supply route into Zululand was secure, Chelmsford found it necessary to attack a Zulu village that threatened the road from Rorke's Drift to Isandlwana. This was the home of the chieftain Sihayo kaXongo – friend of Otto Witt.

At 3.30am on 12 January the force designated to attack the village assembled in the dank darkness of a Sunday morning. It consisted of the 1st Battalion, 3rd Regiment, NNC commanded by Hamilton Browne and four companies of the 1st Battalion, 24th Regiment under Captain Degacher. Lieutenant Colonel John Cecil Russell was to lead all the available cavalry on a reconnaissance, while the 2nd Battalion of the NNC and the remaining companies of the 24th remained in reserve.

To the surprise of many Imperial officers, the attack was a complete success, with the native troops equating themselves well. The Zulu were driven off, their cattle captured and the village burned. As the men returned to camp, they were engulfed by a tremendous thunderstorm that soaked everyone to the skin. As they passed a deserted village, Lieutenant Coghill spotted a wandering fowl pecking at the ground. Ever-mindful of the shortage of fresh meat, he immediately gave chase – only to come to grief when his horse floundered in the wet mud. The fall resulted in the escape of one very lucky bird, while Coghill suffered a wrenched knee which left him almost incapable of walking, but did not affect his riding too much. Therefore, he was allowed to remain as an ADC – a role that was considered as 'light duties' and which would ensure Coghill's way to Isandlwana and history.[1]

Pearson's No.1 Column, with the Naval Brigade in the vanguard, crossed the Tugela River at the Lower Drift on 12 January. The Naval Brigade had stretched a wire hawser across the Tugela, which was used to haul the ponts backwards and

1   Sir Patrick Coghill wrote in his memoir *Whom The Gods Love* that his uncle had injured his knee on 21 January while out riding with Lord Chelmsford. As a result of this, he was unable to accompany Chelmsford on the 22nd. Furthermore, Nevill Coghill wrote a letter home after 12 January and does not mention anything about the incident.

The assault on Sihayo's *umuzi* on 12 January 1879.

forwards across the river. Initially, manpower had been used, but was then replaced by oxen, as these became available. As at Rorke's Drift, a single pont could carry an entire company of infantry, or a wagon and team in the one load – the journey to and from the north bank taking just 30 minutes. Percy Barrow's cavalry came next, followed by the infantry. By that evening, the bulk of the column was across the river.

On the orders of Pearson, Wynne and his Royal Engineers began to construct a fort. This was to be large enough to hold the entire column in the event of a major Zulu attack and was also equipped with an ample storehouse to hold supplies. As this was taking place, Percy Barrow's cavalry patrolled into the surrounding countryside – uncovering little sign of the enemy. One of the patrols came across a small number of Zulu and several were captured. They revealed that while they were few, the British would soon have more than enough enemies.

The construction of the fort was finished on 17 January and was duly named 'Fort *Tenedos*' in honour of the ship that had supplied the 'bluejackets' – a nickname given to the sailors due to their mode of dress. A garrison comprising of one company from the Naval Brigade and two from the 99th Regiment was left to secure the lines of communication. Wynne had constructed this fort where he had been ordered – not where he, an experienced engineer, would have placed it – and its position raised criticism from several quarters.[2]

Since the beginning of the month, the weather had been atrocious. As a result of this, the track leading towards Eshowe had degenerated into viscous mud that clung to boots and wagon wheels. Streams that had been mere trickles had turned into raging torrents and now presented major obstacles. In order to lessen the damage to both track and drift, Pearson decided to split his column into two – each marching one day apart. Hopefully, this would allow repairs to be carried out to the track after the first half had passed and before the second arrived.

Captain Warren Richard Colvin Wynne commanding 2nd Company, Royal Engineers.

Fort *Tenedos*.

2   It was the opinion of Crealock that the fort was ill-placed and would have been incapable of holding off a determined attack. Given Crealock's reputation in South Africa, his opinion does not seem to count for much (see *A Widow Making War*).

Reveille at the fort was sounded at 4.00am on the morning of 18 January. Two hours later, Pearson led the first part of his command north towards the mission station at Eshowe, 37 miles away. This portion of the column consisted of five companies of the Buffs, the Naval Brigade less one company left to garrison Fort Pearson, the 1st Battalion of the NNC, the artillery, half the mounted troops and Wynne's engineers. The column's supplies and ammunition were carried in 50 ox wagons pulled by the faithful oxen – in all, a grand total of 2,400 officers and men. The advance was unopposed and by 2.00pm the column had crossed a small river – the Inyoni – and was encamped on the north bank. Despite the continuing bad weather, this particular river was running at a trickle, but it flowed between a deep gully and its high sides were already damaged by the wheels of the wagons that had previously crossed.

On the morning of 19 January, Colonel Welman led the second part of the column from Fort *Tenedos*. This consisted of four companies of the 99th, the remaining three companies of the Buffs, the 2nd Battalion, NNC and the remainder of the cavalry. Supplies for these men – numbering 2,000 – were again carried in ox wagons (80 in total). Once more, the advance was unopposed – and despite the damage caused by the passage of the previous wagons, progress was such that Welman arrived at the Inyoni while Pearson was still there. As darkness fell on the evening of 19 January, Pearson advanced another four miles and had crossed the Umsundusi – the next river on the route – and was quickly followed up by Welman's infantry. Back at the Inyoni, a traffic

Lieutenant Francis
Hartwell Macdowel.

jam had occurred due to the supply wagons having to be double-spanned to cross the deep (and now very muddy) drift. In the first four days of the campaign, the column travelled a mere 16 miles. This was to be no *Blitzkrieg*.

With the centre column, the following few days were spent in improving the track and moving the supply wagons forward – a slow and often frustrating experience. One of those engaged in this work was Lieutenant Macdowel, Royal Engineers.

Francis Hartwell Macdowel was the son of Professor Macdowel MD of the University of Dublin. Macdowel had been in South Africa since late 1877 – during which time he had been involved in the building of a fort close to the 'disputed territory' and surveying the same region in the event of war. He had distinguished himself in the abortive campaign against Sekhukhune's baPedi in 1878. Here, under difficult circumstances, he had extricated a force of some 80 men from a position that was surrounded by the baPedi to a place of safety. Initially, Macdowel was to have served in Wood's column; however, he was ordered to Helpmekaar, where he was appointed as the Royal Engineer responsible for Glyn's column. It was Macdowel who superintended the crossing at Rorke's Drift, for which he received Chelmsford's personal commendation.

On 20 January, Glyn's centre column – accompanied by Chelmsford and his staff – arrived at Isandlwana. Here, a camp was established at the base of the hill. There were those men among the ranks of the 24th who remarked on the similarity between the shape of the hill and the Sphinx collar badge worn by the regiment; many considered it to be a bad omen. Because of its size – and the belief that they would not be here for long – there was no attempt made to fortify the position. The following reasons were given: the difficulty in circling the numerous oxen-drawn wagons – many of which would be needed to go back to Rorke's Drift to bring up further supplies; the ground was stony and much too hard to dig; there were no tools for digging – and even if the tools were available, it would have meant digging a trench over a mile long! Finally, it was deemed that this would be only a temporary stop – and any attempt at entrenchment would be a waste of time. In lieu of defences, Chelmsford chooses to rely on extensive scouting to give ample warning of any attack. This flew in the face of advice given in his personal instructions on the subject.

On the same day, Wood's column reached the White Mfolozi. Here he established a camp protected by a stone laager on the southern bank. Almost immediately, Buller led his cavalry out across the river – heading north to carry out a further reconnaissance of two likely Zulu strongholds: the Zunguin and Hlobane Mountains. Hlobane Plateau is situated at the southern end of the Zunguin range. It rises from the surrounding plain to a majestic height of 5,300 feet and is encompassed by sheer cliffs some 200 feet high. Its base was thick with rock scree and tangled vegetation – presenting an almost insurmountable barrier. There were two possible approaches to the plateau's summit: one at the eastern end and the other on the western side. Here the cliffs had corroded in such a manner that trails (of a sort) had been formed. On the eastern side, the trail to the top was the easier of the two. It was accessed by way of the Ntensheka Nek – a shoulder of ground approximately one-and-a-half miles long connecting Hlobane to Mashongolola Mountain. While the approach up Ntensheka Nek was steep, there were no serious obstacles to overcome. The final climb onto the plateau was much more severe: the trail at the western end of the plateau was extremely steep; its pitch was about one foot in 10, which in turn, fell onto a ridge only 15 yards wide where it joined the mountain. Where the ridge met a lower plateau called Tendega (or 'Little Hlobane'), it widened out to some 25 yards.

Later that evening, a courier arrived from Buller to say that he had contacted the enemy at Zunguin Mountain, but had been driven back by a force of some 1,000 warriors. During the following night's march – designed to relieve Buller – Wood ordered the remaining cavalry on ahead to act as immediate reinforcements, while Wood followed up with the 90th Regiment, Wood's Irregulars and the 1st Battalion of the 13th Regiment.

The next obstacle for Pearson's column was the Amatikulu, which he reached on 20 January. Here the water was running much deeper and swifter than at the Inyoni, while the drift itself was in a bad state of repair. Pearson ordered a camp to be set up on the south bank of the river to allow the supply wagons to catch up and Wynne's section of Royal Engineers time to effect adequate repairs.

On 21 January, Chelmsford – now encamped at Isandlwana – ordered Dartnell and his mounted volunteers to scout the Nkandla Hills. Lonsdale, with 16 companies of the Natal Native Contingent, was sent south-east to the Inhlazatshe Hills. By late afternoon, the two units had met in the hills near the Mangeni River. Dartnell had encountered some Zulu warriors and Chelmsford gave permission to mount an attack. That evening, it was clear that the Zulu were assembling in some force in the east – perhaps as many as 1,500 men. Dartnell attempted to carry out a mounted patrol, but was confronted by a large Zulu force, which tried to encircle him. The patrol beat a hasty withdrawal and Dartnell sent to Chelmsford for reinforcements; these were refused. Chelmsford carried out a further reconnaissance – this time to the Nquthu Plateau – but by 3.00pm his vedettes had reported only some mounted Zulu scouts. By late evening, Chelmsford was convinced that the Zulu were somewhere either in the Nkandla Hills, or on the eastern part of the Nquthu Plateau. He further realised that Dartnell's call for assistance would have to be answered after all. His force would have to be divided!

Pearson carried out a reconnaissance of the northern bank of the Amatikulu and found the ground to be covered in near-impenetrable brush. Because of this, Percy Barrow's cavalry was ordered to carry out meticulous scouting patrols – pushing forward and to the flanks for several miles. Only when all was reported clear did Pearson establish a camp and bring his supply wagons forward from the Umsundusi.

9

Nyezane: A Close-Run Thing? (The victory no one remembers)

While the history books are charitable in their treatment of both Isandlwana and Rorke's Drift, they are less generous in their treatment of Nyezane: the first battle fought on 22 January. This battle was not only a victory for the British, but was in fact the first major engagement of the campaign. While largely overshadowed by the

day's events elsewhere, the battle was a classic example of how the British columns should have faced their Zulu enemies once they crossed the border.

No.1 Column had, by 22 January, reached a small stream called the Nyezane. Here – four miles from their previous camp – Wynne and his engineers, along with the Natal Native Pioneers, arrived at the drift to prepare it for the wagons of the column. The men were having a short rest and availing of drinking water when the sound of gunfire was heard from the north.

Possibly the first British officer to come under fire in this action was Captain Arthur Fitzroy Hart from County Clare, Ireland.

Captain Arthur Fitzroy Hart, 31st (Huntingdonshire) Regiment, serving with the Natal Native Contingent.

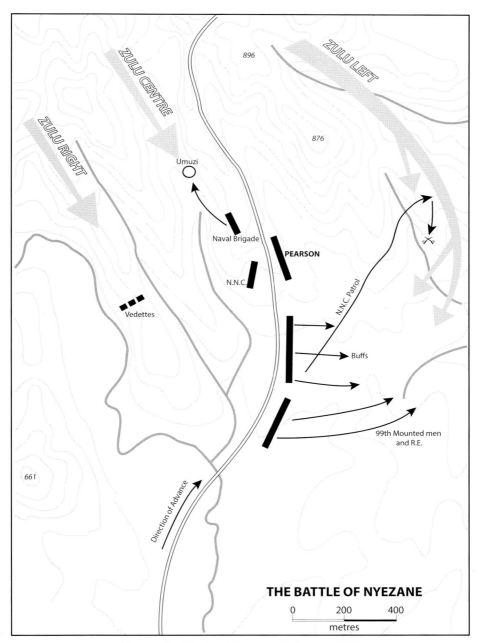

Map 2 – The Battle of Nyezane, 22 January 1879.

Commissioned into the 31st (Huntingdonshire) Regiment in South Africa, he was serving as a Staff Captain with the 2nd Regiment, Natal Native Contingent. Hart was the brother of Lieutenant Reginald Clare Hart, Royal Engineers, who would be awarded the Victoria Cross in Afghanistan at the end of January.

During the action, Wynne's company – consisting of 94 other ranks – advanced in extended line and supported Percy Barrow's horsemen. At the end of the two-hour action, the Engineers alone had expended 1,850 rounds of ammunition. They had suffered no casualties, although one man had the sight of his rifle shot away by a Zulu marksman, or possibly a stray bullet.

This letter from G. Baskerfield of the Royal Engineers to his mother tells of the action at Nyezane (no corrections have been made to the text):

POINT HOSPITAL, DURBAN, NATAL, MAY 10, 1879. – We landed here in Durban on the 3rd January, and encamped until the 5th. We then started on the march for the Tugela, which is 70 miles from Durban; it is the river which separates the colony of Natal from Zululand, and where all our stores are collected for transport up to the columns. I shall never forget the horrors of that march. We started in torrents of rain, over roads which took us up to the knees in mud. There is no exaggeration about it, for these roads are not like English roads, nice and level. They are only mere tracks caused by the great heavy, lumbering waggons, which are continually passing over them with war materials for the front. We march on till six o'clock that night, and then halted at a little village called Verulam, drenched to the skin and smothered in mud. We were then about to pitch our tents – the rain still continuing (for when it rains here, which is once a year, it continues for three months – January, February, and March) – when some of the inhabitants kindly offered us a large hall to sleep in, and so saved us the trouble of pitching them. We accordingly turned in and proceed to take off our wet clothes and wait until dinner was cooked for us, which took about three hours. We soon 'wolfed' that lot, and then prepared to lie down (for it was 9.30pm.), but not to sleep, for we were too cold. We had taken off everything but our shirts, and there we had to lie down, cold and wet, till morning without a single rug or blanket to keep out the intense cold, for they were away on the waggons, which could not get up through the mud. Such was the first day's march and the same with all the others till we reached the Tugela, which was on the 12th January. We then crossed the river on to the enemy's side. We remained there till the 19th January, and then started on the march for old Cetywayo's[1] kraal with the column, which was composed of the 99th Regiment, 3rd Buffs, 2n'D' Company R. E. (which you know is the one I am in), 2,000 native contingent, and about 200 volunteers. We marched twelve miles that day, and encamped at the river Tuyoui, threw out our picquets and

1   Cetywayo is an alternative spelling of Cetshwayo.

videttes, and then retired to rest. About ten o'clock the alarm was given. We were all out in a minute, and remained under arms for about an hour; but it proved to be a false alarm, to the great dissatisfaction of the men, who were obliged to turn in again. On the second day all went well, having advanced another twelve miles. We started again on the third day's march at five a.m., and marched on till seven o' clock a.m., when we arrived at a river, where there was no passage for the waggons. The engineers were then ordered to get out their picks and shovels, and make one. We soon had them out and into it like bricks. We had been working about three quarters of an hour, and had nearly finished, when firing was heard. Two companies of the 3rd Buffs had just crossed the river about ten minutes before. No sooner was the firing heard than we threw our picks and shovels down, and dashed across the river, and then round to the right, into a thick, dense bush, about 800 yards away. We then soon came into action. We poured in a deadly volley into a thick mass of the enemy, which made them "sit up" a bit. We then extended out into skirmishing order, and kept up a well sustained fire on the enemy, who did not show any want of pluck, for on several occasions they came as close as fifty yards of the muzzles of our rifles, but these individuals paid for their audacity with their lives. We then advanced on them, but they got round on our right flank and partly in our rear so we got the order to retire. No sooner did they see us retiring, when they set up a deafening yell, and rushed out of the bush, but we turned round on them and put another volley into them, which checked them for a time. We then had the two ranks reversed – one rank one way and rear rank the other, and did a bit of fighting back to back. After about fifteen minutes in that position, they turned and fled, for the firing was too hot for them. We pursued them right through the bush, picking up any amount of assegais and shields, and some guns, which the enemy had thrown away in their confusion. The enemy's loss was 850 killed and 500 wounded; our loss was twenty seven killed and wounded. Colonel Pearson had his horse shot under him. The action lasted two hours and three quarters – from 7.45 until 10.30 a.m. We then started on the march for another five miles, and stopped there till next day, so as to get away from the dead, for we never buried them. By the time we got our dinner that day we had just been exactly twenty four hours without food, so you see we had our fighting on empty stomachs. The following day we shifted up to Ekowe, which was ten miles. As soon as we reached there the engineers had to start fortifying it. It is only a mission station, with two small houses. We soon had the place completed, and then commenced the greatest hardships ever I have been through in my life. We were completely hemmed in by an army of 30,000 Zulus, and we were running short of provisions. We were the only column in Zululand, Colonel Glyn's having been massacred the same day as we had our battle. We were hemmed in here for nearly three months on half rations – 6oz. of biscuits and 6oz. of Boers' meal. The agony I endured for those three months nobody can tell; actually half starved; then false alarms, continued rain, and no place to sleep only under the waggons, with your one solitary blanket and oil sheet, and the water flowing under, threatening to wash you away if you did not hold tight to the spokes of the wheels. I have been that hungry that when they would take out any mouldy biscuits from the commissary store and bury them, I used to watch them, and go out and get a shovel and dig them out again, and eagerly devour them, thanking God that I was there first to get them, before a whole swarm of men would be down fighting for them. This state of things continued until the 4th of April, when the reinforcements came to our relief. I will just tell you what a few things were sold at auction which the volunteers left behind them when they retired on the Tugela. – Tobacco, 27s per lb; condensed milk, 18s a tin; bottle of pickles, 17s 6d; cheese 12s 6d per lb; So you see how eager the men were for them, tobacco especially, as they had been without it seven weeks before these were sold.

Now, about myself, I am here in hospital with the fever, and am very near well now, so you need not fear for me, for I am alive and kicking yet.

On reaching Eshowe, Colonel Pearson's column split. Part retired to Natal, while the remainder encamped – effectively putting them in a state of self-imposed siege.

10

Isandlwana: 'I regret to have to report a very disastrous engagement ...'

At Isandlwana, reveille had sounded at 4.00am on 22 January and within the hour, Chelmsford had departed from the camp with the following: six companies of the 2nd Battalion, 24th Regiment, four guns under Colonel Harness and a company of the Natal Native Pioneers. These men would be required to clear the track for the guns and accompanying wagons. Breakfast had been a hurried affair.

Colonel Glyn advised Nevill Coghill that because of his knee injury, which prevented him easily mounting and dismounting, it would be best if he remained in camp and acted as a galloper – an officer who would be capable of carrying messages from place to place. During the night, a message had been sent to Durnford to move his command up from Rorke's Drift to Isandlwana, but the orders were unclear just as to what his role was to be. The camp at Isandlwana had been left under the command

The Mountain of Isandlwana – beneath the slopes of which the advancing No.3 Column made a temporary encampment.

of Lieutenant Colonel Henry Pulleine – the officer commanding the 1st Battalion of the 24th Regiment. At his disposal were the five companies of his own battalion, one of the 2nd Battalion, the two remaining guns of 'N' Battery (under the command of Brevet Major Stuart Smith), four companies of the 3rd Natal Native Contingent and approximately 100 mounted volunteers. Added to this were possibly another 100 Imperial soldiers from the various units that made up the column. Smith had, in turn, delegated command of the guns to Lieutenant Curling, while he accompanied Chelmsford's command for the ride.

The military news in the local papers on this day was all about Afghanistan; the following telegram was received by the Central News from the Indian Office:

> From Viceroy, January 20. – Roberts reports all quiet at Khost. Mahaud Mazaris, under Umar Khan, have assembled two or three thousand strong in Zam Pass, near Tonk, and entrenched themselves. Reinforcements have been sent to the spot.

> From Viceroy, 21st January, 1879 – Gathering of Wazins near Tonk dispersed after few trifling attempts in neighbouring villages; easily repulsed.

The Times received the following by telegram:

> Khoost, January 18th. – The Khoost valley is settling down. The inhabitants appear willing to accept the situation. Khost presents a good strategical position, and gives an alternative route into Afghanistan via Ghazi. This route is open all the year round, but has not been properly explored. Some Mangola have come in, but none of much importance. General Roberts is anxious to secure their friendship, as they can create annoyance along the whole line of route to the Shutargardan Pass, and reprisals are difficult. Slight snow has fallen, and the Sufaid Koh natives say if no more snow falls within the next ten days the pass will not be closed this winter.

Another story concerned the attempted assassination of a British officer – one Major St John – as he walked in the bazaar in Kandahar. In a following incident a short time later, a native 'ran a muck' [sic] with a sword and inflicted serious wounds on two officers, a sergeant and a private before being killed by other troops. It was reported that such fanatics – usually under the influence of opium or bhang and ready to face death – should be availed of by 'hanging with the greatest promptitude and publicity'. While it is acceptable that such an act will seem repugnant to Western ideas, 'the prescriptions of the East make it imperatively necessary to carry out such measures to convince the assassin's co-conspirators that he has not earned the reward for those who slay infidels'.

The news from South Africa concerned the ongoing attempts by Sir Bartle Frere to engage Lobengula, King of the Ndebele, in discussions regarding future trade.

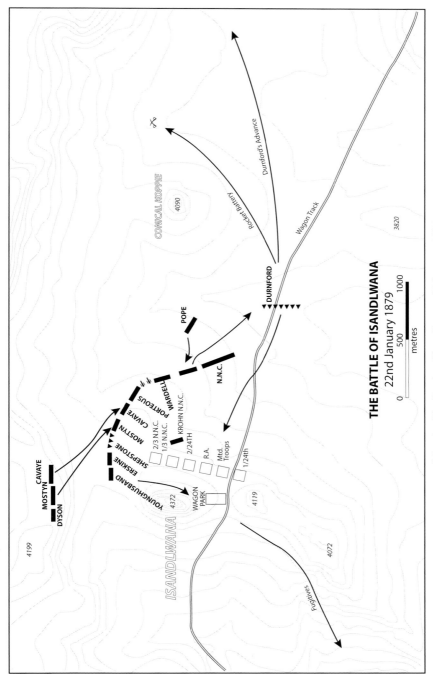

Map 3 – The Battle of Isandlwana, 22 January 1879.

Brevet Major Francis Broadfoot Russell, 11th Battery, 7th Brigade, Royal Artillery commanding the rocket battery of No.2 Column.

At 1030am, Colonel Durnford arrived at Isandlwana with part of his command – approximately 500 men. Trailing along at the end of this column was Captain Francis Russell and his rocket battery – escorted by men of Captain Cracroft Nourse's 'D' Company of the 1/1st Natal Native Contingent.

The rockets used by the battery were not too dissimilar to those used by the British Army during the Napoleonic Wars – and with the accuracy to match! These were 9-pounder Hales, launched from metal troughs. They were extremely inaccurate and made a frightful noise, and frequently had a devastating effect on the morale of natives, but not necessarily on the Zulu. Russell's weapons were loaded on pack mules and crewed by a detachment of nine men of the 1st Battalion, 24th Regiment under the command of Acting Bombardier George Goff of the Royal Artillery.

There is some initial confusion as to Durnford's role when he arrived at the camp: he was under the impression he was to support Chelmsford's advance, while Pulleine assumed he would reinforce the garrison. As the two officers discussed the situation, there is the sound of gunfire from the east. Durnford – fearing an outflanking move by the Zulu to cut the camp off from Chelmsford's force – led his men out to investigate, with Captain Russell and his rocket battery loyally following up behind.

Meanwhile, some four miles to the east of Isandlwana, a mounted patrol under the command of Lieutenant Raw came upon some Zulu cattle and their herd boys. Giving chase, the patrol pursued them for a short distance before the herd disappeared into a fold in the ground. Approaching the edge of what turned out to be a small valley, Raw saw before him – and sitting in complete silence – some 20,000 warriors. The long-sought-for enemy had been found! For an instant, both sides were still; then almost as one, the Zulu rose to their feet and charged towards the horsemen. Raw's men paused to fire a few scattered shots from horseback before beating a hasty retreat back towards Isandlwana.

The Zulu Army discovered by Raw comprised of 12 regiments – and as they advanced towards the British camp, they formed their traditional battle formation known as the 'beast's horns'. Four regiments make up the 'right horn', two the 'chest' and three more the 'left horn'. The 'loins' were formed by the remaining four regiments. As the Zulu 'left horn' approached the camp, they came across Durnford and his command, which had previously ridden out to investigate the sound of gunshots. (These were Raw's men shooting at the Zulu as they first started to move.) Firing from the saddle in measured volleys towards the advancing 'left horn', the troopers began to fall back towards the camp.

Mounted troopers of the Natal Native Contingent come into contact with the Zulu.

The Native Horse fought a futile delaying action as the Zulu rose from their place of concealment.

As Captain Russell brought forward his rocket battery towards the Conical Kop, he received a message from Durnford warning him of the Zulu presence. Almost immediately, Zulu warriors appeared as if from nowhere. Giving the command action 'front', the battery quickly set up the firing troughs. They had time to launch only one rocket before Zulu rifle fire from approximately 100 yards away hammered into the battery with devastating effect. Two of the mules were bowled over by the force of the bullets, while Captain Russell was shot from his saddle – falling to the ground badly wounded. The men of the escorting NNC fired a few scattered shots before fleeing. Private Johnson of the 24th Regiment attempted to rescue the captain, but as he pulled him to his feet, another Zulu bullet slammed into Russell and he was killed instantly. As the Zulu closed in, only four men were able to make their escape – riding off on the surviving battery mules. Those survivors were Privates Grant, Trainer, Johnson and Acting Bombardier Goff.

Meanwhile, back at the camp, Lieutenant Cavaye and his command were on outpost duty on the spur of the mountain. Suddenly, they found themselves heavily engaged with an overwhelming force of Zulu. As it became obvious that the camp was under a major attack, Colonel Pulleine deployed his remaining companies to the front of the mountain.

Stuart Smith had been sent back to the camp, along with Captain Alan Gardner, with a message for Pulleine. This stated that those tents belonging to the men with Chelmsford were to be struck and sent forward, along with a supply of rations for one week. Smith and Gardner had just delivered the message to Pulleine when word was received that a force of Zulu was descending on the camp. This was followed by the sound of gunfire. On the strong advice of Gardner, the order was ignored and Pulleine quickly penned a reply to Chelmsford to the effect that there was the sound of gunfire to the left of the camp and he was unable to move at present. As the attack developed, Smith returned to his command and ordered Lieutenant Curling to

Lieutenant Charles Walter Cavaye commanding 'E' Company, 1st Battalion, 24th Regiment.

Captain Reginald Younghusband commanding 'C' Company, 1st Battalion, 24th Regiment.

Captain William Eccles Mostyn commanding 'F' Company, 1st Battalion, 24th Regiment.

move the two guns forward to a site on a small rise. From here, the guns had a clear field of fire towards the front of the Nquthu escarpment. The artillery went into action and began shelling the Zulu with shrapnel at a range of approximately 3,400 yards. Pulleine was now in no doubt that he had a major battle on his hands, and further realised that the companies were too far apart.

Captain Younghusband was ordered to go forward with his company to cover the withdrawal of Cavaye and Mostyn in an attempt to shorten the line.

From left to right, they were deployed as follows: Captain Younghusband's 'C' Company of the 1st Battalion, next the Natal Native Contingent and beside them the Natal Native Horse. On their right was Captain Mostyn's 'F' Company and next to them Lieutenant Cavaye's 'E' Company. To their right was 'A' Company – under Lieutenant Porteous – and next the two guns of 'N' Battery. To the right of the guns was Captain Wardell with 'H' Company and then 'G' Company of the 2nd Battalion under Lieutenant Pope. There is contention as to what was on Pope's right flank; some writers believe it was more of the NNC.

Back on the right flank, Durnford's men were also retreating back towards the camp. Despite accurate fire from the troopers' carbines, the Zulu were not slowing down one bit. As Durnford reached a donga, at a point where it crossed the trail, he judged it large enough to hold his command and deep enough to shelter the horses. Still being a mile from the camp, Durnford decided to make a stand. The men dismounted, and lining the rim of the donga, proceeded to deliver volleys into the advancing mass. A short time later, other mounted volunteers joined them. With this reinforced skirmish line and added firepower, the Zulu were stopped in their tracks, for a time.

Lieutenant Francis Pender Porteous commanding 'A' Company, 1st Battalion, 24th Regiment.

Lieutenant Charles D'Aguilar Pope commanding 'G' Company, 2nd Battalion, 24th Regiment.

At the camp, despite having such a large frontage to cover, the men of the 24th were putting down a steady fire and the Zulu were being held at bay. Officers were carefully regulating the rates of fire warning the men not to waste ammunition.

A contemporary engraving that rather exaggerates the density of the firing line at Isandlwana.

In the donga, Durnford was forced to order a withdrawal. In truth, he had no alternative; here his men were running low on ammunition – and with this slackening of fire, there was a danger that the Zulu 'left horn' would be able to outflank his right. The riders sent back to the camp for ammunition re-supply were unable to find their own wagons – and any attempt to obtain ammunition from the wagons of other companies was met with a blank refusal. As Durnford's force withdrew, they exposed the right flank of the main British line – a line that was itself running short of ammunition. This was due not only to the distance the men were deployed from the camp ('A' Company runners had to make a round trip of over two miles to their supply wagons), but also to the ammunition boxes themselves.

The question of which mark of ammunition box was present at Isandlwana (and their method of opening) is one of great contention. The majority of available evidence points to the boxes being those referred to as 'Mark Vs'. These are described as having a length of 20.5 inches, a width of 6.8 inches and a depth of 8.5 inches. Their average weight when empty was 12 lbs 4 ozs. With a full load of 600 rounds of Martini-Henry ammunition, the box weighed a little less than 80 lbs. The main difficulty in opening these boxes came not in the removal of screws or the two surrounding copper bands, which were not required to be removed in any case, but in the removal of the opening of the inner tin liner. The following is taken from the Official Records:

> 'List of Changes' no3434 – 'Boxes, Wood, Ammunition, Small Arm, with tin Lining, Service.' 16 October 1878. 'Alteration to lid of tin lining.' It has been found in many instances, when using the handle for opening the tin lining of the above mentioned boxes, that the tin immediately around the handle gives way, and the box is not properly opened; all the boxes will in future be fitted with a large handle, fixed square on the lid, so as to ensure the proper opening of the box.

This defect – discovered three months before Isandlwana – was unlikely to have been rectified in time and would not have applied to boxes already in South Africa. Even if some ammunition had been shipped out in the new boxes, quartermasters (being quartermasters) would have seen to it that old stocks would have been used up first!

Opening the wooden box was only the beginning of the problem for troops under pressure and in a hurry to return to the firing line. Inside the liner, the packets of ammunition were packed so tightly that it was virtually impossible to spill them out by turning the box upside down. It was necessary to prise the first few packets out using a knife or bayonet – and even then the sharp tin liner would have made a bloody mess of the fingers of anyone attempting to remove the remaining packets in a hurry.

This alone did not cause any failure of supply, but it did slow it down. Why did the supply run as short as it did? This must be put down to the fact that more than the normal expenditure of ammunition was experienced. While first-line re-supply at company level was probably sufficient in the beginning, that which was due from the reserves held in the camp was not. The difficulty of moving an ample supply forward to the firing line may well have caused a fatal slowing-down of the volleys that

Zulu warriors pushing home their attack despite sustaining heavy casualties.

were keeping the Zulu at bay. In order to get enough ammunition forward quickly, complete boxes would have had to be carried forward. Even between two men – already burdened with their kit and rifles – was the sheer physical effort involved in carrying a box weighing almost 80 lbs in the extreme heat of an almost midday sun.

On the spur of the mountain, Vereker's company of the Natal Native Contingent were forced back by the press of Zulu. The Honourable Standish William Prendergast Vereker was the third son of Viscount Gort of Limerick and he had been educated at Oxford before coming to Cape Town.

By August 1878 he was in the Transvaal and had enlisted in the Frontier Light Horse as a Trooper. During the following campaign, he proved himself a capable and professional soldier and was offered a commission in the 3rd Regiment, Natal Native Contingent – a position he accepted without hesitation. Now he found himself tumbling down the spur of Isandlwana with the remnants of his company. Spotting Lieutenant Raw's troop close by, he joined with them as they fought their way down the spur, through the camp and onto the saddle. As this command in turn disintegrated, Raw and Vereker decided it was time to go. Vereker had lost his mount in the melee and Raw caught one from some of those loose horses passing by and brought it to him. As Vereker prepared to ride out of the camp, a trooper of the Natal Native Horse came to him and, using sign language, indicated that the horse belonged to him. Vereker was nothing, if not a gentleman. He dismounted at once and handed the reins to the trooper.

Lieutenant The Honourable Standish
William Prendergast Vereker, 2nd
Battalion, 3rd Regiment, Natal
Native Contingent.

Vereker gives up his only chance of escape from the battlefield – an engraving from
The Boy's Own Annual.

Lieutenant Raw made his escape; Vereker died fighting alongside Durnford. The Vereker family continued the tradition of volunteering. In 1940, Private Vereker of the Durham Home Guard was a former High Sheriff for Durham County and the brother of Viscount Gort VC – commander of the British Expeditionary Force. Another Home Guard connection with the Zulu War can be found with Private Gebuza Mungu of the Pennard Platoon, 15th Glamorgan (Gower) Battalion of the Home Guard. His father, Umundela Mungu, allegedly commanded an *impi* in Cetshwayo's Army.

Pulleine then had no choice but to order a withdrawal to the centre of the camp in the hope of presenting a solid formation in front of the mountain. However, the shortages of ammunition had resulted in the lessening of the volley fire, and in turn, the Zulu had managed to come closer. As the men of the 24th withdrew, officers ordered rallying squares, but it was of no use. The Zulu then ran among the red soldiers, stabbing and slashing, seemingly everywhere.

The British resistance at Isandlwana breaks down into small groups of men in 'rallying squares'.

Lieutenant George Hodson,
1st Battalion, 24th Regiment.

Lieutenant George Frederick John Hodson, from Dublin, was killed as 'C' Company fell back towards the camp centre; he was 24 years old. By the time the main body of British troops had withdrawn to the camp, it was a case of every man for himself.

Major Francis Freeman White – recognised as the oldest soldier serving in the 1st Battalion – was killed fighting alongside his men. The two brothers from Cork, Sergeant John Reardon and his brother Timothy (a Drummer), were also killed as the Zulu plunged through the camp. Up on the Nek, Anthony Durnford was killed trying to keep the trail back towards Rorke's Drift open.

Realising that the artillery pieces were in imminent danger of being overrun, Stuart Smith ordered them to be limbered up and for the section to withdraw at all speed. To the men of the Royal Artillery, the guns were as important as regimental colours to the infantry. The loss of a gun was seen as a disgrace, even if the detachment fought to the death.[1] With some of the artillerymen acting as rearguard, the guns galloped across the front of the camp – losing one man to a spear thrust even as they moved off. Smith and Curling led the way –cutting down with deft slashes of their swords anyone rash enough to stand in their way. When the section reached the edge of a gorge, they were unable to stop in time. The inertia of the limbers and guns forced the horses over the edge, where they hung helpless and entangled in the bushes, to be slaughtered by the Zulu. Unable to do anything for the horses, or any surviving members of the gun crews, the two officers rode on towards the river, with Smith suffering a spear slash to his arm.

As Major Stuart Smith – now without his horse and weak from loss of blood – made his way down towards the river, he saw Lieutenant Smith-Dorrien tending to a wounded man. Moving further down the bank, he saw a group of warriors closing in on the two men. Just as he shouted a warning to Smith-Dorrien, the Zulu seemed to be everywhere.

1   In the Royal Artillery, guns have detachments; in the Royal Navy, they have crews.

The black wave
of death.

In the ensuing melee, Stuart Smith, the wounded soldier and Smith-Dorrien's horse all died under the slashing blades of the Zulu spears. Lieutenant Curling, however, made a successful escape from the battlefield. Smith-Dorrien managed to fight his way clear – and reaching the river, he grabbed the tail of a riderless horse that was swimming past. Hanging on for dear life, Smith-Dorrien was eventually washed across to the Natal side of the Buffalo River.[2] Some weeks later, Stuart Smith's body was found – and he was buried where he fell.

2   Horace Lockwood Smith-Dorrien was a 20-year-old Lieutenant serving with the 95th (Derbyshire) Regiment. He had been seconded to Chelmsford's force as a Commissariat officer. In August 1914 he commanded the 2nd Corps of the BEF as it retreated from Mons in Belgium. Disobeying orders, he issued the following: "Gentlemen, we shall stand and fight." This gallant action bought valuable time for the remainder of the BEF to extricate itself intact. His superior, Sir John French, never forgave him for doing

Lieutenant Horace Lockwood
Smith-Dorrien, 95th
(Derbyshire) Regiment.

Captain Younghusband and the survivors of 'C' Company managed to hold out for a time – fighting from the rocks on the shoulders of the mountain. When they had exhausted their remaining rounds of ammunition, they made a last desperate bayonet charge into the surrounding Zulu. Lieutenant Macdowel of the Royal Engineers was killed towards the end of the action. Despite the opportunity to escape, he elected to remain in the camp and was one of those who were attempting to re-supply the firing line with ammunition when they were overwhelmed.

At the headquarters tent, Colonel Pulleine entrusted Lieutenant Teigmouth Melvill, Adjutant of the 1st Battalion, with the Queen's colour and ordered him to carry it to safety.

something that he himself should have done. He hounded him out of France and castigated him in his memoirs. Smith-Dorrien, by far the better man, saw no further military service after the Battle of 1st Ypres and died in 1930 aged 72.

A dramatic engraving from The *Graphic* entitled 'At Bay'.

The last of the 24th: Isandlwana.

Lieutenant Teignmouth
Melvill, Adjutant.

Shaking hands, Pulleine turned away and made ready to die with his battalion.[3] With the flag, attached to a six-foot pole and encased in a heavy black leather case slung across his saddle, Melvill galloped out of the camp.

As he made his way through the devastated camp towards the Buffalo River, the colour on its pole seemed to snag on every tree and bush. Melvill's red tunic was also causing him problems. Prior to the battle, Cetshwayo had ordered his warriors to "Kill the red soldier!" –and it was noticed that those officers wearing their blue patrol jackets were largely ignored as they rode through the camp attempting to escape. While the five Imperial officers who did survive Isandlwana were all wearing blue patrol jackets, many more that were similarly dressed did not. As Melvill crossed the saddle of the mountain, he found his way barred by Zulu – the road to Rorke's Drift was well and truly closed! This left Melvill, along with practically every other potential escapee, no alternative but to strike out across unfamiliar territory towards the Buffalo River.

The *Kaffrarian Watchman* (reprinted in *The Irish Times*, 15 March 1879):

We have received the following extract from a letter of a gentleman whose testimony may be relied upon. 'When the loss of the camp seemed quite certain,

The dash with the Queen's colour.

Colonel Pulleine called Lieutenant Melville, and said – "Lieutenant Melville, you as senior lieutenant will take the colours and make the best of your way." He shook hands with him, and turned round and said, "Men of the 1st Battalion 24th, we are here and here we stand, and fight it out to the end." He was quite cool and collected'.

The gentlemen who wrote this would not pen anything for the sake of mere dramatic effect, and we are glad to be able to publish it to show that an English officer knows how to die when duty hold.

In the camp – as the lines broke – Coghill rode to the camp and ordered Colonel Glyn's groom and cook to strike the tents, load them onto a wagon and take the Colonel's horses to the rear. Just why he should have given such an order at this time is strange to fathom, but as good soldiers should, the order was obeyed. Sometime later, Coghill spotted Colonel Glyn's groom, Private John Williams, still with the horses. Telling him to mount and follow on, both men rode out of the camp.[4]

Why did Coghill leave? In Victoria's day, it was considered right and proper that an officer stayed with his men no matter what – and yet, did Coghill have any men? The role dictated to him previously was that of galloper, a mounted messenger, with the camp descending into chaos and small parties of infantry scattered all over the place; just who was Coghill to command? Post-war, there was a concentrated attack on both men via the pages of the press demanding why these officers did not die with their men. If we accept that Pulleine did order Melvill to carry the colour to safety, then he left Isandlwana with a clear conscience in that he was doing his duty. Coghill's decision to leave has to remain a mystery, known only to him, but one wonders what decision the gentlemen of the press would have made if placed in a similar situation.[5]

As Melvill made his way towards the Buffalo River and safety, he met up for a time with Coghill. Coghill was having a slightly easier time of it – being dressed in his blue patrol jacket, although this had not detracted one Zulu, who was able to wound his horse with a thrown spear. Passing some horsemen who were walking their mounts, Coghill suggested it was not a good time for walking; the enemy were close on their heels. Forcing his way past, he made for the river. When he neared the bank, he again met up with Melvill. As the two riders neared the river, the ground became covered with thick bush and was strewn with large boulders – making progress uncommonly

---

4   Private Williams survived the battle.
5   The attacks did not only come from the press: Sir Garnet Wolseley wrote: 'I am sorry that both these officers were not killed with their men at Isanduly [sic] instead of where they were. I do not like the idea of officers escaping on horseback when their men on foot are (being?) killed. Heroes have been made of men like Melvill and Coghill, who taking advantage of their horses, bolted from the scene of the action to save their lives'. In turn, Chelmsford wrote the following: 'As regards poor Melvill and Coghill, the case is even more difficult. The latter was a staff officer attached to Colonel Glyn, and had every right to leave the camp when he realised that nothing could be done to save it'.

Crossing Fugitives' Drift on the Buffalo River.

Lieutenant Melvill clinging to the Queen's colour (assisted by Lieutenant Higginson).

slow and uncertain. Plunging down the steep gorge towards the river, Melvill was all but exhausted after his struggle to keep hold of the colour, as it seemed to snag and catch at every opportunity. Delayed by this, Coghill again took the lead. When the pair reached the Buffalo River, it was found to be a raging torrent due to the previous rains.

Without hesitation Coghill – a superb horseman – galloped his horse into the foaming water and quickly crossed to the far bank. As Melvill – an equally accomplished rider – attempted to follow, he found himself burdened by his cumbersome charge. With the staff of the colour dragging on the bushes lining the riverbank, he forced his horse through and into the river. Entering the water, Melvill's horse lost its footing on the wet rocks in the riverbed and he became unhorsed – being immediately swept away in the rapidly-flowing river. Still holding onto the colour, he was carried along until he was washed up against a large rock in mid-stream.

Here he was grabbed by Lieutenant Walter Higginson – Adjutant of the 1/3rd NNC and late of the Dublin City Militia – clinging on for all he was worth.[6] Higginson's horse had also stumbled when it entered the river – and together, both men held on for dear life as the current threatened to sweep them away and Zulu gunfire from the bank splattered into the surrounding water; then, with their strength ebbing away, they lost their grip on the rock and were swept further downstream and into a deep pool a short

6   Later the 4th Battalion, Royal Dublin Fusiliers.

Coghill going to the aid of Melvill.

distance from the drift. Here, Melvill – weighed down by his water-filled boots, sword scabbard, revolver and the sodden colour – struggled to stay afloat. Seeing Melvill's plight, Coghill turned his horse – and without a thought for self-preservation, once again entered the river.

As Coghill approached the two men, a shot from a Zulu rifle killed his horse and he tumbled into the water. Despite his injured leg, he was able to assist Melvill from the river, but without the colour, which floated away downstream. As the two men collapsed exhausted on the bank, Higginson emerged from the river and went to find some horses. Once again, Melvill's red coat attracted the attention of the enemy and warriors began to move towards them. Now it was time for Melvill to assist the injured Coghill – and together they began to hobble up the steep slope away from the river. As Higginson left the men in his search for horses, he saw two Zulu closing in on the pair. Calling out a warning, he shouted: "For God's sake, fire; you both have revolvers!"

Charles Fripp's painting 'Dying to Save the Queen's Colour' represents the death of Melvill and Coghill.

Shots rang out and Higginson saw the Zulu fall.[7] Melvill and Coghill had managed to climb approximately 100 yards up the riverbank when they were brought to bay by the pursuing natives; here they were forced to make their last stand. When their bodies were discovered some days later, Melvill's pocket watch had stopped at 2.10pm.[8] Coghill had died just three days before his 27th birthday.

When Higginson reached the top of the slope, he met up with a few mounted Basuto. Taking command, he led them back towards the river. As they made their way

7   In his seminal work *The Washing of the Spears*, Donald R. Morris states that when Melvill pulled his pistol from his holster, he found that the cylinder had fallen out. It was (apparently) later found in the camp and it is presumed that it was dropped while Melvill reloaded before leaving. If the pistol in question was a Colt (entirely possible), then the cylinder found was simply an empty one, as the quickest means of reloading a Colt was to replace the entire cylinder – much as you do with speed loads for modern revolvers. The remark by Higginson seems to imply that both men were able to shoot at the encroaching Zulus.

8   For many years, it has been accepted (and assumed) that this reflected the time Melvill entered the river. As several survivors reported seeing him in the camp at 2.10pm, this is highly unlikely. It is entirely possible that his watch stopped at 2.10 on the morning of the 22nd – and in the ensuing excitement, he forgot to wind it. A more likely explanation is that the watch, being of good quality, survived the immersion in the Buffalo River and simply ran down after Melvill's death.

The grave of Melvill and Coghill above the Buffalo River.

Zibhebhu kaMaphitha – the Zulu commander who may have ordered the deaths of
Melvill and Coghill.

down to the riverbank, they heard a number of shots and the sound of a struggle, but their vision was blocked by a large rock. As they came closer, they were confronted by a large number of Zulu and were forced away.

The Irish Times, 31 March 1879:

A Survivor of Isandula

To the Editor of *The Irish Times*
Sir, – As some further particulars about the late disastrous battle at Isandula may prove interesting to many of your readers, I annex a copy of a letter just received from Rorke's Drift from Adjutant W.R. Higginson of the Natal Native Contingent, dated Feb. 9th, 1879. – A Reader. "Out of 18 officers and 60 non-commissioned officers in camp, only 2 other officers with myself escaped, viz – Lieut. Vaines and Lieut. Adendorf. I will give you an account of the fight as I gave it to Lord Chelmsford. The attack first commenced on our extreme left, where our outlying picket and the Natal Native Contingent were stationed, at about 7a.m. They were driven back on the camp by the Zulus, who came on in clouds. About 20,000 attacked us. They then extended all along our front, and the 24th skirmishers had to fall back. Colonel Durnford was with the Rocket Battery, with Frank McDowell, R.E. (a son of Dr. McDowell of Dublin). They were both killed very early in the battle. Then Colonel Pulleine was shot through the brain, and five companies 1–24th Regiment and one 2–24th Regiment and 23 officers were cut to pieces. Lieutenant Cochrane, 32nd Regiment, and I got away together, and rode right through the Zulus for the Buffalo River. It is very deep, and there was a very strong current. In crossing, my horse threw me, and as I had my pockets full of ammunition I went straight to the bottom. Fortunately I struck against a large rock, and held on tight. Lieutenant Melville [sic], adjutant 1–24th Regiment, was also thrown in the river, and came down the river towards me. He, poor fellow, gallantly tried to save the Queen's colour, and he had it in his hand. I caught hold of it to save him, and managed to get both of us into calm water. Lieutenant Coghill who rode in to try and save Melville had his horse shot under him, but also got on shore. We managed to get about 100 yards up the hill when Coghill called out 'Here they are after us'. They both had revolvers, and I had nothing to defend myself with, so I told them to fire. We waited till they got within 30 paces, and then fired. Two men fell, who were in front. Then Melville, who was very much done up, said he could go no further, and Coghill said the same. I thought I would have one more struggle for life, though my horse had kicked me on the leg very badly; so I got passed [sic] them, and got on top of the hill. I was then about 16 miles from Helpmakaar, my best place to go. Between walking and running I kept ahead of the niggers for about 6 miles, when they stopped. There were about 20 of the Mounted Contingent, 1 other white officer,

and myself safe. We all got into Helpmakaar about 7 p.m. that evening. I there found my good little horse 'Darby', which a carbineer volunteer had ridden in."

Higginson received a fair amount of support in the local press:

Mr. HIGGINSON AND LIEUTENANT MELVILLE [sic]

To the Editor of the *Irish Times*
Sir, – Your correspondent "S.B." in a letter in today's paper, in writing about the "Death of Lieutenant Coghill," says Mr. Higginson, of the Natal Native Contingent, was asked by Lieutenant Melville to help him while crossing the Buffalo. "S.B." may not intend to slight the conduct of Mr. Higginson, but as it might be taken so, would you kindly publish in your paper a letter we had from him written a few days after the fight.
    Yours, &c., Henry Higginson.
    Kingstown, March 26th.

"Ladysmith", January 25th

My Dearest Mother, I suppose by the time this reaches you you will have seen the account of our defeat at Lion's Kop, in Zululand. There were about 25,000 of them, and we mustered about 700, 1,600 of our natives being on patrol. We lost four companies of the 1–24th, and nineteen officers, with Colonels Pulleine and Durnford. By the greatest providence I escaped to Helpmakaar, a distance of 25 miles, on foot, my horse having thrown me in the Buffalo River while crossing. Lieutenants Melville [sic], the Adjutant of the 1–24th, and Coghill A.D.C. were the last white men to cross with me, and as they went up the other side with me they were both shot down. I came on here yesterday with a wounded officer of ours. Lord Chelmsford arrived here this morning with his staff, and I had a long talk with him, and told him all about the fight, and had breakfast with him. There were twelve of our officers in camp, and I only know of two others who got away. I have lost everything – clothes, watch, photos, papers &c., all are gone.

Given what was initially reported, it seemed that Higginson should also receive an award. However, his actions immediately following the river crossing appear to be less heroic.

The battle fought at Isandlwana was over. Of the 1,774 men that had remained in the camp, the Official Records recount that 1,329 had been killed. Of these, 445 had made their escape.[9] Suddenly, the sideshow in South Africa would overtake the war in Afghanistan beyond all expectations for the British public.

9   As in all engagements such as this, the 'exact' numbers will remain in contention.

Many bodies had been disembowelled – a tradition of the Zulu when fighting what he considered to be a brave foe; the disembowelling allowed the spirit to escape.

Their victory at Isandlwana had cost the Zulu nation dear; their losses were in excess of 2,000. When Cetshwayo heard the news, he said: "A spear has been plunged into the belly of the Zulu nation."

All hope is lost as the Zulu forces penetrate the tent lines.

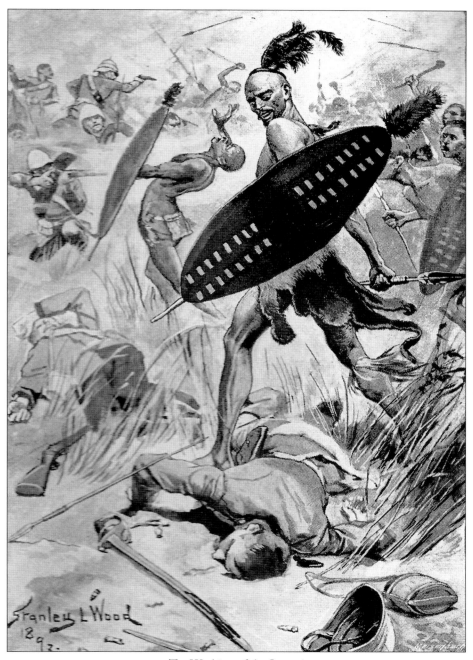

The Washing of the Spears!

11

Rorke's Drift

"Kanti nawe wawukhena?" ("And were you there also?")

With the exception of one regiment, which had done little but cut down a few fugitives that tried to escape across the saddle to Rorke's Drift, the Zulu reserve had not been committed to battle. Their time was still to come!

On 22 January, command of the supply depot established at Rorke's Drift rested with Chelmsford's Deputy Assistant Adjutant and Quartermaster General, Brevet Major Henry Spalding of the 104th Regiment.[1] Apart from command of the post, he was also to keep open the lines of communication and supplies between the advancing column and Helpmekaar. Spalding had previously served in India and had been awarded the Mutiny Medal.

When James Rorke had originally constructed his house, he had approached it more with enthusiasm than with any expertise at architecture. Built from local stone, homemade bricks and thatched with straw, it consisted of 11 rooms and had one very important weakness as far as any defence was concerned: Rorke seems to have had an aversion to doors and windows. Of his 11 rooms, five had no internal doors and opened directly to the outside, while the remaining six were split

Major Henry Spalding, 104th (Bengal Fusiliers) Regiment. (From the collection of Ron Sheeley)

internal doors and opened directly to the outside, while the remaining six were split

---

1   The 104th Regiment, Bengal Fusiliers (later the Royal Munster Fusiliers).

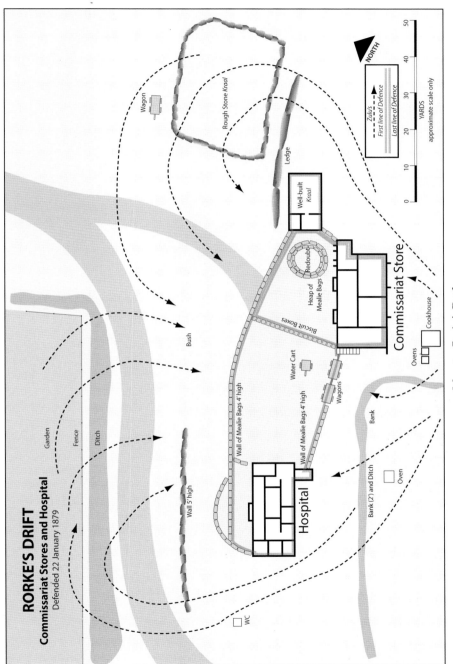

RORKE'S DRIFT
Commissariat Stores and Hospital
Defended 22 January 1879

Garden

Fence

Ditch

Wall 5' high

WC

Wall of Mealie Bags 4' high

Wall of Mealie Bags 4' high

Hospital

Bank (2') and Ditch

Oven

Bank

Wagons

Water Cart

Biscuit Boxes

Ovens

Cookhouse

Commissariat Store

Heap of
Mealie Bags

Redoubt

Well-built *Kraal*

Bush

Ledge

Rough Stone *Kraal*

Wagon

NORTH

Zulu's
First line of Defence
Last line of Defence

YARDS
approximate scale only

0   10   20   30   40   50

Map 4 – Rorke's Drift.

Surgeon James Henry Reynolds,
Army Medical Department.

into two isolated suites – and five of the rooms were windowless!

If the hospital had any advantage as a place of defence, it was the fact that the ground in front of the building sloped away towards a drop of some two feet. Those patients in the hospital were in the care of Surgeon James Reynolds, Army Medical Department and his staff of three assistants and a civilian servant. Reynolds had been born on 3 February 1844 at Dun Laoghaire (Kingstown), County Dublin.

He was the son of Lawrence Reynolds JP of Dalyston House, Granard, County Longford. He was educated at Castle Knock and Trinity College, Dublin, where he graduated BA, MB, ChB in 1867. Reynolds joined the Medical Staff Corps on 24 March 1868 and was attached to the 36th (Hereford) Regiment on 24 March the following year as medical officer. While serving with the regiment in India, Reynolds earned a commendation from Lord Sandhurst for his work during a cholera outbreak. He had been promoted to Surgeon in 1873.

One of the three members of the Army Hospital Corps present on 22 January was Private Michael McMahon. McMahon was a former member of the 64th Regiment[2] and had been born in the village of Rathkeale, County Limerick. Initially recruited in Ireland, he had enlisted at Lanark – the then headquarters of the regiment.

At Rorke's Drift, three of Reynolds' patients were men wounded in the assault on Sihayo's homestead; the remainder were members of the various units in the column and were suffering from assorted injuries and illnesses. The garrison of the post was supplied by men of 'B' Company, 2nd Battalion, 24th Regiment. While the majority of these men were young short service soldiers, many – including their officer – had already seen active service in South Africa. Command of the company had then fallen to 33-year-old Lieutenant Gonville Bromhead. The Bromheads were a Lincolnshire family – and again had strong connections with the army. Bromhead's father had served at Waterloo with the 54th Regiment – losing an eye in that battle. An uncle had

2   Later the 1st North Staffordshire Regiment.

commanded the 77th Regiment at El Bodon on 25 September 1811 in a battle where infantry had made an uphill charge against cavalry. His grandfather had served with General John Burgoyne in the American Revolution. Bromhead's eldest brother had served in the Crimea and was later killed in Burma while serving with the 76th Regiment.

Gonville Bromhead had been educated at Thomas Magnus School, Newark-on-Trent and had proved to be excellent at cricket – a superb left-handed bowler. He had also excelled at boxing, wrestling and singlestick.[3] His surviving elder brother, Brevet Major Charles James Bromhead (also of the 24th Regiment), was considered to be a brilliant staff officer and a member of Garnet Wolseley's 'Ashanti Ring';[4] he was currently on detached duty in London.[5] They were extremely

Lieutenant Gonville Bromhead commanding 'B' Company, 2nd Battalion, 24th Regiment; photograph circa 1872.

lucky to have, as their mother, Judith Christine Wood of Woodville, County Sligo.

Bromhead's future with the regiment was uncertain. He had suffered from hearing difficulties for many years and found it difficult to hear orders on drill or in the field.[6] For a time, he had been attached to the School of Musketry and had earned a reputation as a fine pistol shot; it could also have accounted for his deafness! His nominal

3   A game derived from the early 1700s in which a wooden stick fitted with a hand guard is used to fight one-handed – hence 'singlestick' (basically, a type of fencing).
4   The 'Ashanti Ring' was a collection of officers Wolseley considered to be clever, hardworking, experienced and brave – and he kept them with him whenever possible.
5   Some of the newspaper reports on the defence of Rorke's Drift incorrectly attribute command to Charles Bromhead.
6   His hearing difficulties had first been noticed in 1871. Some authors give Bromhead's deafness as the motive as to why 'B' Company was detailed for duty at Rorke's Drift, but the present-day Brigadier Bromhead claims a clash of personalities with Godwin-Austin as the reason.

Second-in-Command at the post was Colour Sergeant Frank Bourne. Standing only five feet six inches tall and less than 25 years old, the men in the company had nick-named him 'The Kid'.

While the regimental depot of the 24th was situated at Brecon in Mid-Wales – and 'B' Company contained five men named Jones and three named Williams – there were a high proportion of Irishmen serving in the ranks. Among these were one named Jones and another named Williams. Private Evan Jones – real name John Cosgrove – had enlisted in 1877 aged 18 and had previously served in the Royal Monmouth Engineers. He was born in Wales of Irish parents and had changed his name some-time previously due to the anti-Irish feeling that abounded in the country at this time. He picked 'Jones' as it was the name of his landlady when he decided to enlist. Another patient was Drummer Patrick Galgey of 'D' Company, 2/24th. Galgey had enlisted at Cork on 12 March 1865 aged only 14 years (not unusual at this time).

Private John Williams had run away from home to enlist in the 24th – joining the same year as Evan Jones. He was the son of Michael Fielding, who was born in Ireland, and Margaret Godsil, who was also of Irish descent. Michael had arrived in Monmouthshire in the early 1850s and married Margaret at St Michael's Roman Catholic Church, Abergavenny on 21 January 1855. His son, John, was born in Abergavenny on 24 May 1857 – and on leaving school, was employed as a labourer. Some time before his twentieth birthday, he was courting a young lady called Elizabeth Murphy. She fell pregnant and John decided discretion was the better part of valour, and opted for a military career. He attested at Monmouth on 22 May 1877 under the name 'John Williams' and was posted to the 2nd Battalion of the 24th on 3 August 1877.

Private James Bushe had been born at St John's, Dublin; he left his former trade of a tailor and enlisted in the regiment on 14 September 1870.

There was one member of the 90th Regiment present at the mission station – and it is only fitting that he too should have come from Ireland. Corporal John Graham, No.1123, 90th (Perthshire Volunteers) Light Infantry – also known as Private 2202 Daniel Sheehan – was a deserter from the 2nd Battalion, 6th (*Royal Warwickshire*) Regiment of Foot. He was born near Cork in July 1851 and gained a second class certificate of education – becoming a clerk. On 5 December 1870 he enlisted in the 2nd/6th and by January 1876 he was a Sergeant. In June of the same year, he went absent without leave for a week. He was apprehended, tried and was sentenced to be reduced to the rank of Private. On 15 December 1876 – having served six years in the army – he passed to the reserve to serve a period of six years as a reservist in the Liverpool District. Instead, he returned to Ireland and enlisted at Bin under the guise of 'James Graham' – stating he was born at St Mary's (near Dublin) and that he was a labourer with no prior mili-tary service. He joined the 90th Light Infantry with the regimental number 1123. However, someone must have recognised him as Sheehan, for he was arrested on 26 February 1877 and confined whilst awaiting trial. On 2 May 1877 he was tried and convicted of Fraudulent Enlistment. He lost his 29 days' pensionable service and good conduct pay gained whilst with the 90th and was confined in a military prison until 26 June 1877. On 11 January 1878 he arrived in South Africa, where the 90th were deployed against the amaXhosa in the Transkei. On 2 April of that year, he was tried by local court martial, with his rights and privileges gained in the 2nd/6th forfeited. Despite all of this, he still managed to be present at Rorke's Drift and play his part in the defence.

Among the patients in the hospital was Private Garret Hayden of 'D' Company, 2nd Battalion of the 24th. Hayden had attested at Dublin in 1865 aged 18 years and had joined his battalion at Port Blair. He had been appointed as a Drummer in 1868 – a rank he held for seven years before being reduced to Private. Lying close to him was Private John Lyons from Killaloe, County Clare. He was a former member of the 87th Regiment (known as the 'Eagle Takers') – having served for three years before transferring to the 24th.[7]

Wheeler John Cantwell, Royal Artillery, came from Dublin and had left his position as a servant – enlisting in the 9th Foot in 1868 at the age of 23. He transferred to the Royal Artillery four years later on 1 April 1872; by 1 July 1877 he had been posted to 'N' Battery, 5th Brigade. He served for a period on St Helena and arrived in South Africa on 9 January 1878 – being appointed to the position of Wheeler on 29 July of the same year. He accompanied his battery to the Zulu border, but was tasked to remain at Rorke's Drift and be responsible for the battery's supplies – but had he travelled with his battery on towards Ulundi, his chances of survival would have been slim.

Two days previously, Captain Rainforth's 'G' Company of the 1/24th had been expected at the post and had, as yet, to arrive. Waiting to be relieved by 'G' Company was the 2nd Battalion, 3rd Natal Native Contingent under the command of Captain William Stevenson.

Late on the evening of 21 January, Lieutenant Chard had received orders from Chelmsford's headquarters to move his men up to the column at Isandlwana, but it was unclear if Chard himself was to accompany them – therefore on the morning of 22 January, Lieutenant Chard had received permission from Major Spalding to ride up to the centre column's camp and clarify the position. Shortly after 8.00am Chard arrived at Isandlwana, with his men following behind in a wagon. In the camp, all was excitement; the Zulu had been sighted and action was imminent. Chard was told that his men would be attached to the column, but he was to return to Rorke's Drift and prepare an entrenched position overlooking the ponts on the river. With Driver Robson, RE and a mixed-race wagon driver, the three men – with their wagon loaded with tools – made the journey back along the track. On his return to the drift, he had

---

7   The 87th Foot – later 1st Battalion, Royal Irish Fusiliers – were the first regiment in the British Army to take a French 'Eagle' in battle. The 2nd Battalion, under Major Hugh Gough, captured the Eagle of the French 8th Regiment at the Battle of Barrosa in Spain on 5 March 1811.

passed his fellow engineer Durnford making his way towards the camp and had given him the news about the expected Zulu attack.

On arrival at the mission station, Chard reported to Major Spalding – advising him of what was happening at Isandlwana. This caused some concern to Spalding, who decided to ride down to Helpmekaar to see what was keeping 'G' Company. (Unknown to Spalding, 'D' Company, 1st/24th Regiment had, in turn, been delayed by bad weather on its march up-country and had not, as yet, reached Helpmekaar.) He then detailed one NCO and six men as pont guards to be supported by 50 men of Stevenson's NNC company. In his absence, someone had to be designated as Post Commander. Consulting his army list, he discovered that of Bromhead and Chard, Chard was the senior officer by three years. With the remark that it was doubtful if anything was likely to happen by the time he returned, he departed at 2.00pm that afternoon – therefore passing on his chance of everlasting fame and a possible Victoria Cross. Chard returned to his tent down by the ponts and began his lunch. Shortly after 12.30pm the sound of cannon was heard from the direction of Isandlwana. At the mission station, Surgeon Reynolds, Otto Witt and The Rev George Smith[8] climbed to the top of the Oskarberg – and using a telescope, saw what appeared to be the signs of battle at Isandlwana; then from the Natal side of the Buffalo, three riders were observed riding towards the mission station. In the event that they might need medical assistance, Surgeon Reynolds came down the hill and returned to the post.

At the mission station, a rider approached with the terrible, unbelievable news that the camp at Isandlwana had fallen. Meanwhile, at the river, two more riders had arrived at the north bank and called to be ferried across. These proved to be Lieutenant Gert Adendorff of the 1st Battalion, 3rd Regiment, NNC and Trooper W. Sibthorpe of the Natal Carabineers. Their news was the same: the camp had been attacked and overrun by the Zulu – and the majority of the command slaughtered. At this point, Adendorff volunteered to assist with the defence, while his companion rode on to Helpmekaar for assistance.

A messenger arrived from Bromhead calling Chard back to the mission station. Before he left, Sergeant Frederick Millne, 2nd/3rd Regiment (the Buffs) – along with the ferryman Mr Daniells and the pont guard – offered to moor the ponts in the middle of the river and defend the crossing. While heartened by the offer, Chard was forced to deny it. Anyone on a pont in the centre of the river would be terribly exposed to rifle fire from either bank – and it would be impossible to re-supply any defenders with ammunition.

To fight or flee? Chard, being the senior rank, was faced with a dilemma. The post was completely undefended by any sort of fortifications – and the garrison (including Bromhead's men, supernumeraries and those hospital patients capable of holding a

---

8   Smith was an Anglican missionary and chaplain of the Weenen Yeomanry – a local volunteer unit – and was presently serving as a Volunteer Chaplain with the centre column.

Assistant Commissary Walter Alphonsus Dunne, Commissariat and Transport Department.

rifle) numbered just over 100 men. To flee presented difficulties, as there were over 30 sick men in the hospital, and the only transport available was the slow-moving ox wagons. Any attempt to go back towards Helpmekaar would soon be overtaken by the swiftly-moving Zulu. This discussion went on between Chard and Bromhead for some time before Assistant Commissary Dunne and his assistant, James Dalton, tipped the scales in favour of making a stand.

Walter Alphonsus Dunne, Commissariat and Transport Department – with a rank equal to that of Lieutenant – was the officer in charge of the stores held at Rorke's Drift. Described as a tall, pleasant-looking man, he was 26 years old and had been born in County Cork on 10 February 1853. He had enlisted in the Control Department in 1873 – an institution that had been formed to provide officers for the Army Service Corps, which at the time, consisted only of NCOs. In 1875, the Control Department had been renamed as the Commissariat and Transport Department – an improvement on the former, but only just. Since his arrival in South Africa in 1871, Dunne had seen his fair share of action. He had first served on the Cape Frontier before being posted to the North-Eastern Transvaal to take part in the campaign against the Pedi. As this campaign came to a sorry end due to drought and horse sickness, Dunne made his way to Natal to join Chelmsford's invasion force. Such was his keenness to take part that a journey of over 100 miles through hostile territory was made alone. Details of this journey were recorded in a letter home written on 20 January 1879, which was published later that year in *The Irish Times* of 5 March:

I have not had a moment I could call my own to tell you of my adventures on coming here on horseback from Luneburg, how I had to swim a river, how the next day my horse sank up to the girths in mud, and how finally I completed in safety the ride of over one hundred miles. When I got here I was so done up that I could do nothing for two or three days, but I soon came round again, and now feel as well as ever. As has been long expected war had begun with the Zulus, and we are beginning another campaign with greater difficulties to face than the last. I am in charge of the commissariat of the column, which is a very serious responsibility entailing a great amount of work and anxiety, the roads and transport are so bad. So far things have gone well. In addition to this column are two others of about equal strength entering Zululand. This column crossed the River Buffalo this morning, taking food, &c., for fifteen days. I remain here in charge of the depot, which is protected by some of the 2–24th Regiment and 400 natives. This is the first quiet day I have had for some time, and I was very glad when they moved off from the camping ground. It was a busy and picturesque scene to look on, the rows of tents and wagons, with crowds of oxen and men winding to and fro. The wagons were carried across the river on pontoons; the men went in boats. From our side of the river the view was very fine and impressive, as the strains of the band and the notes of the native war song were wafted on the breeze. Now the spot is deserted. There is a large farm house for commissariat stores, outside of which grain is raised high in bags, covered with tarpaulin. Inside boxes of biscuits are piled to the roof, with tea, coffee, meal, sugar, flour, &c. we are in the middle of a fine country, and the weather is cool, but there has been a great deal of rain, which is a disadvantage, as it cuts up the roads and damages our supplies … A part of our column had a small engagement the other day, the first of the war, and captured 400 head of cattle, some sheep and goats and horses. Some of the 4th Foot are expected here shortly …

Dunne pointed out to Chard that the post was supplied with an adequate supply of mealie bags – beef and biscuit boxes – with which to construct a perimeter wall. There was also an ample supply of ammunition, some 20,000 rounds; Dalton supported this argument to the full with the now immortal phrase: "Now we must make a defence!"

Acting Assistant Commissary James Langley Dalton was a former Sergeant in the 85th Regiment and had brought with him a distinguished reputation from his time on the Cape Frontier; he was also the possessor of a commanding personality. In a time of indecision, such a man can work wonders.

The third member of the Commissariat at the mission station was Acting Storekeeper Louis Alexander Byrne (formerly of the Natal Civil Service),[9] who was

9   *The Irish Times*, 21 February 1879.

Acting Assistant Commissary James Langley Dalton, Commissariat and Transport Department.

Acting Storekeeper Louis Alexander Byrne – a locally recruited member of the Commissariat and Transport Department.

an assistant to Dalton and Dunne. Byrne had been born in Ireland in 1857 – and at 22, was just beginning his career in the Commissariat.[10]

By now, some of the few survivors of Isandlwana were arriving at the post, but none were stopping, with the exception of Lieutenant Alfred Henderson and a group of approximately 100 native horsemen of the Natal Native Horse; now he requested orders for his men. Chard asked them to provide a cavalry screen towards the drift and the slopes of the Oskarberg, and to attempt to delay any Zulu advance to allow the post more time to build its barricades. The time was now about 3.30pm.

The Rev Witt and Smith came down from the hill and reported that the Zulu were approaching in force. Witt, concerned about the safety of his family, harnessed his wagon – and taking a wounded NNC officer (Lieutenant Purvis) with him, made a speedy egress. To protect the hospital and those patients remaining, Bromhead detailed a guard of six men: Privates Alfred Henry Hook, Robert Jones, William Jones, John Williams, Joseph Williams and Thomas Cole. Those patients able to hold and fire a rifle were also armed. Loopholes were dug in the walls and material was gathered to barricade the doors.

Picquets from 'B' Company were deployed on the lower slopes of the Oskarberg and the pont guard was ordered up from the river to join the small garrison. Some

10   Byrne's father was apparently from Cardiff and was possibly a second-generation Irishman.

members of the garrison – along with the men of Captain Stevenson's command – set about building Chard's planned barricades under Dalton's direction, with some of the 24th standing over them.[11]

Mealie bags weighing up to 200 lbs each, equally heavy two-foot-square pine biscuit boxes and two transport wagons were incorporated into the walls. These eventually rose to a height of approximately four feet – the height of two of the heavy biscuit boxes – and in places, these had been topped by a layer of mealie bags. The spaces between the wheels of the two wagons had also been filled with boxes and mealie bags, with a further layer of bags laid across the bed of the wagons. At 4.20pm there was the sound of scattered firing from the Natal Native Horse, rapidly followed by the unit itself, as it galloped past the post. Henderson reined in his horse to tell Chard that the men would not stand and fight. They had performed well at Isandlwana, where they had seen a much larger force destroyed. Now they were practically out of ammunition and saw little prospect of a biscuit-box fort doing any better. As they rode by the post, a hospital patient heard one of them call out: "Here they come, black as hell and thick as grass!"[12]

As the horsemen disappeared into a cloud of dust, the men of the NNC also decided that discretion was the better part of valour, and took off into the bush. Sad to say, they were led by both the good Captain Stevenson and his European NCOs. This prompted a degree of outrage among the remaining defenders and several shots rang out, with one bullet finding its mark in the back of Corporal W. Anderson of that unit.[13] Now with a reduced garrison, Chard and Bromhead realised that there were not enough numbers to man the entire perimeter in any great strength – therefore he planned and ordered the construction of an inner wall running from the corner of the storehouse out to the north wall. In the event of not being able to hold the outer wall, this would serve as a fall-back position. This was not as strong as the first wall and contained gaps to allow the withdrawing men to pass through. Within this wall, Walter Dunne began to build a final redoubt from the unused mealie bags – described as a 'hollowed-out tea cosy'. When all was ready, or at least as ready as it was likely to be, what force did Chard have to defend Rorke's Drift?

It is impossible to say exactly how many men were present that day; various sources give varying numbers. Some writers quote only the men of the 24th; some quote only

11   R.J. 'Bob' Hall – a meat contractor attached to the Natal Mounted Police – mentions in his account that men of the 24th Regiment stood over the men of the NNC while the laager was built under the direction of Mr Dalton. It is the authors' own view that 'standing over' the NNC was coercion – and history has proved that there is nothing like a long, shiny, sharp piece of metal on the end of a loaded rifle to ensure that people do as they are told!

12   Credited to Bob Hall – meat contractor with the Natal Mounted Police.

13   Despite this desertion, there is little doubt that the precarious situation of the garrison would have been much greater but for the assistance of those members of Stevenson's company of the NNC who built most of the barricades before the arrival of the Zulu.

those deemed to have fought in the defence. If you take into account those sick and injured in the hospital, as well as able-bodied defenders, then a number of either 154 or 156 comes up. The attacking force was in excess of 4,000 men and drawn from the amabutho regiments of the uThulwana, the iNdlondlo and the uDloko. All of these warriors were in their forties and wore the *isicoco* of a married man. The iNdluy-engwe were an unmarried regiment, with their ranks filled by men in their late twenties. These regiments had formed the uNdi Corps and had been the Zulu reserve at Isandlwana; their only contribution in that battle had been the hunting down and killing of fugitives attempting to escape towards the Buffalo River. The commander of the corps was Prince Dabulamanzi kaMpande – the half-brother of King Cetshwayo. The warriors were anxious to obtain their share of the fame that would be generated by those who had attacked and fought at Isandlwana – therefore Dabulamanzi heeded the cry: "Let us go and fight at Jim's!"; and contrary to Cetshwayo's explicit order to act only in defence within the borders of Zululand, he led his warriors across the Buffalo River and into Natal.

The first Zulu attack began at 4.30pm – just two-and-a-half-hours from darkness. A band of warriors from the iNdluyengwe surged towards the rear of the hospital – only to be cut down in droves by the combined fire from the hospital rear, the wagon wall and the storehouse. As a result of this, some of the Zulu were forced to ground some 50 yards from the rear wall – taking whatever cover was available. The remainder continued to move forward and to the left – turning to attack the west gable end of the hospital.

Prince Dabulamanzi kaMpande.

Zulu forces crossing a river, as they did the Buffalo River in order to attack Rorke's Drift.

With odds of approximately 30 to 1, the Zulu would seem to have enjoyed a marked superiority, but with the small frontage offered by the perimeter, this was not so. The presence of a chest-high barrier between defender and attacker – coupled with the longer reach of the Martini-Henry and its 22-inch bayonet against the stabbing spear of the Zulu –gave the defenders every advantage in the close-quarter fighting.

As Surgeon Reynolds (between treating patients) made one of his many tours around the perimeter – handing out ammunition – he was struck in the helmet by a Zulu bullet. While the helmet suffered detriment, Reynolds did not. Chard took a place on the wall for a time, armed with a rifle, while Bromhead (apparently a fine revolver shot) did his bit in keeping the enemy outside the perimeter.

Inside the hospital, conditions were getting serious. The small rooms were filling with smoke from the black powder cartridges of the rifles and the heat was intense. Private Cole – allegedly overcome by an attack of claustrophobia – fled from the room he was sharing with Hook. Coming out onto the front veranda, he was faced by warriors attacking the front wall. As he moved forward, a Zulu bullet caught him in the head – killing him instantly. The same bullet continued on its way and hit Private James Bushe – smashing into his nose. Bushe – the ex-tailor from Dublin – continued to fire. The Zulu appeared to be making some progress at this part of the defences, and warriors were seen climbing onto the top of the wall. A well-timed bayonet charge – led by Lieutenant Bromhead – put paid to this incursion and the

Zulu forces probing the defences of the mission station at Rorke's Drift.

The initial assault on the barricades at Rorke's Drift.

enemy were beaten back. Almost immediately, they charged again – and again, good bayonet work pushed them away from the wall. This happened several times in quick succession, as did increased attacks against the gable end of the hospital – the warriors being reinforced all the time; then a determined rush brought the warriors over the barricade at the western end of the hospital – compelling the defenders to retire along the front of the building. With indecent haste, another barricade consisting of boxes was erected from the eastern end of the hospital out to the north wall. Those men who had withdrawn from the front of the building took up position here and poured a deadly flank fire into those Zulu attempting to get into the hospital. As the warriors swarmed over the walls, they were cut down almost immediately, with few surviving to get inside the building.

Elsewhere, the Zulu were attempting to leap over the wall and make attempts to grab the bayonets of the defenders. All were shot. On the rear wall, the Zulu rifles scored another hit, as a musket ball thumped into the neck of Corporal John Lyons from County Clare. As he fell, he cried out to fellow Corporal, William Allan: "Give it to them Allan, I'm done; I'm dying."

Corporal William Allan – photographed post-1881 – holding the rank of Sergeant.

Private Frederick Hitch photographed in the uniform of the Corps of Commissioners, circa 1880.

As Corporal Allan replied in the affirmative, another Zulu bullet smacked into his right arm! As Lyons lay on the ground calling for assistance, Lieutenant Chard and some others pulled him away from the wall and took him to the care of Surgeon Reynolds. The construction of the first fall-back position was still under way and being supervised by James Dalton. Suddenly, he was felled by a gunshot wound to the upper body. Within this position was Lieutenant Bromhead, Private Hitch and five other men.

The garrison was receiving sustained rifle fire not only from the slopes of the Oskarberg, but from those warriors that had come in close to the defences. While many of these firearms were of antiquated vintage, they were still capable of inflicting terrible wounds. The home-made bullet that slammed into the back of Private Frederick Hitch shattered his shoulder blade into 39 pieces before exiting through the front! After having his wound patched up, Hitch continued to distribute ammunition to the riflemen on the walls, while armed with Bromhead's revolver for his own defence.

Such was the amount of small arms fire sweeping the ground between the hospital and storehouse that it was deemed untenable – and Chard reluctantly ordered the remaining defenders back behind the inner wall. As the men fell back, Corporal Schiess (a Swiss, of the NNC) crept out along the now abandoned front wall – and dropping down over the barricade, shot three Zulu riflemen, whose fire had been more than usually accurate. This now meant that the hospital defenders were cut off from the remainder of the garrison! As darkness began to fall, some of the defenders reported seeing a cloud of dust from the direction of Helpmekaar; this could only mean one thing: a relief column was on its way! It was, in fact, Major Spalding leading the two companies of the 1st Battalion. Some three miles from the mission station, Spalding saw the flames rising in the evening air. At the same time, a force of Zulu barred his way and attempted to outflank his column. With less than 200 men against an unknown number of enemy warriors, Spalding assumed that the post had met the same fate as those at Isandlwana and turned back to Helpmekaar.

There then began the battle within a battle. Inside the hospital, a group of soldiers – neither officer nor NCO among them – began to fight. Not for Queen, country or regiment, but for their very existence.[14] The Zulu made a concentrated assault on the western end of the hospital – making a determined effort against the room held by Privates John and Joseph Williams. In the room were three patients: Private William Horrigan and two other men. Holding the only exit from the room – a door leading to the outside and the waiting Zulu – Horrigan and Joseph Williams held off the enemy with bullet and bayonet, while John Williams began to dig a hole in the interior wall with a pickaxe. Suddenly, the Zulu managed to grab hold of Joseph Williams and quickly dragged him outside, where he was spread-eagled on the ground and stabbed

---

14   Sergeant Robert Maxfield was a patient, but was delirious with fever and played no active part in the defence.

The darkness of night is illuminated by the burning thatch of the hospital roof.

Whilst Private Alfred Henry Hook holds off the Zulu attackers, Private John Williams
prepares to evacuate a patient.

repeatedly – so much so that his body was all but dismembered. As this was done, John Williams broke through to the other room. The Zulu flooded into the room and killed the two patients lying on the floor.

As they were doing this, Williams and Horrigan were able to scramble through the hole to the next room. Here, Horrigan turned to the left instead of right and stumbled into warriors that had come in through the front of the hospital, and he was killed. Williams turned right and found himself in a room with nine patients. Next door, Private Hook was forced from his room by the heat and smoke from the now burning thatched roof. He was forced to leave behind an injured private of the NNC; Hook heard the Zulu questioning the man before killing him.

Private Alfred Henry Hook.

In this room, there now was Hook, Williams and nine sick men. Once again, John Williams went to work with the pickaxe, while Hook held off the encroaching enemy. A thrown spear struck Hook's helmet – glancing off and doing little damage.[15]

In the confined space, the Zulu could only force their way into the room one at a time – and Hook was able to deal with them with bullet and bayonet. In the confined space – choked with smoke from the burning roof and the repeated discharge of the Martini-Henry – Hook fought for his life and the lives of the nine sick men, while John Williams hacked a way out. As the struggle went on, Williams forced his way into the next room and began to drag the sick men through the hole. All but one man, Private John Connolly (suffering from a dislocated knee), was safely through when Hook was eventually forced out by the burning roof. Turning, he dragged the injured Connolly to safety – dislocating his knee for the second time.[16]

Other soldiers decided to take a chance and make a run for it out through the press of surrounding warriors. After hiding for a time in a large wardrobe, Privates John Waters and William Beckett ran outside. As Waters left the hospital, he was spotted by a Zulu, who stabbed him in the stomach with a spear as he passed. The wound

---

15   While the blow did little at that time, Hook was troubled by headaches in the years to come.
16   His actual injury was synovitis due to a partial dislocation of the left knee that had been caused while in the process of loading a wagon. (See *The Silver Wreath* by Norman Holme)

A battle within a battle: Private William Jones keeps the Zulu at bay to enable Private Robert Jones to escort the patients to safety.

would prove fatal. Beckett – a black cloak around his shoulders – ran outside and lay concealed among some Zulu. Another patient, Private Arthur Howard, leapt over the parapet at the front of the hospital and lay among a pile of Zulu corpses.

Inside the hospital, all rooms were now full of thick acrid smoke. Hook and Williams had arrived in a room held by two of the Jones's of 'B' Company. Privates Robert and William Jones had held their room against all comers – and Robert had suffered a wound to his abdomen from a Zulu spear. Now there was nowhere else to go but out of the hospital. It was apparent that the only exit from the burning building was through a small high window in the rear south-eastern room and out into the

Private John Williams – the assumed name of John William Fielding.

Private William Jones.

Private Robert Jones.

bullet-swept yard. The men inside the hospital scrambled out of the window, or were assisted by Jones and Jones. All these men made it across the yard to the inner perimeter.

The remaining patient in the hospital was the fever-ridden Sergeant Maxfield. Robert Jones made a last gallant effort to save him, but as he entered the room, he saw the Zulu stabbing the Sergeant as he lay on his bed. With the hospital now fully ablaze, Jones had no option but to leave immediately. At this point, John Williams and Hook broke through the remaining wall with their patients and began to hoist them out of the window. As they were lowered to the ground, Private Hitch and Corporal Allan were waiting to give them cover as they made their way across the open space to the inner wall. One of the patients – Private Robert Cole, who had been suffering from fever – stumbled just a few feet short of the wall. Private Michael McMahon at once leapt over the wall and with little grace, but with startling proficiency, manhandled him to safety.

As Sidney Hunter of the Natal Mounted Police crawled across the yard, a Zulu leapt the barricade, ran over and thrust a spear between the Trooper's shoulder blades. A split-second later, the Zulu was hurled to the ground by a hail of bullets from the defenders behind the inner wall. Those members of the garrison still on their feet were now ensconced behind the inner wall, with the badly-wounded men sheltering in the eight-foot-high tea cosy of mealie bags constructed by Dunne. Surgeon Reynolds was treating the wounded on the veranda and continuing to pass out ammunition to those men still on the walls.

Padre Smith was also engaged in passing out ammunition – and prayers – in equal measure. He was also quick to rebuke any man he heard uttering an oath. The Zulu had taken possession of the cattle *kraal* – and from here, and on all other walls, their incessant attacks continued. By now, the defenders' rifles were almost too hot to hold from the continuous firing – and some men wrapped pieces of torn shirt around the barrels to protect their hands. In some cases, the Boxer cartridge jammed in the breech – the base being torn off by the extractors. This meant a frantic few minutes' work with a pocket knife to dig out the jammed round. Fouled barrels meant that the hearty kick from the Martini-Henry was now increased many fold – and all riflemen were suffering from badly-bruised shoulders. Some men fired their rifles from the opposite shoulder, the waist or braced against their chests to lessen the effect of the recoil. Through all of this, they suffered a terrible thirst – thirst generated by stress, fear, gun smoke and the stench of burning flesh coming from the burning hospital. As the night wore on, the Zulu attacks decreased in their ferocity, until by about 10.00pm the charges against the walls ceased.

The first light of Thursday, 23 January dawned on a sight of utter devastation. The defenders looked out from their small battered fort across a carpet of hundreds of Zulu dead. Everywhere they looked, there were bodies – some still writhing in agony from the wounds caused by the Boxer cartridge or well-thrust bayonet. Every defender had some injury or other, from bruised arms, burnt and blistered hands to serious stab wounds and Hitch's shattered shoulder. Across the mission station drifted smoke from the now burnt-out hospital – mingling with the disgusting odour of roasted flesh.

The Zulu had gone. In the remaining hours before dawn, they had begun to slip away back across the Buffalo River and into Zululand; now only the dead and wounded remained – laying siege to the mission station with their bodies. Privates Waters and Howard emerged from their hiding places – much to the surprise of the garrison, who had assumed them dead. Lieutenant Chard ordered out patrols to assess the situation and confirm that the enemy was no more. Henry Hook and Trooper Lugg both had close calls when they were separately attacked by warriors feigning death. Hook settled his with a swift thrust of the bayonet, while Lugg dispatched his assailant with a knife.

Zulu forces attack the ramparts, whilst in the background casualties are evacuated from the window of the hospital.

The relief of Rorke's Drift, 23 January 1879.

Chard called an officers' conference. In the event of another attack, it was decided to pull down the remains of the hospital to give a clear field of fire. A count was made of the remaining ammunition – and it was discovered that out of 20,000 rounds, only 900 remained.[17] At 7.00am a large body of Zulu were spotted to the south-west of the post – and Chard ordered all those fit men to stand to. The Zulu ignored the mission station and made their way back towards the Buffalo River. These warriors could see something denied to Chard: the remains of the centre column returning from a very uncomfortable night at Isandlwana. Lookouts perched on the roof of the storehouse peered towards the drift and saw a group of horsemen approaching. These proved to be Mounted Infantry of Chelmsford's column.

Losses to the garrison amounted to 15 killed during the action, while a further two died of their wounds. Among the dead were Acting Storekeeper Louis Byrne and Dubliner Private Garret Hayden, who was killed while a patient in the hospital. Byrne had been shot through the head while giving a drink of water to Corporal Scammel.[18]

17   Accounts vary in the actual number of rounds left, but it can be assumed that ammunition was at a premium.
18   *The Irish Times*, 17 May 1879.

What of the Zulu casualties? According to an account written by Lieutenant Chard, 351 warriors were buried on the day after the battle, with many more being found later in the surrounding countryside. Approximately 50 bloodstained shields were discovered on the banks of the Buffalo, and it was believed that the Zulu had dragged the badly-wounded to the bank and tipped them into the water. When the surviving garrison were met by Chelmsford's force retiring from Isandlwana, they manned the walls of the mission station not as Welshmen, Englishmen, Irishmen or heroes, but as soldiers – professionals who had simply done their duty as they had done so in the past, and who would continue to do so in the future.

Chelmsford withdrew his force back across the Buffalo River, while Rorke's Drift was properly fortified against any future attacks. It was named 'Fort Bromhead', which seemed only apt. It would be several months – and many reinforcements – before Chelmsford was ready to try again.

The left-hand column, under command of Colonel Evelyn Wood VC, had engaged a Zulu force at Hlobane on 21 January. Here the Zulu were defeated, but Wood was forced to break off any further action on hearing the news of Isandlwana.

Colonel Henry Evelyn Wood VC – commander of No.4 Column.

The mission station photographed in late 1879 after the position had been fortified and named 'Fort Bromhead'.

Some members of the 2nd Battalion, 24th Regiment, who defended Rorke's Drift.

Fort Bromhead from the rear of the position; note the walled cemetery, with its obelisk memorial, in the centre of the photograph.

The storehouse at Rorke's Drift with the thatched roof removed and the position loop-holed.

12

With Wood on the Offensive

Having heard the sound of firing from Isandlwana on 22 January – and assuming Chelmsford had found the battle he had been looking for – Wood decided to move against those Zulu in the area of Hlobane. A patrol Wood led out from camp came under fire from the slopes of the mountain – and the 13th Regiment, along with the Mounted Burghers, was sent to drive the enemy riflemen away. The Zulu refused to stand and decamped to both the heights and down to the plain. The men of the 90th Regiment left to garrison the camp at once took off after them – leaving said camp in the hands of a – few drummer boys and other supernumeraries. Those warriors on the mountain saw this – and at once a party was on its way to the supply wagons. Fortunately, Wood (from his position) also observed the rash movement of the 90th, and swiftly dispatched the Frontier Light Horse to intercept the enemy.

Camp of the 13th (1st Somersetshire) Prince Albert's Light Infantry and 90th (Perthshire Volunteers) Light Infantry on the Zulu border.

As all of this was happening, a messenger arrived from Chelmsford with the news of the disaster at Isandlwana. To Wood, what was to follow was all too logical: with Chelmsford forced to retreat back into Natal and Pearson besieged at Eshowe, his own column was the only remaining threat to Cetshwayo – and Cetshwayo knew it! At any time, he could expect the full force of the Zulu Army to fall on him – and his present campsite was not the position to fight a major battle. Wood immediately ordered the column to a spot some 20 miles to the west of Hlobane. This was Khambula – a saddle connecting the Zunguin Range to the Ngcaba-ga-Hwane.

The *Belfast News Letter*, 25 January 1879:

> Again the news is of happenings in Afghanistan. The local papers report news received from St. Petersburg that states Shere Ali will not come to St. Petersburg, but will remain at Tashkend. The *Golos* admits that England is *de facto* Sovereign of Afghanistan, and has every chance of success in Asia Minor. The *St. Petersburg Gazette* hears that Yakoob Khan has fled from Afghanistan.
>
> In the English Channel a French fishing smack was found with the crew of eight men frozen to death.

The *Belfast News Letter* of 27 January carries a report from the Special Correspondent of the Standard at Lord Chelmsford's headquarters; it is dated 3 January:

> Cetywayo, the Zulu King, refuses all the demands made upon him, and has assembled a corps of eight thousand fighting men on the border.
>
> General Lord Chelmsford and his staff leave Cape Town to-day for the front.
>
> The British troops will advance during the present week, all the necessary preparations having been completed. The British reinforcements have arrived.
>
> Maritzburg, January 6, – A *Gazette Extraordinary*, published today, announces that the High Commissioner has placed all matters connected with Zulu affairs in the hands of General Lord Chelmsford, but gives Cetywayo, the Zulu King, to the 11th January to make full and unconditional submission.
>
> A Reuter's Telegram dated 17 January from Cape Town reported the following. [sic] Official information reached here on the 3rd inst. that John Dunn had crossed the frontier and reported that Cetewayo intended fighting. General Lord Chelmsford has been instructed to take steps to compel the Zulu King to comply with all demands, but is willing to wait till the 11th for a final answer. Preparations are being made to cross the Jugela.[1]

---

1   The name 'Jugela' is how the Tugela is spelt in the original newspaper report.

13

At Eshowe

On 28 January, Pearson and his command was now firmly ensconced at Eshowe (referred to as 'Fort Ekowe' in original documents) and effectively under siege. He received a message from Chelmsford in which he explained that the unfortunate disaster experienced by No.2 Column at Isandlwana now placed Pearson in 'a very awkward position' – an understatement to say the least. As a result of this, Pearson held a Council of War with his officers – and a decision was taken to evacuate the fort. Wynne objected to this; his view, like that of Dunne and Dalton at Rorke's Drift, was to hold firm. Supported by Brevet Colonel Walker, AAG and Captain MacGregor, AQMG, Pearson gave the order to hold their ground.

In order to lessen the drain on food supplies at Eshowe, it was decided that Percy Barrow would take his horsemen back to Natal on 29 January. He left that afternoon accompanied by the 2nd Regiment, Natal Native Contingent. Eshowe was now in a state of siege. A total of 1,357 troops and 337 civilians were packed into an area of only 10,000 square yards – a space much too small for so many men. According to *The Soldier's Pocket-Book for Field Service* (3rd edition), which was written by Major General Sir Garnet Wolseley, a space of 150 x 120 yards (18,000 square yards) was recommended for an infantry battalion using tents in a restricted space. At Eshowe, more than double that number of men was to be housed under the supply wagons in a

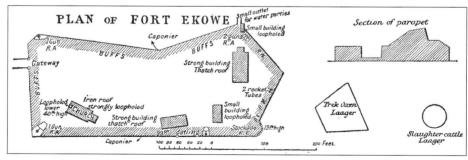

The plan of 'Fort Eshowe'.

The fortified kwaMondi mission station at Eshowe.

space of 10,000 square yards. As a result of the overcrowding and unsanitary conditions, Wynne was one of those to fall sick with chronic diarrhoea. It was the beginning of a downward spiral of illness and overwork that would eventually kill him.

On 30 January, the Zulu War rated only three lines in the local press. In a telegram dated 'Cape Town, January 7' it is stated: 'The rivers in Zululand are very full, and it is thought possible Cetywayo has not had time to communicate the British ultimatum to minor chiefs'. Also of note was a report of a meeting held in Berlin to discuss the plague sweeping Russia.

Under siege at Eshowe: 'Jack's Response'.

By March, it was evident to Cetshwayo that the war was about to enter its second phase. The white man had gathered his strength and was one again prepared to take on the black man for this small part of Africa. Evelyn Wood – entrenched at Khambula – was perceived as the most dangerous enemy at present. Since the defeat of Chelmsford in January, Wood had been a near-constant thorn in the side of the Zulu. After the reversal at Rorke's Drift, Cetshwayo was implicit with his instructions to his warriors: on no account were the British to be engaged if they were positioned behind any type of fortification. Instead, they must be drawn out onto the open ground, where a proper battle could be fought. If the British would not oblige, then the Zulu Army was to refuse to attack and proceed on into the Transvaal and hope that the 'red soldiers' would follow them. The Zulu Army assembled for the attack against Khambula was equal in size to that present at Isandlwana and contained many of the warriors that had fought there. Despite the severe losses they had suffered on 22 January, they believed themselves unbeatable. Certitude was reinforced by the large number of Martini-Henry rifles now carried by the warriors.

From the previous January, Wood had occupied a series of entrenched positions along the saddle connecting the Zunguin Range and the Ngcaba-ga-Hawane Range. South Africa was now in its summer months and the weather was hot and humid. Ever careful of his sanitary arrangements, Wood enforced the strictest protocol in the removal and disposal of both human and animal waste. All manure was carted from the laager to a dump some distance away and deep latrine trenches were dug for the garrison.

Despite all of this, Wood was forced to move the entire camp on several occasions – each new camp being fortified in the now normal manner. After the attack on Moriarty's column at Ntombe River, the Frontier Light Horse had given a vigorous pursuit, but despite an all-night ride in atrocious weather, they had been unable to catch up with the enemy. Shortly after this, Wood received a communication from Chelmsford informing him that he, Chelmsford, was going to make a relief march to Eshowe and suggested that Wood could carry out a diversion in an attempt to draw the Zulu away from Chelmsford's line of advance. Wood, ever ready to engage the enemy, agreed to this at once.

Since his initial repulse at Hlobane in January, Wood's command had not been idle. A force of mounted men had been sent to assist Rowlands at Luneberg. When, in turn, Rowlands had been dispatched to Pretoria to deal with a threat from the Boers, some of his men were attached to Wood's column. Added to this were troops that had survived the debacle at Isandlwana: the Edendale Troop, Natal Native Horse and the 1st Squadron, Mounted Infantry. In the ranks of the Mounted Infantry was Private John Power, 24th Regiment, from County Kilkenny. Power had survived Isandlwana and was to be awarded the Distinguished Conduct Medal for his actions at Gobatse and Hlobane – it being presented to him by Queen Victoria the following September at Windsor Castle.

In the following weeks, Buller and his riders raided far and wide – capturing cattle and burning Zulu homes – yet Wood had wanted to engage the Zulu in a major battle; and the request from Chelmsford gave him just such an opportunity. He decided to attack Hlobane. Wood had carried out a careful reconnaissance of the plateau and had estimated that the enemy presence was not less than 2,000 men.

The offensive was ordered for 27 March. Lieutenant Colonel Russell was tasked with creating a diversion by taking a force of some 600 men to the top of Tendega (Ntendeka) in order to block any escape attempt from the western end of the plateau. He was only to advance on to the plateau itself if in receipt of a direct order for assistance from Buller. Buller would lead the main assault, with just under 600 men advancing up the slightly easier route on the eastern side of the mountain. With the greater distance to travel, Buller left first. Among his force was the Frontier Light Horse, now led by Captain Robert Barton, while Knox Leet still led Wood's Irregulars. Attached to the force – and acting as 'artillery' support – was a Royal Artillery rocket detachment.

By the time the sun was setting, they had covered some 30 miles and had reached the base of the mountain. Here, Buller ordered a campsite to be prepared. Fires were lit, horses were unsaddled and preparations were made to settle down for the night. The prying eyes of any enemy would have been well-deceived. Shortly after darkness had descended, the horses were re-saddled and Buller led his men up the mountain. Within a few paces, it was obvious that this was to be no walk in the park. The hillside – much steeper than first realised – was covered in loose stones of varying size, which caused the horses to slip and slide. Some horses lost their footing completely and fell from the sides of the steep pathway to their deaths; others suffered broken legs and had to be shot. The reaction of

Private John Power, 1st Battalion, 24th Regiment.

Irregular forces on a cattle raid.

the Zulu to these gunshots in the dead of night have not been recorded, but is says little for a clandestine advance on an enemy position.

At 10.00pm Buller called a halt for a rest. Those men previously forced to shoot their horses collapsed under the weight of bridle and saddle (expensive items not to be left behind), while those still with mounts wrapped the reins around their wrists and settled down for a brief nap.

14

Hlobane, 28 March: 'Run like the Devil'

Just before dawn, Buller's men once again began their climb towards the plateau. As the party neared the top of the climb, a thunderstorm erupted from the still dark sky. It soon became obvious that this path – steep, treacherous and, at times, simply not there – was also something else. As the rain began to fall in torrents, the path became a riverbed for water spilling from the top of the plateau. Through the confusion of thunder, lightning and the falling waters, the Border Horse became separated from the main party. As they reached the summit, they were greeted by a defended barricade and concealed riflemen in caves that covered the slopes of the mountain. A volley of rifle fire then greeted Buller's men. This resulted in the deaths of two officers and two privates of the Frontier Light Horse, along with several horses.[1] This was not the position for a withdrawal – strategic or otherwise – and Buller immediately gave the order to attack. Quickly driving off those warriors who held this part of the summit, the horsemen rode towards the centre of the plateau.

As this was happening (approximately), Lieutenant Colonel Russell and his diversion were having trouble of their own. While they had successfully scaled Tendega, the path onto Hlobane was deemed difficult for men on foot and impossible for any mounted force – therefore Russell halted his command at the foot of the pass and sent Lieutenant Edward Browne, 24th Regiment, with 20 men of the Mounted Infantry up the slope on foot to attempt a rendezvous with Buller.[2] Wood, who had spent the night with Russell, decided to try and make his own way onto the plateau, using Buller's route. Riding around the base of the mountain – and accompanied by his personal staff (an escort of Mounted Infantry from the 90th Light Infantry and some 'loyal' Zulu) – he had almost reached the track when he met the Border Horse lost from the previous evening. Both the Horse and their commander, Colonel Weatherley, seemed to be in a state of near-panic. Weatherley was a well-experienced

---

1 The officers were Lieutenants Otto von Stietencron and George Williams.
2 This was a local rank, Browne was in fact a lieutenant.

officer – ex-regular army and well versed in fighting natives. Nevertheless, he and his men displayed a severe lack of enthusiasm for any further action.

As both parties neared the base of the plateau, a number of rifle shots were directed at them from behind fallen boulders and the caves in the hillside. One bullet shattered the spine of Mr Llewelyn Lloyd, Wood's political assistant and interpreter – causing a mortal wound.

A second shot felled Wood's horse, but Wood managed to escape injury.

An abaQulisi rifleman narrowly misses Wood, but mortally wounds Mr Llewellyn Lloyd.

Colonel Wood pinned beneath his horse.

The men of the Border Horse immediately scattered for cover – and when Wood ordered Weatherley into the attack, his men, with the exception of two officers, refused to advance.

At this point, Lieutenant and Captain The Honourable Ronald George Elidor Campbell, Coldstream Guards – Wood's staff officer – volunteered to go and, with some men from Wood's personal escort, advanced towards the enemy.

The majority of the fire seemed to be coming from one particular cave – and Campbell, accompanied by Lieutenant Lysons and Private Fowler, made a determined advance towards the entrance. The path towards the enemy was narrow and contorted – allowing passage in single file only. As Captain Campbell reached the mouth of the cave, a single shot rang out and struck Campbell in the head – killing him instantly.

Lysons and Fowler immediately ran forward and fired into the cave – killing the Zulu rifleman and, in turn, driving away others back up the hillside (killing several more in the process).

While Lieutenant Lysons remained to act as a rearguard, Captain Campbell's body was retrieved and brought back down the slope. Wood decided to bury Campbell and Lloyd at the base of the hill, despite being under fire from those warriors now gathering along the top of the plateau.

Lieutenant and Captain The Honourable Ronald George Elidor Campbell, 1st Battalion, Coldstream Guards.

Ronald Campbell assaults the cave containing the enemy riflemen only to be slain in the attack.

Second Lieutenant Henry Lysons, circa 1886, in the uniform of the Cameronians –The Scottish Rifles.

Private Edmund Fowler – photographed after 1882 when serving with the Royal Irish Regiment.

For their actions at Hlobane, both Lysons and Fowler would be awarded the Victoria Cross. Edmund John Fowler had been born in County Waterford in 1861 and would receive his Victoria Cross from the hand of Queen Victoria at Windsor in 1882. By this time, Fowler had taken his discharge from the 90th and had re-enlisted in the Royal Irish Regiment – serving in both the 1st and 2nd Battalions. In the same year he was awarded the Cross, he faced a court martial and was sentenced to lose all his medals – including his VC.

However, Her Majesty declined to approve this – perhaps feeling that such an action would be unjust, given the short time after his award being presented, and Fowler had his medals restored. He seems to have had less of an attachment, and sold it at Sotheby's in 1906 for the sum of £42. Today, it is held by the Cameronians Museum. He died at Colchester in Essex on 26 March 1926 and is buried in Colchester Cemetery.

By now, Weatherley had managed to not only get his own nerve under control, but had also managed to galvanise his command back into action – setting off to find Buller's trail up Hlobane.

After the burial service, Wood decided that it was too late to attempt to follow Buller and decided instead to return to the west side of the mountain to find out the situation with regard to Russell.

Meanwhile, on top of Hlobane, Buller and his men were busy rounding up Zulu cattle. The top of the plateau was largely flat, with several streams running across it and disappearing over the side. Here and there, areas were marshy – and some care had to be taken when riding. Those warriors found guarding the cattle were easily driven off. About halfway along the plateau, at its narrowest point, there was a slight rise covered with a scattering of boulders.

Here, Buller detailed a detachment of the Frontier Light Horse to act as a rearguard. The enemy were massing

Brevet Lieutenant Colonel Redvers Henry Buller, 60th (King's Royal Rifle Corps) Rifles.

on the eastern side of the plateau and had again blocked off the route Buller had used to gain access to the top. As Buller led his men along the plateau towards the west, he met up with Captain Browne of the Mounted Infantry. Browne's message from Russell was that it would be impossible to ascent the near-vertical escarpment with his command. On hearing this, Buller detailed Captain Robert Barton to take his Frontier Light Horse – some 30 men in total – and bury those men killed earlier. He was also to locate Weatherley. Shortly after, Barton had left Buller's attention was drawn to the plain below Hlobane to the south-west. The black mass that was some 20,000 Zulu warriors was coming – and it was coming fast!

Down on the plain, Wood was also aware of the approaching enemy. Lloyd had been the single Zulu-speaker in the party, and he was dead, but it required little in the way of interpretative skills to convey any warning to the waiting horsemen.

Back on the plateau, Buller immediately dispatched a note to Barton to 'return by the right of the mountain' – meaning that Barton should withdraw in the direction of Khambula. When the message reached Barton, he had already met up with Weatherley – and the outcome spelt disaster. In using the word 'right', as opposed to giving a specific geographical direction, Buller inadvertently sent the commands of Barton and Weatherley straight into the advancing Zulu *impi*. The outcome was in no doubt. As the *impi* advanced, it seemed to swallow up the horsemen; few escaped. Weatherley died fighting alongside his 15-year-old son, who had joined his father's unit as a Sub-Lieutenant. Captain Barton was almost clear when he saw that

Buller's rearguard action.

Lieutenant Pool had been unhorsed. Returning, he picked up the fallen officer – and after a fierce melee, managed to fight his way clear and make off towards the British camp. Hotly pursued by a number of Zulu, Barton managed to keep just ahead of the running warriors, but after some seven miles, his horse collapsed under the weight of two riders and the warriors closed in for the kill. It was all over very quickly.[3]

3   In a hand-written report, Buller blamed himself for the tragic loss of life due to his misinterpreted dispatch. However, another hand (possibly Wood's) struck out the self-accusation, censoring the transcript, which admitted the error.

The warriors on the plateau – seeing that reinforcements were at hand – now began to seriously harass Buller's men. Ordering the captured cattle to be left, Buller sent his native levies down the mountainside first. As the levies made it to the veldt below, they took to their heels, but were quickly outpaced by the fleet-footed Zulu and all were slaughtered. As the horsemen dismounted and began to make their way down the slope, encroaching warriors menaced them on all sides. Expected assistance from Russell was not forthcoming; another misconstrued message, this time from Wood, had seen Russell evacuate his position. Buller's only assistance was that offered by Browne and a modest party of Mounted Infantrymen. In the confusion of the descent down what would become known as 'The Devil's Pass', Buller formed a rearguard in an attempt to hold off the Zulu.

For a while, the tide was held – and there is no doubt that many men owe their lives to this action, but soon the press of enemy became too strong and Buller was forced to order back the rearguard. In an instant, all was chaos – and the withdrawal became a race against certain death.

As the Zulu fought with the retreating horsemen, some were dragged from their mounts and thrown to their deaths over the side of the mountain.

A magic lantern slide depicting the chaos on 'The Devil's Pass'.

A modern-day photograph of the lower plateau of Hlobane and 'The Devil's Pass'.
(Courtesy of Paul Naish)

Others, not wishing to meet the same fate, turned their weapons on themselves. Buller, Browne and Knox Leet all returned to the fray on many occasions to rescue those men who had become unhorsed in the descent. During the retreat from the mountain, Knox Leet saw Lieutenant Smith of the Frontier Light Horse fall from his mount. As the warriors closed in on the fallen man, Knox Leet rode in amongst them – firing his pistol with commendable accuracy – thus enabling Smith to climb up behind him. This action earned him the Victoria Cross.[4]

When it was obvious that any further action was futile, Buller order the men back to the camp at Khambula; the time was about noon. The action had cost the British and Colonials 17 officers and 82 white troops, along with approximately 100 African levies. Zulu losses were not recorded. One of those to survive Hlobane was Private J. Power from County Kilkenny; he had also survived Isandlwana and would survive the war to return to his home in Ireland.

4   Knox Leet received his VC from Queen Victoria at Windsor on 9 December 1879. He went on to command the 1st Somerset, Light Infantry and later exchanged to the 2nd Battalion, which he commanded in the Burma War of 1885-87. He retired in July of that year and was awarded the CB. He died the following year and was buried at Great Chard in Kent – and his name is listed on the Burma War Memorial in Taunton, Somerset.

A depiction of one of the rescues executed by Buller.

Buller rescues Cecil D'Arcy on 'The Devil's Pass'.

15

Khambula

The hammering received by Wood's cavalry on the previous day at Hlobane had, at least, served to act as a warning that further action was imminent. Reveille was sounded early at Khambula on the morning of 29 March and the garrison arose to make their final preparations. The British position was a classic one for defence against a native enemy: situated on a ridge – giving a clear field of fire for both rifles and artillery. Wood had constructed an earthen redoubt, which was connected to a wagon laager by a wooden palisade. Inside the latter were the transport oxen. Some 200 yards to the west of this was another laager. The wagons were chained together and surrounded by an outer ditch, with the spoil piled to the outside to form a breastwork.

Wood's scouts sight the Zulu advance towards Khambula.

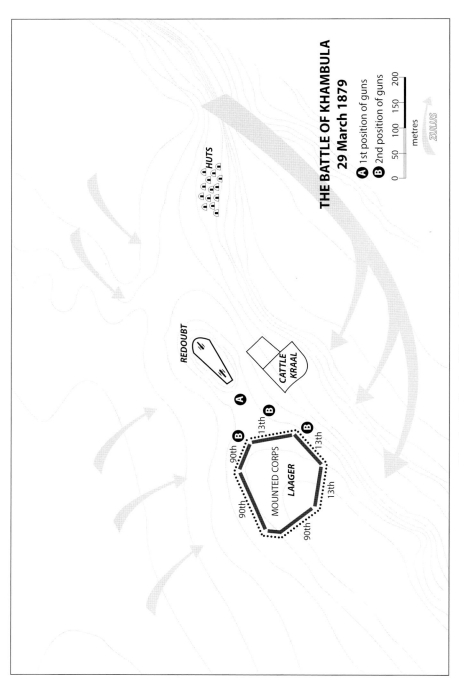

THE BATTLE OF KHAMBULA
29 March 1879

Ⓐ 1st position of guns
Ⓑ 2nd position of guns

0   50   100   150   200
metres

ZULUS

HUTS

REDOUBT

CATTLE KRAAL

Ⓐ

Ⓑ

90th

13th

Ⓑ

Ⓑ

13th

MOUNTED CORPS

LAAGER

90th

13th

90th

Map 5 – The Battle of Khambula, 29 March 1879.

Zulu amabutho assault the positions at Khambula.

The defences were garrisoned by just over 2,000 men. There were 15 companies of Imperial infantry: eight from the 90th Regiment and seven from the 1st Battalion of the 13th. Buller was also there with his ragtag and bobtail collection of Colonial cavalry – some of whom had fought at Isandlwana. The largest unit within Buller's command was the Frontier Light Horse (157 men), who despite their losses the previous day, were still in the mood for a fight – not to say revenge. Almost 200 of Wood's Irregulars remained in the camp; the others had dispersed after Hlobane. Artillery support came from six guns: four from 11/7 Battery, Royal Artillery, while the other two were unattached. Two of the guns were placed in the redoubt along with one company of the 90th, while one-and-a-half companies of the 13th were in the cattle laager. The other four guns were in the open space between here and the main wagon laager, with a 360 degree arc of fire if necessary. The remainder of the infantry and the cavalry were inside the main wagon laager.

One of Wood's mounted patrols spotted the Zulu leaving their camp on the White Umfolozi River[1] at approximately 10.30am. At first, it appeared as if the warriors would obey Cetshwayo's instructions and bypass Khambula – leaving Wood with no option but to follow them into the Transvaal.

1   Modern spelling: Mfolozi.

Nevertheless, pride and overconfidence won the day and the Zulu Army halted about four miles south of the camp and deployed for battle. The Zulu appeared to be in no great hurry and moved at their leisure about the surrounding hills.

Wood decided there was time for lunch; the British soldier, like many others, fights best on a full stomach. Reserve ammunition was positioned directly behind the barricades and the surgeons laid out the tools of their trade. Some surgeons also loaded their revolvers in case there was the chance of a pot-shot at the enemy; the Geneva Convention would seem not to have been applied too rigorously in South Africa! Just before 1.00pm the call to arms was sounded and the tents struck to clear the fields of fire. Those men who had been at the tail end of the dinner queue were faced with the choice of throwing their meal away, or somehow saving it for after the battle. 'Old soldiers' opted for the latter. By now, the enemy were almost ready. The Zulu 'left horn' was to the south of the camp, while the 'right' was to the north. The 'chest' was positioned on the eastern side of the ridge. Despite having the greatest distance to cover to arrive at their attack position, the 'right horn' elected to attack first. At 1.30pm the iNgobamakhosi Regiment advanced towards the waiting redcoats on top of the ridge. They were almost a mile distant at this point – a mile of open ground, sloping up towards the laager; ground bereft of cover, save for a few scattered ant-hills. Hoping to bring the iNgobamakhosi ahead of the other regiments, Wood ordered Buller out from the laager to try and provoke an early attack. The irrepressible Buller galloped out at the head of about 100 men and rode to within easy range of the Zulu. Dismounting, they fired a stinging volley into the waiting ranks. The result was almost predictable: screaming their war cry '*Usuthu!*' the mass of warriors surged towards the skirmish line like a tidal wave.

Springing into the saddle, the riders quickly fell back a mere 50 yards or so before dismounting to repeat the performance. Each time the charging warriors looked as if they were going to catch the horsemen, they galloped back a little further. No matter how quickly a Zulu can run, a horse is just that little bit quicker – well that's the theory anyway! Nevertheless, it took a cool head and a steady command to carry out such manoeuvres – and Buller had both.

With the cry of "We are the boys from Isandlwana!" ringing in their ears, Buller's men retired onto the wagon laager. However, a portion of the cavalry declined the safety of the laager. The men of the Natal Native Horse (approximately 70 men) had been at Isandlwana – and not unnaturally, had a certain distrust of British-defended positions. They elected to remain outside for the remainder of the battle – causing a fair degree of annoyance and harassment to the Zulu flanks throughout the action. Inside the laager, the redcoats held their fire, while the artillery opened a salvo of shrapnel shells towards the oncoming enemy. At a range of 400 yards, the Martini-Henrys in the laager and redoubt fired almost as one. The leading ranks of the iNgobamakhosi disintegrated as the heavy lead slugs tore into them. Some warriors, hit by several bullets, seemed to almost come apart. A few warriors, both incredibly brave and lucky, survived long enough to reach the wagons, but there was no way inside – and all were ruthlessly shot or bayoneted as they struggled over the defences. For the

'We're the boys from Isandlwana': Zulu warriors charging into the attack.

remainder, there was nothing to do but lie on the ground and seek such scant cover as was available. Wherever they moved to, the rifle fire searched them out – and they were forced back into more solid cover offered by a fold in the ground to the north-east. All that remained in front of the wagon laager were the dead and the dying. It had taken just 45 minutes.

A Mounted Infantry officer under fire.

Wood's plan had worked. With one of the Zulu 'horns' blunted, there was now little chance of a combined attack on all sides of his defences at the one time. Nevertheless, the 'left horn' now had to be dealt with – and here the Zulu had a distinct advantage. A steep valley covered the advance towards the southern flank of the camp. Here, hidden ground allowed the Zulu to approach to the base of the hill – and on its western end, a streamlet had formed a trail that allowed access to the top of the plateau (emerging practically in the middle of Wood's position). As the mass of warriors swarmed up the slope, they were met with volley after volley of concentrated firepower. By mid-afternoon, these charges had not slackened – and there was a moment when it looked as if the Zulu might just be successful. A group of warriors made it into the cattle *kraal* fighting hand-to-hand with the men stationed there – the fighting going on under and above the cattle still penned in the *kraal*. Wood immediately ordered the men out of the *kraal* and back to the main position. The warriors poured into the vacated position – and those armed with rifles began a fierce (but inaccurate) fire against the British. Encouraged by this success, the warriors renewed their charges from the dead ground up against the plateau. Unable to bring any degree of fire against these warriors as they assembled for their charges, Wood ordered Major Robert Hackett to advance with two companies of the 90th Regiment to the edge of the plateau and to direct their fire down into the valley.

Without hesitation, Hackett and his men left the relative safety of the laager and advanced in extended line to the rim of the valley. Here they poured accurate and

Brevet Major Robert Henry Hackett, 90th (Perthshire Volunteers) Light Infantry.

Hackett's sortie.

rapid volleys into the surprised Zulu. In a few minutes, large numbers of warriors were felled by the concentrated rain of heavy lead slugs pouring into the packed masses from above. Perceptibly, the Zulu fell back deeper into the valley – taking cover in the rocks.

Hackett had little time to enjoy his success: Zulu rifle fire from the captured cattle *kraal* on his left flank began to have an effect on his men. Seeing this, Wood ordered the four guns and those infantry in the redoubt to concentrate their fire on the cattle *kraal* in an attempt to drive out the enemy riflemen. As this was happening, warriors of the extreme 'left horn' of the Zulu force had managed to gain a foothold on the top of the ridge – and they too began to fire into the right flank of Hackett's men. 'E' Company of the 13th Regiment were dispatched from the main laager – and they managed to prevent them from forming up for a charge, but were unable to drive them from the ridge. The Zulu fell back a little way and took possession of the camp rubbish dump! Here was a large pile of horse and ox manure – liberally grown over with fresh grass – although 'fresh' is probably the wrong word to describe it! From here, a number of Zulu riflemen opened fire on Hackett's line and the southern flank of the laager. Receiving fire from both flanks, the men of the 90th soon started to suffer casualties. Lieutenant Bright was bowled off his feet by a bullet that passed through both of his legs. Hackett fell next – a bullet through the temple. His two companies were recalled – and picking up their wounded, fell back to the main laager. Hackett survived this horrific wound, but was left blind. Lieutenant Bright bled to death before the surgeons noticed the seriousness of his wounds.

Second Lieutenant Arthur
Tyndall Bright.

Back in the main laager, the fire from the dung heap had come to the notice of
Buller. Gathering a party of riflemen, he ordered them to fire directly into the pile of
manure. Horse and ox manure – even that which has baked in the South African sun
for a time – is no barrier against the bullet of a Martini-Henry. The following day,
over 60 corpses would be discovered behind the dump. By late afternoon, it was clear
that the Zulu attack had failed. They surrounded Wood's position on three sides – and
their attacks, even those delivered in the late afternoon, had come perilously close to
success. At 5.00pm Wood ordered a contingent of the 13th Regiment to clear any
surviving Zulu from the cattle *kraal*, while men from the 90th again advanced to the
rim of the valley and drove off with the bayonet any who lingered there. Once more
delivering volleys into the bottom of the valley, they forced the warriors to retreat –
and a retreat only; this was no rout. The warriors went slowly – occasionally turning
to fire back at the British and, as usual, taking away their wounded. Now it was time
for the *coup de grace*. Buller and his cavalry tore out of the laager and had their revenge
for Khambula, Isandlwana and any other grievance real or imagined. As the horsemen
emerged onto the open veldt, the Zulu withdrawal disintegrated. Exhausted by the

battle, many warriors had no strength left to flee and simply stood waiting for death; some committed suicide. The cavalry showed no mercy – shooting from the saddle and even using abandoned Zulu spears to kill the fleeing warriors. For 12 miles the slaughter continued; some men only stopped killing when they ran out of ammunition, or their arms were too tired to use the spears.

How many died in this carnival of death is not known, but it must have easily exceeded a thousand. Almost 800 were recovered from the immediate area of the camp; they were buried in mass graves. Losses to the Zulu for the entire action probably exceeded 3,000. British losses were a mere trifle in comparison: 18 other ranks killed, with eight officers and 57 other ranks wounded – of whom 10 later died.

For the Zulu, an ample supply of guns and ammunition was not enough. A lack of proper instruction and practice ensured that the warriors still fired too high – and much of their firepower was wasted. At both Khambula and Gingindlovu, most of this fire went into the wagon laager and hit wounded men waiting to be treated by the surgeons.

The following letter is from Private John F. Henry, 1st Battalion, 13th Regiment of Wood's column, to his brother in Belfast. It was published in the *Belfast News Letter* on 19 May:

Camp Khambula, Zululand,
April 7, 1879.

I take the earliest opportunity of informing you of my safety, and sending you a few particulars of our latest fighting.

On the 27th March, a patrol, consisting of the whole of our mounted volunteers and a portion of the Imperial mounted infantry, the whole being under the command of Colonel Wood, V.C., C.B., started for the Insandani Mountain, which is known to be a great stronghold of the renegade Umbelini. Our patrol arrived safely on the top of the mountain, and, after skirmishing for some time, began to retire slowly, our own native levies driving away all the cattle. Immediately after the retiring movement they were surrounded by a large "impi" of Zulus, who butchered everyone that came in their way. Our loss was ten officers and eighty men killed. There were very few wounded, as most of the men were assegaied. The remnants of the patrol returned to camp the same evening, and the rumour quickly spread that nearly the whole of Cetywayo's available force intended attacking our camp. Preparations were at once made to give them a 'suitable reception', but the night came and the morning also, yet still no attack. About 11 a.m. on the 29th, scouts brought the information that this main impi, in conjunction with Umbelini's, were advancing quickly on the camp. The 'alarm' was shortly after sounded, the cattle driven in, and everything was done to make all 'taut'. The first shot was fired at seventeen minutes to two; and the steadiness and determination with which the serried battalions of the Zulu King came to the assault was a sight to be seen once in a lifetime. Zulu spies estimate the number engaged at 25,000. The firing was terrific, the artillery doing great execution with the 7-pounders. The fighting lasted till fifteen minutes to six, when the Zulus retreated in the greatest disorder, pursued by our mounted men, and shelled by the guns. The number of dead Zulus found in the immediate vicinity of the camp amounted to about 3,000, while the roads for miles in all directions are literally strewn with dead and wounded. Our loss was 2 officers and 25 men killed and 45 wounded, some fatally. Among the killed were three Belfast men, named respectively Hayes, Montgomery, and Duncan, while three or four more belong to the North of Ireland. So you will see that the Belfast men were doing their duty. The total Zulu loss is fully 5,000 killed and double that number wounded. So ended the great victory at Khambula, in which 2,400 men (of every colour and branch) fought the flower of the Zulu army, numbering 25,000 men, and after four and a half hours' desperate fighting succeeded in revenging their comrades at the ill-fated Isandula.[2] This should silence the croakers at home who talk about the British soldier having deteriorated. Fatigue parties have been engaged for the last two or three days in burying the dead, who are taken away in waggon loads. A great many of the rifles taken from the 24th Regiment were recovered, and an immense amount of Martini Henri [sic] ammunition has been found lying on the battlefield.

Our column has not received any reinforcements yet, but I believe they are on their way up. We have not been annoyed since they attacked the camp, and everything in this direction is quiet. Five or six of the wounded have died since the engagement.

We have had plenty of hard work, and the food we get is of the worst description-but, of course we cannot complain as the answer is 'You are in the field!' and that means that you must put up with everything. It is over two years now since we have lain in a bed, and during that time we have had nothing but tents and two blankets. We have had our clothes on for nearly four months, in addition to sleeping with our belts on, and our rifles at hand, ready to turn out at a moment's notice. But our men enjoy pretty good health through it all. I do not believe the war will last long when the reinforcements are to the front, and hope (God willing) to see you all again.

The following letter from Private William MacDonald – also serving with Colonel Wood's column – to his parents in Belfast again describes the action at Khambula:

Dear Parents – It is with grateful thanks to Almighty God that I am spared that I now write to you after one of the greatest battles that ever was fought in South Africa. The first of the engagement took place about eighteen miles from the camp, between our volunteers and the Zulus. The volunteers left the camp on

2   An alternative spelling of Isandlwana.

the 27th of the month, and they engaged the Zulus on the morning of the 28th. The volunteers were defeated, with the loss of 100 men. They came back that evening in great confusion, many horses without riders, shouting that the Zulus were after them. Well, we put our camp in the best state of defence we could. You may be sure that we did not sleep much that night. Our out-lying picquets were on the alert, looking and expecting them all night. They did not come; so the next morning we thought that they had taken another direction; but we were mistaken. About half past ten our mounted vedettes came flying in with the news that there were about 25,000 Zulus marching on our camp. Well, in another hour we could see them coming in all directions over the hills. It was an awful sight, as we were only about 2,300 strong, and thinking on the massacre of the poor 24th at Isandula, we were in rather an excited state, but only for a short time, for British pluck is not to be cooled by the appearance of savage hordes. So on they came, column after column. All this time our men were working away strengthening our waggon laagers. One we have for the cattle, and the other for the volunteers, with their horses who were camped inside. There was one company of ours in charge of the cattle laager; they were very weak, only about forty men. The 90th Regiment were on the rear face of the laager, with some of the volunteers, and the 13th Regiment and volunteers took charge of the remainder of the laager. Well, the dinner bugle sounded, and we thought that we would have time to have our dinner before the Zulus would get within range of us. I was bringing my accoutrements up to the laager to be ready when the alarm was sounded, with my dinner in my hand. Before I got the length of the laager "To arms" was sounded, so the dinner was put to one side, and every man hurried to his post, some poor fellows never to eat any more. Well, the Zulus tried the same move with us as with the 24th; but Colonel Wood is too old a soldier for them, so he sent out the mounted men to meet them. They engaged them until they got within range of our guns. Then the battle commenced. We were mowing them down in hundreds; but still they came on in the face of a most deadly fire. They were very brave men. On they came. Well, we get them broken a little, and then charged out of the laager. They retired, and we followed, cheering and firing all the time, the 7-pounder guns shelling them as they ran over the field, and we following them with a raking fire of rifles. They were well armed, as they got all the rifles of the 24th, with the ammunition. There were 28 men on our side killed, and I think 80 wounded. There were three Belfast men killed. Their names are Duncan, Hayes, and Montgomery. I am afraid that some of the wounded will not recover. There was a poor fellow named Sam Redpath from about Tandragee shot. He was some friend of the Redpaths that lived in Gamble Street. He was shot on my left. I had some very narrow escapes, but, thanks to the Almighty, I did not receive a scratch.

Both of the articles below took up less than three column inches in the paper of 3 February. Twice as much space was devoted to the happenings in Afghanistan, and

The Currie Line ship *Dublin Castle*, which was used as a hired troop transport.

twice as much again to an ice-skating excursion onto the frozen waters of Lough Neagh in County Antrim.

A Central News telegram printed in the *Belfast News Letter* announces that hostilities have commenced in the Zulu War! 'Advices of the 14th January from Cape Town per Messers. [sic] Donald Currie & Co.'s steamer Dublin Castle, state that the fighting had commenced with the Zulus and the Imperial troops'.

A Reuters telegram in the same paper gives a little more detail:

> Cape Town, January 14 (by telegram from Madeira), – Cetywayo not having replied up to the 11th inst., the British troops crossed the Umgena and Tugela Rivers on the 12th, and encamped on Zulu territory. The British force has hitherto encountered no opposition. Cetywayo is reported to be afraid of the peace party which is strongly amongst the Zulus. It is expected that but feeble resistance will be offered.
>
> Major Lanyon[3] has been appointed Lieutenant Governor of the Transvaal.
>
> Sir Bartle Frere is at Pietermaritzburg, and will leave on the 20th for the Transvaal.

3   Major William Owen Lanyon (1842-1887) was born in Antrim. The son of Sir Charles Lanyon, Member of Parliament for Belfast, Lanyon was one of Wolseley's 'Ashanti Ring'. He served as a colonial administrator in Southern Africa from 1873 after being invalided out for the Ashanti War.

16

The War Continues

On 4 February, a patrol led by Brevet Lieutenant Colonel Wilsone Black of the 1st Battalion, 24th Regiment found the bodies of Melvill and Coghill lying where they had been killed; several dead natives were lying close by. The two men had not had their stomachs slashed. Either they had killed all of their attackers in the melee, or these natives were not Zulu.[1]

The men were buried in a grave in the shelter of the rocks near where they fell. The Rev George Smith, who had served in the defence of Rorke's Drift, carried out the funeral service.[2]

The patrol then carried out a search of the river for the lost colour. Since 22 January, the river had subsided by three feet – and the staff was found within a short time. Close by, the flag was also found – ripped from the colour pole by the force of the water. The ragged flag and staff were taken back to Helpmekaar and presented to Colonel Glyn in what many describe as a very moving ceremony.

1   The Zulu are not known as a nation of swimmers, and it is a tradition taken from oral Zulu sources that Sothondose – a local headman – and some of his people were watching the struggle being enacted on the riverbanks. A Zulu *induna*, Zibhebhu kaMapita, is supposed to have called across the river to Sothondose – urging him to kill the white men, or he would cross at a drift upstream and kill not only the whites, but also the headman and his people.
2   On 14 April, the bodies were exhumed and reburied in coffins about 10 paces from where they fell.

Brevet Lieutenant Colonel
Wilsone Black, 1st Battalion,
24th (2nd Warwickshire)
Regiment.

The recovery of the Queen's colour of the 1st Battalion, 24th (2nd Warwickshire) Regiment
from the Buffalo River.

The burial of Melvill and Coghill.

The graves of Melvill and Coghill.

The return of the lost colour; men wept.

The following appeared in the *Belfast News Letter* of 18 March 1879:

THE ZULU WAR
THE RECOVERY OF THE 24th COLOURS

The route by the downward course of the Buffalo River was strewn with dead bodies, those of the natives composing the majority, these being members of the Natal Native Contingent or loyal natives who believed in the supreme power of the Government, or the magical effect of the boundary line even to the last. When the steep path leading down the precipitous rocks to the river was reached scouts were posted. A descent was made, and half way down, nearly half a mile from the river, lay the bodies of Adjutant Melville [sic] and Lieutenant Coghill. These were decently interred, and service was performed by the chaplain. Lieutenant Coghill's ring, Adjutant Melville's spurs, and other articles belonging to the brave fellows being carefully taken charge of by their comrades. The path thence to the river, was strewn with dead Zulus and various paraphernalia of savage warfare. Arrived at the river the dead horses, saddles, stirrups, spurs, leggings, charms, and articles of native dress, accidentally or purposely cast off, lying by the roaring stream, foaming over huge boulders, passing between precipitous cliffs covered with bush and aloes, showed the spot where the rushing torrent and savage foe alike overwhelmed many brave men. About 500 yards below, at the crossing place, Mr Harbour, of Commandant Lonsdale's corps, succeeded in finding the Queen's colours of the 1–24th Regiment, with the pole complete, injured by the action of the rapid stream but otherwise untouched. The gilt lion and crown surmounting the pole and the colour case were found by two other of Lonsdale's men a few yards lower down. These colours were borne back at the head of the little cavalcade in triumph, and when Rorke's Drift was reached the soldiers left their dinners, or whatever occupation they were engaged upon, overjoyed at the sight of their lost colours regained, and gave the heartiest cheers for the old flag and for Major Black and the volunteers who had recovered them. Major Black, in a few, well-chosen words, then handed the colours to Colonel Glyn, amidst loud huzzas, and the colonel, with heartfelt emotion, on behalf of himself and his regiment, thanked the little band for the noble work they had voluntarily undertaken and successfully performed.

Even allowing for a degree of artistic licence on the part of the reporter, this article reinforces the distance covered by Melvill and Coghill after they had crossed the Buffalo River. Mention of the path being 'strewn' with Zulu bodies between the two men and the river is also evidence that some form of fighting withdrawal was made.

The same article reports in a telegram dated 'Cape Town 24 February' that General Chelmsford claims the disaster at Isandlwana was caused by tactical errors on the part of those in command and the difficulty of procuring ammunition:

IN MEMORIAM.

Lieut. N. J. A. COGHILL.

Lieut. T. MELVILL.

Killed whilst Saving the Colours of the 24th Regiment at Isandhlwana.

In Memoriam.

THE ZULU WAR

TERRIBLE ENGAGEMENT

DISASTROUS DEFEAT OF THE BRITISH

RETIREMENT OF LORD CHELMSFORD

These were the headlines that appeared in the *Belfast News Letter* of 11 February 1879.

The local papers of 12 February reported that the 88th Connaught Rangers have been ordered to embark immediately from Mauritius and other reinforcements are ordered from Bombay, 13 days' distant.

In *The Irish Times*, there was a report from Aldershot:

The news of the British disaster was received here with astonishment and consternation. Many officers declare that bad general-ship [sic] must have been shown somewhere or the convoy attacked by the Zulus would not have been so exposed to so formidable an attack. Mess conversation was strong on what should be done, firstly a change of command, Lord Napier of Magdala or Sir Garnet Wolseley to take charge of the British forces.

Belfast newspapers of 18 February reported that the previous day, Major General Bell VC – commanding the Belfast District – inspected the volunteers of the 104th Fusiliers previous to their departure to join their new regiments:

> The men underwent a searching medical examination on Saturday, and later in the day received their foreign-service equipment, excepting the tropical helmet, which they will receive immediately on joining their respective regiments. The major general expressed himself as highly satisfied with the appearance of the men and their qualifications for active service, and congratulated the officer commanding on the promptitude displayed by his men in volunteering for the front. The draft for the 21st North British Fusiliers at present quartered at the Curragh Camp will leave Belfast by the 10.00am train to-day en route to head-quarters, which will embark at Queenstown on the 24th. As we have already mentioned, the draft for the 94th will proceed to Aldershot, but at what date is yet uncertain.

It was also reported that the War Department had decided to equip the 'M' and 'N' Batteries of the 6th Brigade, Royal Artillery with 9-pounders in lieu of 7-pounders. As well as this, workmen in the Woolwich Royal Arsenal were busy preparing and packing one million ball cartridges destined for Zululand:[3]

> These along with other armaments and equipment are being transported from Woolwich to the ports of Southampton and Plymouth by special trains. These special war trains run at high speed directly from the depots to the dockside and all other rail transport, even the Royal Mail, being subservient to them.

The same newspaper carries the story that 3rd Battalion, 60th Rifles – in preparing to depart for South Africa – had disposed of the regimental property (including the billiard table and the contents of the library, which had been sold at public auction).

A certain vicious theme was beginning to appear in the newspapers. In *The Irish Times* of 18 February, the following was printed:

---

3   Such was the demand for cartridges that factories in both Belgium and France supplied ammunition.

JAM FOR THE ZULUS

In the *Sporting Gazette*, the 'Man about Town' says: – I trust that amongst the loot stores seized by these fellows they found plenty of blister ointment as did their predecessors during the later war. Some of the most adventurous discovering pots of it amongst the medical stores mistook it for 'real jam', and the effect upon their constitutions cost many of them their lives, being far worse than that of an embrocation which a colleague friend of mine took internally, and nearly lost his life by doing so a few years since.

Surgeon Major William Elgee, Army Medical Department (from County Armagh), received orders on 19 February to hold himself in immediate readiness for service in South Africa. He would arrive on 30 March and be appointed to serve aboard the hospital ship *Pretoria* until January 1882. (Elgee died on 11 April 1910 – having been awarded the South African Medal for 1879.)

The first casualty lists from Isandlwana were published in the local press on 7 March, while the *Belfast News Letter* of 14 March carried this report on the actions of Surgeon Reynolds at Rorke's Drift:

BRAVERY OF A MEDICAL OFFICER

Dr. Reynolds shares the honours of defending Rorke's House when attacked by the Zulus and it is hoped that this heroic conduct will receive suitable recognition. One of the wounded men states as follows: – "After the niggers surrounded us we fought like tigers. I saw Dr. Reynolds, A.M.D., blazing away at them, cheering the ones that were hit; running to the fellow, dressing his wounds, then fighting away like a hero. He and the Hospital Corps men defended the hospital to the last moment. When the Zulus got in they charged through them and got into the laager behind waggons and mealie bags, where they fought like true Britons until daylight. They made several sorties, and drove them off splendidly."

Surgeon Reynolds, writing the next day, reporting the loss of hospital stores, never mentions a single word about himself, but simply states – "I am glad to say that the men behaved splendidly."

17

Myer's Drift, Ntombe River

Five companies of the 80th Foot were stationed at the town of Luneberg under the command of Brevet Major Charles Tucker.

In late February, an ammunition and supply convoy had left from Lydenburg bound for Natal. On 3 March, Tucker dispatched Captain David Barry Moriarty and his company to escort the convoy into the town. Moriarty had been born in Killmallock, County Limerick in 1837; he was the younger brother of John Moriarty, solicitor of Mallow. Another brother, Surgeon Major Thomas Moriarty, was currently serving in Afghanistan.[1] David Moriarty had joined the army during the Crimean War – gaining an Ensigncy in the 6th Foot (Royal Warwickshire Regiment). He was present during the siege of Sebastopol and had later served in the Indian Mutiny.[2] He had spent five years on half-pay prior to 1879. His party consisted of two lieutenants, Surgeon Cobbins, a civilian and 103 other ranks.

Within two hours of leaving Luneberg, the column had reached Myer's Drift on the Ntombe River. Here they found the river had spread its banks to a width of some 50 yards – swollen by the recent heavy rains.

Seven wagons of the expected convoy had arrived at the north bank, but were unable to cross the drift due to the swiftly-rushing river. The remainder of the day was spent constructing a raft – and by the following morning, the company (less two platoons) had crossed to the far bank. Moriarty detailed one of his lieutenants and the two platoons to remain on the southern bank and work on the approaches to the

---

1   Thomas Moriarty was born at Grange, County Limerick on 26 May 1837. He had gained his BA from RUI in 1858 and his MD in 1860. He had served in the Jowaki campaign of 1864 – being awarded the Campaign Clasp. From here, he had been posted to Afghanistan. He retired on half-pay with the rank of Brigade Surgeon on 3 January 1881 and died at Cork on 14 October 1912.

     On the same day that David Moriarity's death was reported in the local press, there was news that the British reconnaissance in Afghanistan had pushed forward as far as Gundamuk.
2   *Belfast Morning Telegraph*, 11 April 1879.

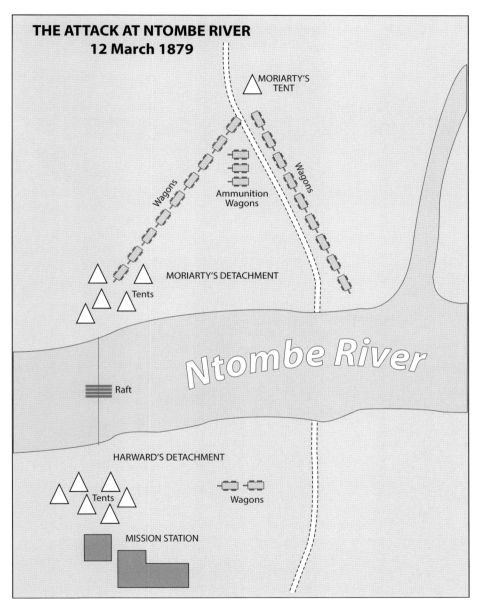

Map 6 – The attack at Ntombe River, 12 March 1879.

Major Charles Tucker, 80th (Staffordshire Volunteers) Regiment; photograph circa 1896.

Captain David Barry Moriarty, 80th Regiment.

A wagon convoy under escort by the 80th Regiment.

drift, which were quickly dissolving into thick glutinous mud. A further detail was ordered to remain on the northern bank to establish a campsite, while Moriarty led the remainder in search of the missing wagons. The convoy was found some several miles to the north. It had halted – and the 11 civilian drivers were more than glad to see Moriarty and his men. When their escort had abandoned them, they had laagered the wagons and settled down to await rescue. Natives from close-by *umuzis* had driven off some of the oxen and managed to plunder several of the wagons.

With the remaining oxen, it was impossible to move the entire convoy at once and the wagons had to be moved a few at a time down to the drift. This task was completed by 9 March, but still the river was in full flow – running with a 7-knot current, which made it impossible to take the wagons across. During a previous lull in the weather, those men left behind had managed to get two of the first wagons across, but the river had risen again and now there was nothing to do but wait for it to subside. Moriarty arranged his 16 wagons in an inverted 'V', with the legs of the 'V' resting some 20 yards from the riverbank. There was a large gap between each wagon – and no attempt was made to fill them with thorn, scrub or any other form of barricade. While the ammunition carts and remaining oxen were taken inside the laager, for some reason, Moriarty chose to pitch his own tent outside (on the road at the apex of the laager).

Myer's Drift today – looking across from Booth's position to where the main convoy was encamped. (Courtesy of Paul Naish)

Lieutenant Henry
Hollingworth Harward,
80th Regiment.

On 11 March, Major Tucker arrived from Luneberg to see how operations were progressing. Another officer of the 80th Foot, Lieutenant Henry Hollingworth Harward – a veteran of the Ashanti campaign – accompanied him.

Tucker was unhappy with Moriarty's layout north of the river. In his opinion, the wagons provided little or no protection in case of attack, but his comments fell on deaf ears. It would appear that like lemmings, some of Victoria's officers were slow to learn. Moriarty was confident that he would be able to get the remainder of the wagons across the Ntombe the following day. Tucker departed – taking the two lieutenants with him and leaving Harward in their place.

Harward took command of the wagons and men south of the river. Like Moriarty, he posted no advance pickets – being content with a single sentry on either side of the camp. As darkness fell, it began to rain – and as the night wore on, a thick mist developed, which brought visibility down to almost nil. At approximately 4.00am, a single rifle shot was heard from the direction of the north bank. Lieutenant Harward immediately had his men stand to and sent a runner across the river to ascertain the situation on the far bank. Within a short time, the runner returned – informing the Lieutenant that Captain Moriarty had been told of the gunshot and had turned out his men. In fact, Moriarty did no such thing; apparently, he went back to sleep without giving his men any orders whatsoever.

By 5.00am the rain had ceased and the mist began to clear. The morning silence was suddenly broken by the crash of gunfire. The men on the south bank watched in trepidation as a horde of approximately 800 Zulu charged from less than 70 yards into the laager. Even as Moriarty emerged from his tent – calling "Guards out!" – his men were being slaughtered. The Zulu were everywhere – cutting and stabbing at men still asleep and those struggling to grab rifles and equipment. South of the river, Lieutenant Harward ordered his men to open fire in an attempt to provide some support. As the Martini-Henrys blazed out from the south bank, a group of some 200 Zulu broke off from the main attack and charged into the river towards Harward and his men.

Back on the north bank, Moriarty was seen by one of the wagon drivers – Josiah Sussens – to be surrounded by Zulu. The Captain fought like a cornered tiger. Killing

Prince Mbilini waMswati's attack on the encamped convoy.

the first three Zulu with shots from his pistol, he seized a fallen warrior's *assegai* and began fighting his way down towards the river. As he bulldozed his way along the side of the laager, a spear thudded into him, but still he fought on – slashing his way through Zulu as if they were ripe corn. Abruptly, a musket ball smashed into his chest – knocking him off his feet. As he fell, he called out: "I'm done! Fire away boys! Death or glory!" The Zulu swiftly moved in for the kill – and the spears ended the life of an officer who while he may not have known the value of a wagon laager, certainly knew how to fight.

South of the river, Lieutenant Harward and his men were fully engaged with their own fight for survival. Josiah Sussens emerged from the river – stark naked – and in the middle of a battle as bad (if not worse) than the one he had just escaped from. The remainder of the two platoons under Harward and those men who had escaped from the north bank were gathered into isolated groups; they had formed into rallying squares. In this formation – resembling ragged circles – they were attempting to fight their way clear of the chaos of the campsite. Sussens decided to make a run for Luneberg. As he made his way along the side of the road – dodging scattered groups of Zulu – he came across a Sergeant and a number of the 80th that seemed to be retiring in good order. The NCO was Sergeant Anthony Clarke Booth from Brierley Hill, Staffordshire. He had with him Lance Corporal Burgess and seven other men. They were properly equipped, had full pouches of ammunition and were pouring deadly volleys of fire into any Zulu that came too close for comfort. Sussens joined them – and was grateful for the offer of a greatcoat to cover his embarrassment! Lieutenant Harward had remained with his men until close to the end. It was he who

A cigarette card depicting Sergeant Anthony Booth rallying the survivors of the attack.

ordered Booth to retire to a deserted farmhouse some two miles away across flat open veldt, while he rode for help.

By 6.00am, he was at Luneberg – and within a short time, Major Tucker had assembled a mounted force (along with two of the three garrison companies) and was heading for the drift. When they arrived at the battle scene, Sergeant Booth[3] had lost four men from his command. The camp had been thoroughly ransacked of anything valuable – including all arms and ammunition. Captain Moriarty and the bulk of his command lay dead – and the Zulu were long gone. Another disaster did not sit well with the high command in Natal: while a well-deserved Victoria Cross was awarded to Sergeant Booth, a scapegoat was required. With Moriarty dead, Lieutenant Harward was tried before a court martial. Nevertheless, he put up a good defence and he was acquitted on all counts. The proceedings of the court martial were sent to Sir Garnet Wolseley for review – and his comments (on the orders of the Duke of Cambridge) were read to every regiment in the British Army:

> Had I released this officer without making any remarks upon the verdict in question, it would have been a tacit acknowledgement that I concurred in what appears to me a monstrous theory, viz., that a regimental officer who is the only officer present with a party of soldiers actually and seriously engaged with [the] enemy, can, under any pretext whatsoever, be justified in deserting them, and by so doing, abandoning them to their fate. The more helpless a position in which an officer finds his men, the more it is his bounden duty to stay and share their fortune, whether for good or ill. It is because the British officer has always done so that he possesses the influence he does in the ranks of our Army. The soldier has learned to feel that come what may, he can in the direst moment of danger look with implicit faith to his officer, knowing that he will never desert him under any possible circumstances.
>
> It is to this faith of the British soldier in his officers that we owe most of the gallant deeds recorded in our military annals; and it is because the verdict of this Court-martial strikes at the root of this faith, that I feel it necessary to mark officially any emphatic dissent from the theory upon which the verdict has been founded.

Given the outcome, Harward had little option but to resign his commission, which he did so in May 1880.

The Belfast *News Letter* of 16 April 1879 reported the following casualties for the 80th Regiment in its action at the Ntombe River:

---

3   Sergeant Booth was married to Lucy O'Brien of Doneraile, County Cork; not many people know that!

Killed
Captain D. B. Moriarty, Sergeant Earnest Johnson, Corporals Geo. Hanson and John McCoy, Privates John Anthony, Arthur Banks, George Brougdon (?), Henry Brownsoa, James Christie, Henry Dutton, Wm. Fox, Edward Gittings, Joseph Green, George Haines, Thomas Hodges, John Ingham, John Lafferty (?), George Mitchell, Robert Moore, Wm. Moran, Henry Night, Joseph Tibbet, Joseph Weavery, James Brown, Wm. Findley, Henry Jacobs, Ralph Wiese, Arthur Middaw (?), Henry Ruffle, Jonah Adey, John Chadwick, Thos. Tucker, John Robinson, James Vernon, Henry Hill, John Hughes, Bernard M. Sherry, William Phipps, Henry Meadows.

Missing
Sergeant Henry Fredericks, Drummer John Leather, Privates John Banner, Alfred Day, John Dodd, Wm. Farelly, Wm. Flyfield, John Farneaux, George Headley, Eli Harker, Thos. Healey, Henry Lodge, Joseph Silcock, Henry Smith, Jubin Hart, Charles Pritchard, Arthur Pannell, Richard Tomlinson, George Tucker, Herbert Woodward, Michael Sheridan.

The public in Britain were quick to offer advice on how best to combat the Zulu warriors.

This letter – dated '3 March, Dublin' – is one example:

Meeting the Zulu Assegai
To The Editor Of *The Irish Times*

Sir, – In reference to my letter to you of yesterday, suggesting that our infantry engaged in savage warfare should be armed with a short sword as well as a bayonet, I would further suggest that the blade should be a broad double edged one, [in] which form, for close cut and thrust, is the most deadly.

As to the desire expressed in Lord Chelmsford's despatch about shortening the cavalry sabre, [I] wish you would allow me to make a few remarks. We all of us know the manner in which a cavalry soldier's sabre jumps and clatters about when riding, and even when walking, with it hooked up to his belt, how he has generally to grasp it in his left hand to prevent it swinging and banging. Now in a country like the Cape, when cavalry will, as occasion requires, have to act as infantry, it would be impossible for a man to move quickly on foot with a long, heavy, steel scabbard turning and twisting from a hook at his side. I would suggest that the scabbard be leather, fixed to the belt like the ordinary bayonet, and that the sword be straight, as in fighting on foot the straight sword has a superiority over the curved one, no matter how slight the curve. All the better if it were made so as to fix on the carbine if necessary. By this means the soldier would have a comparatively steady scabbard, and a noiseless one, and the sword would be more efficient for foot fighting. As for length, about one-sixth shorter than the ordinary one might do. – Yours, &c.,

An Ex-Light Dragoon

Chelmsford assumed command of the Eshowe relief force at Fort Pearson on 23 March. Five days later, all those troops involved in the operation had been ferried across to the north bank of the Tugela and were encamped near Fort *Tenedos*. The weather was atrocious; it rained with such ferocity that it proved almost impossible to keep a campfire lit – and the men slept in sodden blankets in a sea of mud.

The relief column was to advance in two divisions: the first was commanded by Lieutenant Colonel F.T.A. Law, Royal Artillery and consisted of two companies of the Buffs, five of the 99th, a complete battalion of the 91st and some 300 men of the Naval Brigade.

The second division – led by Lieutenant Colonel Wykeham Leigh Pemberton – had six companies of the 3rd Battalion, 60th (KRRC) Rifles, his own regiment; the complete battalion of the 57th (West Middlesex) Regiment and 190 men of the Royal Marine Light Infantry. The former 2nd Regiment, Natal Native Contingent had been reformed as two separate battalions – and as was the army way, had numbered them the 4th and 5th;[4] it was split between the two divisions – and the Royal Navy supplied artillery support for the column. They had landed two 9-pounder field guns, two 24-pounder rocket troughs and two Gatling guns – complete with crews. Percy Barrow would make his second advance to Eshowe – leading 70 men of the No.2 Squadron, Mounted Infantry; 130 mounted Natal Native Horse and 150 of John Dunn's mounted scouts. There was also the Natal Volunteer Guides – drawn from the Natal volunteer regiments and corps (50 men in total).

Chelmsford would not repeat the mistakes of the previous January. Each wagon in the column would carry ammunition, with the box lids unscrewed and close to hand. At the evening's halt, the wagons would form a laager – a square formation approximately 130 yards on each side. Around this square – at a distance of nine feet from the wagons – was dug a ditch three feet deep, with the spoil thrown up in front to form a breastwork. Within the laager would be positioned the natives, horses and draft oxen, while the Imperial infantry were between the wagons and the trench. No bugle calls, with the exception of the alarm call, were to be sounded – and extensive and aggressive patrolling went on at all times. Chelmsford forbade all luxuries, such as officers' personal kit – and, despite the weather, tents for the men. Nevertheless, it still required in excess of 100 wagons to carry the ammunition and rations for the column, and a month's supply for the garrison at Eshowe.

---

4   This would seem to be a particular army 'thing'. In 1915 – during the defence of Kut in Mesopotamia – the British had three defence lines around the town: the first line, the middle line and the second line! (No, we don't know why they do it either.)

Lieutenant General Frederic Augustus Thesiger, 2nd Baron Lord Chelmsford.

Troops crossing the Tugela River from Natal into Zululand.

Below is an appeal which was printed in the *Belfast News Letter* of 24 March:

APPEAL ON BEHALF OF THE WIDOWS AND ORPHANS OF THE 24th REGIMENT AND OTHER FORCES

TO THE EDITOR OF THE *BELFAST NEWS LETTER.*

Sir – I have been requested by Major Streatfield, who, when adjutant of the 24th Regiment, lost his leg during the Indian Mutiny, and has been appointed one of the central committee, to collect donations to the "fund for the relief of widows and orphans of all men belonging to the 24th Regiment and Queen's troops killed on the 22nd and 23rd January at Isandula and Rorke's Drift."

Any subscriptions, no matter how small, will be thankfully acknowledged by your obedient servant,

J. Blakiston Houston.

Orangefield, Belfast, March 24.

(It is hoped this appeal will meet a generous response in Belfast and its neighbourhood. The widows and orphans of those who fell nobly defending the cause of the Crown in Zulu Land [sic] deserve universal sympathy. – Ed. B.N.-L.)

The *Daily Telegraph* reported that a 'brief and despondent letter addressed to the Secretary of War read like that of an almost broken-hearted man'. Another report in the same paper described Chelmsford as looking 'prematurely aged and haggard'.

18

The Eshowe Relief Force

At last, the column was ready to go – and at 6.00am on the morning of 29 March, men and oxen began their soggy tramp to the besieged garrison at Eshowe.

By 12.00pm the vanguard of the column had reached the Inyoni River (nine miles away). Unfortunately, darkness was falling by the time the last of the wagons had arrived at the campsite. With the falling darkness, the wagon conductors (many of them inexperienced) failed to guide their charges into the correct positions – and consequently, there was only space for one third of the cattle inside. Thankfully, the night passed without incident.

The Eshowe relief column in adverse weather conditions.

19

Gingindlovu (He who swallowed the elephant)

From 1 April, the relief column had hugged the open coastlands; now it struck inland – heading for the safety of the British entrenchments at Eshowe. Somopo, the Zulu leader, realised he had to strike before Chelmsford made it to safety – and near the abandoned village of Gingindlovu, the Zulu made their move.

At dawn on 2 April 1879, Somopo, with Dabulamanzi acting as his Lieutenant, sent his 10,000 strong *impi* charging through the misty dawn towards the northern side of the British laager at Gingindlovu. This force was made up of five regiments: the uVe, inGobamakhosi, umHlanga, uMbonambi, umCijo and the uThulwana. Although they had received reinforcements, all of these regiments had suffered under shattering volleys from Martini-Henry rifles in the hands of Imperial soldiers at Isandlwana and Rorke's Drift. Three of them had been at Khambula along with the uNokhenke.

Chelmsford had drawn up his entire force in a square situated on a slight rise. Once again, he was risking no chance of failure. A formidable laager had been formed, with the wagons and a perimeter trench dug. The Imperial infantry manned the four sides, while the Naval Brigade, with their artillery and Gatling guns, were positioned at the corners. The surrounding terrain was bereft of any cover that would be useful to an enemy. Eyewitness reports say that the Zulu advanced dressed in full regimental regalia, and used the charge famous from the days of Shaka: the 'Horns of the Beast'.

At 1,000 yards, one of the Gatling guns opened fire. A short (but effective) burst cut into the advancing line of warriors – and they immediately went to ground. Those warriors armed with rifles – and there were many – returned a heavy fire on the laager and the others continued to advance. At 400 yards, the Martini-Henrys opened fire – controlled volleys making their way up and down the firing line. By now, the Zulu had surrounded the laager, but the firing from within was keeping the enemy at bay. While the attacks came in on all sides, they lacked any co-ordination – and only in a few places did the warriors make a determined effort (in one case, the bodies were found within 20 yards of the perimeter).

Towards the end of the action, the Zulu ceased their futile charges against the laager and took cover in the grass and clumps of bushes. From here, they opened a concentrated (but inaccurate) fire on the defenders – yet even inaccurate fire can find

Prince Dabulamanzi kaMpande – one of the Zulu commanders at Gingindlovu.

Zulu warriors advancing into position, as drawn by Charles Fripp, who was present
at Gingindlovu.

targets: Lieutenant Johnson of the 99th, being a skilled marksman, had procured a rifle and was firing at one particular Zulu who was doing much mischief. Johnson had fired several shots when he suddenly grasped at his chest and exclaimed: "I am shot!" He collapsed immediately and lapsed into unconsciousness. He was swiftly taken to the hospital tent, but died after about 10 minutes. He was 28 years old.

The result of the battle was predictable. The Zulu hurled themselves against the square and were hurled back as if by an invisible hand. The massed rifle fire and the merciless chattering of the Gatling guns cut them down in droves. Within a short time, it was obvious that the assault had failed – and the enemy began to melt away. When this became obvious to Chelmsford, he ordered out the Natal Native Horse under Major Barrow (along with a troop of Mounted Infantry) to move out of the square and harry the retreating Zulu. By the end of the day, over 1,000 warriors lay dead – both around the square and in the veldt beyond. Chelmsford's losses amounted to two officers and 11 other ranks killed, with a further 48 men wounded. In contrast to the ammunition expenditure at Isandlwana, the defenders at Gingindlovu had fired between six and seven rounds per man in carefully-controlled volleys.

The following letter records one man's view of the action and reveals a certain sense of humour not normally expected of a Victorian professional, but then again, he was Irish. The writer is Doctor Henry Cooke Linden – a civilian surgeon from Belfast.

The landing brigade from HMS *Shah* manning the barricades at Gingindlovu.

The spelling and grammar in the letter are as per the original, which appeared in the *Belfast News Letter* of 27 May 1879:

<u>Herwin Hospital, April 16 1879</u>

I have just returned from the front with the senior medical officer, in charge of about forty wounded and a number of sick. I am happy to say that I escaped from my first baptism of fire without a scratch, and without any exaggeration it was a thorough one. The column for the relief of Ekowe started from the Tugela on Saturday morning, 30th March, at about three o' clock, after a fearful night of rain and lightning. The men rose up half-starved − (I speak for myself as well, being on the same rations) − and looked very little like warriors before whom the Zulu nation was to fly like dust before the wind. As the orders were that no luggage was to be taken except what we could carry ourselves, we were obliged to dispense with beds, tents, and other acceptable luxuries. I took shelter as best I could, with my rug wrapped round me, under a bullock waggon, but the rain came down in such torrents that it soon made the little refuge I had even more uncomfortable than outside on the grass, as I was awakened by the flood of water rushing over me down the hillside, where we were encamped. It being only eleven o' clock I turned out with great difficulty, owing to the stiffness of my legs and back, and, a few of us collecting in groups here and there, we threw our wet rugs on the ground, and sat conversing on various topics to pass the time till dawn, so you may imagine that neither myself nor my horse were in the best form for marching. Dawn came at last, and with it the reveille, which was unnecessary on this occasion, as most of us had been pretty well roused already, and then the bustle and shouting of the mule and oxen drivers began. The unfortunate oxen seemed to have felt the previous night's inclemency, and those of them whose waggons got into holes could hardly pull them out again.

However, at last the grand flying column got on the move. The *flying* column consisted of a convoy of heavily laden waggons, from four to six miles long (no one knows what was in them all, as we were put on quarter rations from the start, and no sugar or coffee was brought at all) and it moved at the rate of two miles per hour. After a long and tedious march, we arrived at the Umnait Mulu river, where we encamped for the night, and where I got another wetting, after having had my clothes dried on me by the sun. I was in such a hurry to quench my thirst at the river that I unfortunately stepped on a deceitful piece of grass, which I thought was solid earth, and fell head foremost into the water, out of which I scrambled, my ardour very much cooled.

Most of the next day (Sunday) was spent in getting the oxen across the river, so that we only marched one mile and again halted for the day. We arrived at Gingindlovu on Tuesday where we made an entrenched camp as usual. At about six o'clock there was a fearful thunderstorm, and also a false alarm of "the Zulus". During the night I believe another false report was raised, but I slept in blissful unconsciousness of alarm or rain, although on waking, I found the water an inch deep around me. My poor horse was looking down from the wheel of the waggon to which he was tied, his mane dripping wet and well above the hoofs in mud. I had just time to have a look around me, and was watching our cattle being driven out of the laager, when there was again an alarm raised that the enemy were coming, which proved this time to be a reality.

The cattle were hastily driven in again, some however, were too far out to get back in time, and had to be pursued by the native scouts, who soon turned with the picquets and made hastily for the laager. Round in the trenches were the men of the 60th rifles, the 57th came next, and the Naval Brigade, consisting of men from her Majesty's ships Shah, Boddicea, and Active; next to these were the men of the 39th Regiment, the 91st Highlanders, and part of the 3rd Buffs; then behind them were the two Natal Native contingents, under commandants Barton and Nettleton, to the former of which I was attached. It was a little after 6 a.m. when the alarm was given, and about five minutes later we were all in the laager and the Zulus coming forward in their usual mode of advancing; the main body quickly forming a horseshoe, the horns of which were rapidly thrown out, surrounding the laager quickly in skirmishing order. We opened a heavy volley of fire on them when about 1,000 yards off the trenches, the two 14-pounders being quickly brought to bear on them, but notwithstanding the heavy fire kept up on our side, it was warmly returned, the bullets coming over our heads and in among us in showers. The enemy still came on with undaunted bravery, some of them approaching so near as twenty yards to the Gatling guns, of which we had two. The battle lasted about an hour and a half, the firing being kept up most energetically on both sides. It seemed to me scarcely five minutes as we had plenty to do, the wounded crowding in on us. The hospital was formed by the waggons being drawn up in the shape of a square, the trenches in which the soldiers stood being some distance outside them; so the medical staff was more exposed, owing to the ground in the laager being elevated; and as the Zulus fired high, the bullets came over the top and through the wheels of the waggons amongst us. We fortunately had only one doctor wounded – Surgeon Major Longfield, R. N., of H.M.S. Tenedos, who is a great friend of mine, and an Irishman. I am glad to say he is doing very well, although the bullet passed through his right arm, shattering the bone greatly, and lodging itself close to the shoulder blade. We lost altogether eight – six men and two officers – named Lieutenant Johnston, of the 99th Regiment, and Colonel Northey, of the 60th Rifles – and about thirty three wounded, including the blue jackets.

We also lost a number of natives and waggoners. As soon as the Zulus began to retreat our mounted men charged out, followed by the Native Contingent, and overtaking some of the enemy, surrounded them and cut them to pieces, the natives assegaing the wounded in the excitement. I ran out too, with my revolver in my hand, and just got up to a bush in front of the trenches where there were two hidden; I had hardly time to think before some of the contingent ran in on them and assegaied them almost at my feet, where they were lying wounded. Behind another bush close by there were seven lying on top of each other. I heard from some wounded prisoners who were taken next day after the men had cooled down a little, that the Zulus who attacked us were Cetywayo's picked men – the flower of his army – which, I am sure, was true, as I never saw such powerful-looking fellows, every man of them being young and over six feet. It seems they had come down to cut our throats in anticipation of the feast they were to have after they had done so, as they were not allowed anything to eat, by the King's orders, for some days previous. I am happy to inform you they did not succeed in carrying out their humane intention, and so lost their promised collation.

We buried 471 Zulus that day (Wednesday 2nd April), and for several days afterwards we were kept busy burying them round about the encampment. I can assure you the odour was something fearful, especially from the bushes they were lying in. I rode out two days after, about half a mile from the camp, and every now and then I came on a dead Zulu, lying in all sorts of positions. The supply of water being very scarce, what we drank we got in an old ditch; and for some days after the battle it was noticed that the water had a greasy look, as if there were tar in it, and on examination it was found that two or three dead Zulus were lying in the bottom of it. I am glad to say that through all I had excellent health and a good appetite, only very little to appease it, sometimes a dry biscuit and a cup of tea without sugar or milk and containing the essential essence of Zulu. Half of the column still remains a few miles from Gingindlovu; the other

Brevet Lieutenant Colonel Francis Vernon Northey, 3rd Battalion, 60th Rifles, mentioned by Dr Linden in his letter.

half came with us as an escort for the wounded. I will not trouble you further with an account of the return march; suffice to say, we were glad to get back to the Tugela; only I am afraid, had we been attacked again, there would have been none of us left to tell the tale. I was the last man of the column returning, being in charge of the rear guard, and I shall not soon forget that march. The poor soldiers staggered along with their tongues hanging out of their mouths, and every now and then they fell flat on their faces. Being medical officer, it lay with me as to whether they might ride on the waggons or not. You may be sure none met with a refusal from me. Colonel Pearson was able to come out after the battle of Gingindlovu, and I am not sorry to get back to decent quarters again. We have had two more deaths this week here, but, on the whole, everything is going on very well.

Lieutenant George Charles Jeffreyes Johnston, 99th Duke of Edinburgh's (Lanarkshire) Regiment, photographed at the School of Musketry, Hythe, Kent.

The 'Lieutenant Johnston' mentioned above was George Charles Jeffreyes Johnston – the son of William Jefferyes Johnston DL – of Woodland, County Cork.

He had been educated at Cheltenham College and was 28 years old – and was buried on the battlefield. There is a memorial inscription to him in St Finbarr's Cathedral, Cork and he is further commemorated at RMA Sandhurst and Cheltenham College Chapel.

Lieutenant Johnston was also mentioned in *The Irish Times* of 12 May in a published extract from a letter written by the Colonel of the 99th to the Duke of Edinburgh:

Ginghelovo 3rd April 1879

We got here on the 1st, after a tedious march, during which we expected attack. Just after arriving we had a terrific thunderstorm, which drenched us to the skin and landed us in a sea of med. At night an alarm, and then three hours' sleep in our wet clothes, with more rain; but, of course, sleeping out in the rain is becoming too common to be thought of. We had four wet nights, as we packed our tents two days before the rest of the force. Yesterday morning we were attacked. The boldness of these fellows daring to attack nearly 4,000 Englishmen is astonishing. They came on most pluckily, but our fire was too

From within the laager at Gingindlovu, a wagon driver fires over the ranks of infantry.

The 91st (Princess Louise's Argyllshire) Highlanders on the south face of the laager, whilst a Royal Navy Gatling gun and rocket battery anchor the corner of the position.

much for them. They seemed fair shots, but aimed too high. We lost one officer, three men killed and four wounded. I was talking to young Johnston, the officer who was killed, and had just complimented him on keeping his men steady, when he fell by my side, shot through the heart. He, of course, poor fellow, never spoke again – just one cry.

Another letter telling of the advance to Eshowe; it was printed in the *Belfast News Letter*:

LETTER FROM A SOLDIER IN ZULULAND

TO THE EDITOR OF THE *BELFAST NEWS LETTER*.
Sir – I would be glad if you could afford space in your newspaper for the following letter, received a few days since by the governor of the Malone Reformatory from a boy who was formerly an inmate of the institution as it shows the benefit he derived from the training he got there. The letter is in part almost illegible, as it was written with a sharpened bullet, but with the use of a magnifying glass I have had it carefully copied, and give it in its exact words.
   Yours truly,
   C. Wolfe Shaw.

Fort Crealock, Zululand, May 22, 1879
My Dear Sir – I suppose you will be surprised to hear that I am at the seat of war in South Africa, but such is the fact. I have at last had an opportunity of earning a decoration before I leave the service. When the news reached England of the disaster at Rorke's Drift volunteers were called for by the Government to make up the six infantry regiments sent out to war strength. Although I had got on very well in my own regiment, I could not resist the temptation of obtaining a medal; and, of course I shared in the general feeling of the army and nation at large that somebody must avenge the slaughter of the 24th, so I volunteered for active service into the 91st Highlanders. Of course I lost my appointment, and had to go out as a private; but I do not mind that, as I have lots of time to get up again, and the medal is worth fifty stripes. We were inspected by the Duke on the 18th February, and embarked in the Pretoria on the 19th, at Southampton, amidst great cheering, & c. I hope you will approve of the step I have taken.
   Before I proceed I must tell you that, not being able to obtain a pen and ink or pencil to write, I had to improvise a rifle bullet for the occasion, so that I cannot write very plainly. We had a good deal of rough passage on the voyage, but after a very fast passage we landed at Durban on the 17th of March, and commenced our march to the front to join lord [sic] Chelmsford's column at the Tugela River. We arrived at the front on the 25th March, after a very hard period of marching with seventy rounds of ammunition and accoutrements and rifle &c. Of course, the heat was excessive. On the 29th March, Lord Chelmsford's

column, consisting of the 91st Highlanders, the 60th Rifles, 57th Regiment, part of the 3rd Buffs, 99th Regiment, the Naval Brigade, and a regiment of the Native Contingent, commenced the march to the relief of Colonel Pearson at Ekowe, about sixty miles distant. On the third day, when we had marched about thirty miles into the enemy's country, dense masses of Zulus were seen hovering about us by the scouts, and on our taking up a position on a height at Ginghelovo on the evening of the 1st April, the enemy's camp fires were only about two miles off. We threw up trenches under a regular downpour of rain, and lay down on the wet ground, but not to sleep, for we were constantly standing to our arms, prepared to repel attack.

As the day broke the Zulus slowly encircled the camp and advanced to the attack, opening on us a very brisk musketry fire. We poured a most terrific storm of missiles on them; the two howitzer guns and a 9-pounder mowed them down in dozens, but they still kept advancing. When they were within one hundred yards of our trenches we commenced file firing, but they stood it bravely; and it was not until they had seen their comrades riddled by the fire of our Gatling guns that they threw up their spears and returned completely beaten.

They lost at least 1,300 men. We buried about 1,000, besides hundreds killed by the mounted infantry who pursued them. We only lost about −; a lieutenant of the 99th, a sergeant of ours, and about four privates killed, and about twelve

Prince Magwendu kaMpande after his surrender to the British, as mentioned in the letter by E. Stewart: 'Johnny, I have grown old in a day'.

wounded. I escaped safe, thank God, but there were several bullets came very close to me in the trenches.

The next day we started for Ekowe, to the relief of Pearson. We left at about six in the morning, and, after a dreadful march up hill [sic] of about twenty-three miles, we arrived at midnight. We did not receive our day's rations till we got in, and all I had to eat was about half a biscuit I had saved from the previous day. It was certainly the hardest piece of work we had before or since. The next day Fort Ekowe was abandoned. Colonel Pearson's column with about 400 sick men, marched to Tugela to enjoy a well-deserved rest, after being half starved and worked to death for about ten weeks. We marched down through the country after the evacuation, meeting with no Zulus, and have since been employed building forts and escorting convoys. I find my experience obtained with Mr. Jamnison (Jamison?) in the field to be of great advantage here, as I am picking and digging from morning till night. I hope you have got a little settled after your bereavement. I assure you, many a time lying on the ground at night, I lie thinking for hours about you, and the mistress and boys. I shall settle down to soldering [sic] properly when I go home as I think I have had enough adventure. Dear sir, I should like very much if you would send my present address to E.S., and ask him to write to me. It will only be a penny to a soldier. I should like very much to hear from him. I hope you will remember me to all in the house. Dear sir, if you would be so very kind, I should like you to send me a *Belfast Weekly News* to read, as a newspaper is worth any money here, and, as I do not write to my friends, you are the only person I can ask. I expect to be at home about November, and I shall be able to thank you.

You hear nothing here concerning the war, although we sleep every night with our clothes and ammunition on and our rifles in our hands. It seems rather funny that we should be in such a state of ignorance about the campaign, but such is the fact.

One of the Zulu chiefs – Macquandy – one of Cetywayo's half-brothers, surrendered the other day, and came into camp with his wives, &c. After inspecting the cannons, rockets, and Gatling guns, the wretch exclaims, "Johnny, I have grown old in a day." They call every white man 'Johnny'. Dabulamanzi, the chief who commanded the division, about 12,000, that attacked us wanted to surrender with his beaten force, but the King sent a force to watch him, and we hear that, after a hard fight, Dabulamanzi has been killed. Cetywayo is a most determined man; he is said to have sent to Colonel Wood, the other day, after Wood had gained a victory, telling him he was not a bit afraid of him; that he would fight him any day if he would not get behind ditches; that he would kill Lord Chelmsford, Colonel Wood, Oham (one of the King's Brothers who surrendered to Wood), and every white man in Zululand, as he had plenty of men to do it. We also hear that he has abandoned Ulundi, his capital, and taken up a very strong position, stating that he defies the English to drive him out.

Men of the 2nd Squadron, Mounted Infantry, harrying the retreating Zulu at Gingindlovu.

Months after the action at Gingindlovu, the remains of the Zulu dead lie scattered across the battlefield.

A contemporary sketch of the British memorial at Gingindlovu.

When he heard from his spies of the Scotch regiment landing, he exclaimed, "Oh, I have beaten the English and they have got the Scotch to help them."

The cavalry have got ten days' rations to make a forced march on him, and the other columns advance on the 28th to cut off his retreat. Our column (General Crealock's) is employed building two forts between the sea coast and Ekowe. We follow in a few days.

Dear sir, I had to scribble this letter now and again when I got the chance, and I hope you will excuse it being hardly legible. I will have to wait a day or two to get a pen to address it. I hope you will be kind enough to send Eliss my address, and if you would send the paper I would be so thankful. I have not got any more time at present, so, hoping you will give my regards to all my friends, Mr. Williams, and the children, I remain yours respectfully,

E. Stewart.

On 11 April, the local press carried an obituary to Captain David Moriarty, who was killed at the Ntombe River. There was more news from Afghanistan, with British reconnaissance forces having pushed as far ahead as Gundamuk. A *Daily News* telegram from Rangoon reported that the Burmese Government wishes for peace – and a report from *The Times* of yesterday (16 April) reported an unsuccessful assassination attempt on the Czar in St Petersburg.

On 18 April, an Irish officer died at Pietermaritzburg. Captain Marmaduke Stourton was the son of William Stourton of Yorkshire and Catherine – daughter of Edmund Scully, Esq. – of Bloomfield, County Tipperary. Born on 14 January 1840, he was educated at Downside College, Bath before travelling to Namur in Belgium. He finally attended Stonyhurst College, Lancashire before being gazetted to an Ensigncy with the 8th Foot in 1861. He served with that regiment on Malta, Gibraltar, in India and at the home depot in England. He became a Lieutenant in 1864 and was further promoted to command 'A' Company in 1870. This year also saw him marry Marie – daughter of William Franks, Esq. In the same year, he exchanged into the

Captain Marmaduke Stourton, 63rd (West Suffolk) Regiment.

Prince Hamu kaNzibe – King Cetshwayo's half-brother – who surrendered on terms he agreed with Colonel Wood.

63rd Regiment. Shortly afterwards, he embarked for service in India – serving on various stations for several years.

Stourton had returned to England by 1879 and was stationed at his regimental depot in Ashton-under-Lyne. When the disastrous news of Isandlwana reached home in February, he immediately volunteered for service in South Africa. He was selected as a special service officer for duty with the 24th Regiment and sailed on 1 March aboard the army transport *Clyde*. During a storm, this ship was wrecked in St Simon's Bay, but owing to the admirable discipline of those on board, there was no loss of life. On arriving in Durban, Captain Stourton was given command of

Lieutenant General Sir Garnet Joseph Wolseley – appointed by the Home Government as the High Commissioner and Commander-in-Chief, Natal, Transvaal and Zululand.

Herwen Hospital.

John Dunn – 'The Zulu Organiser'.

a draft of men for the 24th Regiment and ordered to proceed to Pietermaritzburg.

During the morning of 18 April, Stourton and his men marched a distance of some 12 miles – and during this time, he was remembered as being of the cheeriest form (singing and keeping up the spirits of the men in every possible way). On recommencing the march after lunch, the party had to make their way up a steep incline – and on reaching the top, Stourton was gasping for breath and remarked to an accompanying artillery officer: "I feel my life-blood ebbing away. I am nearly done." He refused to fall out of the march and continued with the column – and once again, was forced to climb a hill in order to reach the camp.

When the bugle sounded 'Halt', Stourton had just enough strength to order the men to fall out before fainting from exhaustion. Despite immediate medical treatment, Captain Stourton died and was buried with full military honours in the camp cemetery.

In May, Both Evelyn Wood's 'Flying Column' and the main column under Chelmsford moved again into Zululand – patrolling, reconnoitring, establishing supply bases and burying the dead at Isandlwana. At all times, they took the proper precautions in defence. Chelmsford would make no mistake this time: in his eyes, another 'enemy' had appeared on the horizon. Wolseley had been appointed as High Commissioner and Commander-in-Chief, Natal, Transvaal and Zululand with complete civil and military power.

Chelmsford could not afford to wait for the arrival of Wolseley, but was determined to finish the war while he still retained command; there was a reputation to think of.

The following letter appeared in the *Belfast News Letter* of 1 May 1879. It is signed only with initials, but the writer claims a fair degree of knowledge on the life of John Dunn and makes no apology with regard to Dunn's supplying of firearms to the Zulu prior to 1879 – firearms that were used with good effect at Isandlwana, where they destroyed the rocket battery; and at Rorke's Drift, where Hitch's shoulder was shattered and Cole received a bullet through the head. The spelling and grammar in the letter are as per the original:

"JOHN DUNN, THE ZULU ORGANIZER."

TO THE EDITOR OF THE *BELFAST NEWS LETTER*.

Sir – With reference to the article which you quote in to-day's *News-Letter* from the *Cork Examiner*, would you allow me to state that from a recent conversation I had with a friend of mine in Scotland, who is personally acquainted with John Dunn, and knows much of his history from his own lips, that he is simply the son of a Scotchman-born in Natal; was fond of a roving and wild life; left his father; settled among the Zulus; became one of themselves, and through his early teaching, such as it was, and the *perferridum ingenium Scotorum*,[1] so asserted his superiority over the simpleminded but brave Zulus that he ultimately found himself chief adviser to the King.

The importation of firearms into Zululand came about in this manner. When the Cape diamond diggings were in full operation thousands of Zulus appeared on the scene, who became to the whites the "hewers of wood and the drawers of water," getting a handsome return for their work and saved money. By and by there also appeared at the diggings large importations of rifles sent out from Birmingham, which were readily bought by the Zulus and taken home with them to their own country. John Dunn, seeing this, thought he might as well do a stroke of business on his own account. Accordingly, he made his arrangements so satisfactorily to his own wishes that large supplies of firearms reached him at Delagoa Bay-the finest bay on this part of the coast of Africa-and were forwarded into the interior to the natives, who greedily bought them, yielding a handsome profit to the said John Dunn.

The story of John's connection with the American civil war, Franco-Prussian war, and Portugal, may be dismissed as only existing in the imagination.

Only a word more as to his personal appearance. He is a middle sized, broad shouldered, full chested man, with nothing exceptionally intelligent in his expression further than having, as Scotch people say, "common sense," but so changed by his dress, the mode of wearing his hair and climate, that he would, to an ordinary observer, at once pass as a nigger.

His Imperial Highness the Prince Imperial of France, Eugene Louis Jean Joseph Napoleon Bonaparte.

---

1   'The intensely earnest character of the Scotch'.

My friend has travelled in Africa and Asia for over twenty years, and is intimately acquainted with Zululand, as well as the present seat of war in Afghanistan – I am, &c.,

N.M.G.

High Street, Belfast, 30th April.

A telegram to the *Standard* from Durban – dated 'April 21' – remarked on the following:

Experienced colonists believe the sending of cavalry from England is altogether a mistake. Light cavalry regiments from India would have been far better. The keenest intellects and best brains that England can produce are wasted there. This will not be a war of gallant actions and heroic deeds, but a struggle in which the issue depends upon management, organisation, patience, and the commissariat and transport departments. A difficulty is rising with the ox-drivers and leaders, who decline to go further. They are afraid of the Zulus, and it is feared will all desert.

Brevet Lieutenant Colonel Richard Harrison, Royal Engineers.

Lieutenant Jahleel Brenton Carey, 98th (Prince of Wales's) Regiment.

At 9.15am on the morning of Sunday, 1 June 1879, a patrol of horsemen under the command of His Imperial Highness Eugene Louis Jean Joseph Napoleon Bonaparte – exiled Prince Imperial of France and son of Napoleon III – left the camp of the Second Division. They were on a reconnaissance from this camp on the left bank of the Blood River to find a new campsite – and the Prince's skill as a draughtsman was being put to good use.

In the wake of the defeat of his father's armies in the Franco-Prussian War, Louis had been living in exile in England with his mother, the Empress Eugenie. When Louis was 16, he had been admitted to the Royal Military Academy, Woolwich. He graduated in 1875, but because of his status, was not commissioned. However, he was permitted to serve as an Honorary Lieutenant in the Royal Artillery. With the outbreak of war in Zululand, Louis made several applications to serve in the campaign, but again, wary of his social position, the War Office declined. Nevertheless, Louis' perseverance was eventually compensated and he was given permission to serve on the staff of Lord Chelmsford as an additional ADC. He sailed from England in February – arriving in the Cape the following April. He rapidly succumbed to a bout of fever and was unable to join Chelmsford until the beginning of May.

Louis quickly tired of the humdrum life of an ADC and again pleaded for a more active role in the war. As a result of this, he was seconded to the staff of Brevet Colonel Richard Harrison, Royal Engineers.

Louis' mentor in this post was Lieutenant J.B. Carey of the 98th (The Prince of Wales) Regiment and Deputy Assistant Quartermaster General of the division.

The Prince Imperial's party languish in the *umuzi* unaware of the impending danger.

Zulu warriors break from cover and ambush the party.

For the remainder of that month, Louis carried out several patrols – making numerous sketches, which provided enough details to compile a map. In the early morning of 1 June, Louis made preparations for what was to be another standard reconnaissance. His escort for the day was to be six men of No.3 (Bettington's) Troop, Natal Horse; six men of Captain Shepstone's Troop, Native Horse; and Captain Carey (recently promoted), who had asked permission to accompany the patrol. There was also a 'friendly' Zulu guide.

As the patrol made its way out of the camp, it was without the Native Horse. They had failed to parade with the remainder of the escort – and Louis, impatient to be away, refused to wait for them. At the camp perimeter, they met with Colonel Harrison, who suggested that perhaps their numbers were insufficient if they ran into any opposition. Louis' reply was that they were plenty enough – and with a final wave, he rode out onto the veldt.

For the following six hours, all went as normal: the patrol rode from place to place; Louis sketching the ground, as they searched for a suitable site or the next camp. At approximately 3.00pm the patrol arrived at a Zulu village (*umuzi*). At first, it appeared deserted, but closer inspection showed signs of recent human habitation. The Prince ordered the men to dismount and unsaddle their horses for resting and feeding. The Zulu guide was sent to bring water for coffee, while the men prepared some lunch.

Louis lay down to relax by one of the huts, but he did not post any sentries. At approximately 3.40pm the guide returned and reported seeing a Zulu warrior on a nearby hill. At once the horses were saddled and the men prepared to mount. At

A French photo-montage depicting the death of the Prince.

An engraving of the death of the Prince Imperial.

FINDING the BODY of the PRINCE IMPERIAL 2nd JUNE 1879.

On 2 June the body of the Prince Imperial was discovered.

this point, the Prince asked: "Are you all ready?" and received an affirmative reply. Suddenly, a volley was fired from the nearby scrub – instantly followed by a wild charge of Zulu warriors (estimated to have been between 15 and 40 in number).

One trooper – left behind when his horse bolted – managed to fire a single shot from his carbine before falling under the Zulu spears. As the remainder of the patrol made for the riverbank, another trooper tumbled from his saddle as a rifle bullet slammed into his back.

Meanwhile, in the village, the Prince was struggling to mount his own horse. Attempting to vault onto the animal by grabbing hold of the saddle holster, he fell heavily as the leather tore in his grasp – his horse trampling on his right arm as it ran

The Prince Imperial's death site.

The destruction of the *umuzi* where the Prince was killed.

off. Struggling to his feet, he made off on foot – closely followed by seven warriors. As the Zulu closed, one hurled a spear that struck the Prince in the thigh. Stopping to withdraw the spear, he turned and fired two shots from his revolver – both of which missed their intended targets. Another spear struck him in the left shoulder and he was forced to his knees. With this, the pursuing warriors closed in around him and it was all over very quickly.

With rank comes not only privilege, but responsibility. While no one expected Carey to have stood and fought alone, he should have been the last man to leave, or made some attempt to go back. While there is no doubt who was in charge of the patrol, someone had to be found to take the blame – and Carey was the obvious choice. There was a court martial – and when the outcome was sent to the Deputy Judge Advocate General for ratification, it was discovered that the officers of the court martial had not been sworn in, and therefore the proceeding had been invalid.

Captain Jahleel Brenton Carey later went to India with his regiment and died of peritonitis in Karachi in 1883. He is listed on the regimental memorial. Carey received quite a lot of support in Irish newspapers at the time; this was due to his name and people assuming he was Irish.[2]

When the Prince's body was being prepared for the return to the Empress Eugenie for burial, it was her wish that a priest of her own faith accompany the body. This duty fell to The Right Rev Rooney, who had studied at All Hallow's College, Dublin and the Propaganda College, Rome.

A letter from the son of a Belfastman – unfortunately unnamed – tells of the reaction to the death of the Prince Imperial and shows that politics and religion are, as usual, never far from the mind of an Irishman:

> PORT ELIZABETH, JUNE 4th, 1879 – Before this reaches home you will have heard by telegram of the awfully sudden death of the Prince Imperial, killed by the Zulus whilst attending his duties on the staff. I need not here enter into the sad particulars, beyond that he was killed in the execution of his duty with two of his troopers. I can hardly realise such a thing. I am personally, deeply grieved, for I admired him as a noble-hearted chivalrous young Prince, who in return for the hospitality and respect shown to his family by the English nation, when exiled from their native land, was not contented to sit down and eat the bread of idleness, surrounded by wealth and luxury, but like a high-spirited gentleman loyally volunteered to help fight that country's quarrels, which had shown him and his such kindness. But independent of his exalted birth was liked by all with whom he mixed. All South Africa is in mourning. It is in everybody's mouth, and the telegraph office is surrounded by small knots of people, who eagerly scan the telegraphs as they arrive. All the shipping in the bay have their flags half mast

---

2   The 'Irish' connection with the Prince Imperial lies with his half-brother, Alexandre Louis Eugene, who was Vice Consul in Belfast in 1866.

'All South Africa is in mourning': the Prince Imperial's body is received in Pietermaritzburg.

Specialist wagons of 'C' Troop, Royal Engineers, carrying their telegraph equipment.

high. The town flag over the Town Hall and other private flags in the town are all half mast high. The poor Prince's death has cast quite a gloom over us all; it seems so sad. What terrible news to his poor widowed mother! He was killed on Whit Monday (last Monday), and we had the news next day. For a long time people refused to believe it, but to-day it has been officially confirmed. It was unwise on the poor fellow's part to trust himself in or near a mealie field, for this stuff grows shoulder high, and affords excellent cover to the wary Zulu, who, with the skill and subtlety of serpents, glide noiselessly through and then fall on their victim, suddenly pinning him to the ground with their assegais. Fancy, the poor fellow had seventeen assegais through him. He was too unused to the habits and ways of warfare of the Zulus, and I think he must have been a little too venturesome. As yet we don't know the exact particulars. His body is now at Maritzburg. I suppose it will be sent home; and thus he has been cut off, in the prime of his youth, just at the commencement of a brilliant career, one of the finest and bravest fellows that ever fought in freedom's cause. Some may not term this war as being in freedom's cause, but it is. It is to free a black, brave, blood-thirsty nation from a monster of blood and villainy in the person of King Cetywayo. I declare this bad news has given me quite a turn; it is so sadly dreadful. How anxiously people are looking forward to a big battle, so that our soldier may be able to revenge their comrades' cruel death. It is not like ordinary warfare, where men are satisfied with killing each other, but these brutes do hack and mutilate and torture all that fall into their hands, which make death more dreadful in its self [sic].

We have just received bad news from Basutoland. The Basutos have surprised and killed a number of burghers up there, all men in good position in business. It is very dreadful, and it goes to show that the gentle Kaffir is a match for the white people when armed with good rifles. What would it have been if Sir Bartle Frere had not disarmed all these outlying tribes? Like a wise man, he saw the danger and compelled the Kaffirs to give up their guns, and really that was one of the causes of this outbreak; but, had he not done so, they would have gradually armed themselves, and at a given signal there would have been a general massacre of whites; and yet there are people at home who find fault with Sir Bartle Frere's policy, when everyone here looks up to him as their colonial saviour. He was quick to see and quick to act, and yet his name is dragged through the dirt. I can assure you there are no Liberals here, and it is quite refreshing to my Conservative feelings to find South Africa such a stout, constitutional, practical place; it covers a multitude of shortcomings, in my mind.

I have not heard from T. S. yet. I suppose he is still up country. Last Sunday, being Whit Sunday, I attended Trinity Church as usual. In the evening I went up to St. Peter's, and was agreeably surprised to see the Bishop of Grahamstown and his chaplain there. G. looked sensible of the dignity imparted to his Church by their presence, and he read prayers. The chaplain preached an exceedingly good sermon, but the bishop did not take part in the service beyond giving the benediction at the close. The service was nicely rendered. The bishop carries in his hand a large wooden pastoral staff, a sort of shepherd's hook, and they wear the bishop's mitre, but I did not see this bishop had one. The bishops themselves are very moderate men, but I think some of their clergy go ahead where they can. G. S. has a great tendency that way, but his Ritualistic longings are stopped for want of funds.

7 June: The *Morning Post* says: 'At a meeting held yesterday at Stafford House of the South African Aid Fund it was resolved to send at once £1,000 to Lady Frere; and it is hoped to dispatch by next mail a first instalment of six trained nurses, able to teach others how to attend the sick'.

The same paper announces that the following Irish officers had received orders to proceed to South Africa: Surgeon Major Jackson and Surgeons

Brevet Colonel George Pomeroy Colley CB, Wolseley's Chief of Staff.

Fulvey, Groghergan, Jennings, Martin, Stokes, Usher, Ward and Wood – also that Brevet Colonel George Pomeroy Colley CB was to have the local rank of Brigadier General while serving as Sir Garnet Wolseley's Chief of Staff in South Africa.

Up to this time, Colley had enjoyed a varied military career. Born on 1 November 1835, he was the third son of George Pomeroy Colley of Rathangan, County Kildare and was the grandson of the 4th Viscount Harberton. Colley had attended Sandhurst and had been commissioned into the 2nd Queen's Royal Regiment in 1852. Between 1854 and 1860 he had served in South Africa – carrying out surveying duties and acting as a magistrate in the Bashi River area of Kaffraria.

At the beginning of 1860, Colley accompanied his regiment to China as part of the Anglo-French expedition and participated in the attacks on the Taku Forts and occupation of Peking. After this, he returned to South Africa to take up his previous duties. In 1862, Colley entered the Staff College and left a year later – having gained an honours pass. He served as Brigade Major with the Regiment at Devonport for the next five years, and then in 1870 was attached to the War Office to assist in preparing the Cardwell Army Reforms.

The following year, he was appointed as Professor of Military Administration at the Staff College, which was followed by a post with Sir Garnet Wolseley in his campaign against the Ashanti on Africa's Gold Coast in 1873. Colley's exertions in arranging all transport during this campaign was, to a great degree, responsible for its success

– and as a result, he was promoted to Brevet Colonel and awarded the CB. In 1875, he accompanied Wolseley to Natal and hence was known as part of the 'Wolseley Ring'. On his return to the United Kingdom, he was appointed as Military Secretary to Lord Lytton, Governor General of India, and later as Private Secretary. Now he found himself accompanying General Wolseley to Natal as Chief of Staff.

In the *Belfast News Letter* of 9 June, a Reuters telegram dated '20 May, Cape Town' announced the death of Captain Chard. The same paper tells its readers that the assassin who attempted to kill the Czar has been found guilty and will face death by hanging. The paper also informs us that the price of calling out the Army Reserve for the year 1878 cost the country a net sum of £589,434. The number of men of the First Class Army Reserve was 13,019 – and the average period during which they served with the colours after being called out was 96 days. Their pay amounted to £67,795 and the cost of their maintenance to nearly £164,000, whilst £188,602 was paid for clothing. A sum of £8,687 was disbursed in allowances for subsistence on discharge.

A telegram to *The Times* – reprinted in the *Belfast News Letter* on 17 June – tells the following:

> A raid made by the Volunteers and the Native Contingent from the Krantz Kop was partially successful. The Zulus opened fire when our men were half way across the river, but retreated before the heavy covering fire of our own natives. A few kraals were burned. There were no casualties on our side. Captain Walker has destroyed the headman's kraal and captured 2,000 cattle at a higher drift.
>
> The report as to a Zulu raid on this side in reprisal is contradicted. Major Chard and Colonel Pearson are both well. According to accounts, the health of the troops is better. The necessity of the complete subjugation of the Zulus is everywhere insisted upon to avoid future wars.

The following – taken from a Reuters telegram – was printed in the *Belfast News Letter* of 20 June:

> Cape Town, June 3 (via Madeira), – Prince Louis Napoleon, the Prince Imperial, is dead. On June 1st he left General Wood's camp on a reconnaissance. The party dismounted in a mealiefield [sic] near the Hyotoyozi, when the enemy crept up, and assegaied the Prince and two troopers. Their bodies have been recovered. The Prince had just returned from a three day's [sic] patrol under General Buller.

The *Belfast News Letter* carried this tribute to the Prince Imperial on 26 June:

LOUIS NAPOLEON
Obit June, 1879.
When I have ponder'd how that some die young,
And yet so old that they can scarce recall
Their youth, then I have truly seen that all

Colonel Hans Garrett Moore VC, 88th (Connaught Rangers) Regiment – photographed after his transfer to the 93rd (Sutherland) Highlanders.

Do live in deeds, not years. Poets have sung
Full oft of genius perished ere its prime;
Of promised fruit that sickened in the bud,
Or fell a prey to a chance wind or flood.
Else love-sick maids have graced the lofty rhyme.
But tells me, Muse, if e'er illustrious Time
Hath given thee, through paltry be the rhyme,
A nobler, faiere sacrifice than mine,
Where manliest youth and mellow'st age combine?
Napoleon! Name in which these twain did blend,
Thy land a hope hath lost, and ours a friend.
    Belfast.   C.A.K.

London *Times*, 28 June:

THE VICTORIA CROSS
(By Telegram)
London, Friday, – The London Gazette this evening announced that the Queen has signified her intention to confer the Victoria Cross on Major, and Brevet Lieutenant Colonel Hans Moore, of the 88th Regiment, for his courageous conduct in attempting to rescue a private of the frontier-armed mounted police, in action with Ngqikas near Komgha on the 29th December 1877.

This belated award was for Moore's attempts at rescuing a trooper of the Frontier-Armed Mounted Police during the Ninth Cape Frontier War at an action known as the 'Battle of Draaibosch'.

Moore was the son of Captain Garrett Moore of the 38th Regiment and had been born in Richmond Barracks, Dublin on 31 March 1834.

His mother was Charlotte Butler of Drum, County Tipperary. Commissioned into the 94th Foot (later the 2nd Battalion, Connaught Rangers), he was with them on 29 December 1877 in action against the Gcaleka people near Komgha. The FAMP had been skirmishing ahead of the 94th when Moore noticed Trooper Giese knocked off his horse. Moore immediately rode forward – and using his revolver, attempted to hold off the natives as he tried to get the injured man back on his horse to escape. Giese was not able to mount and was killed. When Moore returned to his lines, he discovered he had been wounded in the arm by a spear thrust. He later left the regiment and, on returning to England, joined the 93rd Regiment. In 1879 he wrote his own warrant and recommendation for the Victoria Cross – and despite this unusual approach, it was awarded.

Moore retired from the army in 1888 and returned to his home in Tipperary. Here he died on 7 October 1889 – drowning during a sailing accident. He is buried in Mount Jerome Cemetery, Dublin.

Members of the Border Guard stationed at White Rock on the Tugela River.

20

The South African Field Force and the End of the War

The troops Lord Chelmsford had at his disposal for the destruction of the Zulu Army at Ulundi were as follows: Major General Henry Hope Crealock's 1st Division – incorporating two brigades and a number of divisional troops. The 1st Brigade was commanded by Colonel Pearson and consisted of the 2nd Battalion of the 3rd Foot (Buffs), the 88th Regiment (Connaught Rangers) and the 99th (Duke of Edinburgh's) Regiment. The 2nd Brigade – commanded by Lieutenant Colonel Clark – had the 57th (West Middlesex) Regiment, the 3rd Battalion of the 60th (King's Royal Rifle Corps) and the 91st (Princess Louise's Argyllshire Highlanders). His divisional troops consisted of the Naval Brigade, the 4th and 5th Battalions, NNC; John Dunn's scouts and 564 various mounted troops. There was also 'N' Battery, 6th Regiment, RA, containing six 7-pounder guns; 8th Battery, 7th Regiment, RA, containing two 7-pounder guns; 11th Battery, 7th Regiment, RA, with two 7-pounder guns; 'O' Battery, 6th Regiment, RA, Ammunition Column and the 30th Field 'D' Company, RE.

Major General Henry Hope Crealock – commander of the 1st Division; he was the elder brother of Chelmsford's Military Secretary.

The 2nd Division was commanded by Major General Edward Newdigate and also contained two brigades and divisional troops. The 1st Brigade – commanded by Colonel Glyn – contained the 2nd Battalion, 21st Regiment (Royal Scots Fusiliers) and the 58th (Rutlandshire) Regiment. The 2nd Brigade – commanded by Colonel Collingwood – contained the 1st Battalion, 24th Regiment, which was brought up to strength by drafts from

Isandlwana revisited.

The wagons that remained at Isandlwana were necessary for the re-invasion plans.

Members of the Cavalry Brigade returning from Isandlwana having recovered some of the wagons.

the depot in England and the 94th Regiment. His divisional troops consisted of 'N' Battery, 5th Regiment, RA, with six 7-pounder guns; 'N' Battery, 6th Regiment, RA, with six 9-pounder guns; and 'O' Battery, 6th Regiment, RA, Ammunition Column. There was also the 2nd (Field) Company, Royal Engineers; No.3 Troop, Natal Horse; Shepstone's Basuto Horse and the 2nd Regiment, Natal Native Contingent. The command was completed by detachments from the Army Service Corps, the Army Medical Department and an attached Cavalry Brigade under Major General Marshall – consisting of the 1st (King's Dragoon) Guards and the 17th Lancers.

There was also a brigade – designated as a 'Flying Column' – under the irrepressible Evelyn Wood VC. This contained the 1st Battalion, 13th (1st Somersetshire) (Prince Albert's Light Infantry) Regiment – henceforth the 1/13th. There was also the 80th (Staffordshire Volunteers) Regiment and the 90th (Perthshire Volunteers) Regiment. Artillery support was the 11th Battery, 7th Regiment, RA, with four 7-pounder guns and the 10th Battery, 7th Regiment, RA equipped with Gatling guns. There was also the 5th Field 'D' Company, RE and 95 Mounted Infantry. The cavalry were the Frontier Light Horse, Transvaal Rangers, Baker's Horse (also known as Baker's Light Horse), Natal Native Horse and the Natal Light Horse; attached was a unit of the Natal Native Pioneers.

Major General Edward Newdigate commanding the 2nd Division.

Chelmsford's main supply wagons were formed into a laager at Mtonjaneni on 29 June. Here, the men discarded their packs and tents and prepared to move out the following morning – carrying rations for only 10 days. A garrison was to remain to secure the camp and Chelmsford decided to leave the 1st Battalion of the 24th Regiment – this despite aggrieved pleas from the officers who wanted their revenge for Isandlwana. Chelmsford knew that the ranks were filled with men who were mostly new recruits – brought out from the regimental depot to fill the ranks after the debacle of 22 January – and he was not prepared to take any chances in this (his last) attempt to regain something of his reputation.

The following morning, Chelmsford marched his cavalry, infantry and artillery into the valley of the White Umfolozi. This force consisted of most of Newdigate's 2nd Division and Wood's Flying Column. The day was spent marching across a parched sandy plain dotted with cactus and thorn bushes. That night, the troops spent the hours of darkness without cover and only cold rations to eat.

By the morning of 3 July, Chelmsford had concentrated his forces into a laager surrounded by a trench. For added security, he had ordered the construction of a small stone redoubt on a low hill close by. Directly across the river was a low bluff, with a drift situated at either side. This position was held by a number of Zulu riflemen, who took pot-shots at the watering parties as they made their way down to the riverbank. Brevet Lieutenant Colonel Buller VC was ordered out from the camp at 1.30pm to carry out a reconnaissance of the ground between the river and Ulundi. One of those accompanying the patrol was Captain Beresford of the 9th (The Queen's Royal) Lancers.

Captain Lord William Leslie de la Poer Beresford had been born in Mullaghbrack, County Armagh on 20 July 1847 and was the third son of The Rev John de la Poer, 4th Marquis of Waterford. He was not the first Beresford to fight in South Africa: George de la Poer Beresford, 1st Marquis of Waterford, had served there in 1806. Beresford had spent December 1878 in India – serving at that time with General Sir Sam Browne's Peshawar Field Force wintering at Jellalabad. Here, he had Christmas dinner with the headquarters staff and his friend Archibald Forbes, correspondent of the *Daily News*.

The following day, they made their way down to Umballa – from where Beresford was to return to Simla and his duties as ADC to the Viceroy of India. Beresford and Forbes had intended to meet again during the advance on Kabul, but news of the disaster at Isandlwana changed the plans of both men. Beresford had hoped to serve on the staff of his old friend Major General Marshall – commander of the regular Cavalry Brigade that had been sent out as part of the much-needed reinforcements.

Fate decreed that this was not to be. Buller's staff officer had been killed in a recent skirmish with the Zulu, and Beresford was offered his post.[1] When Forbes had met

1   Archibald Forbes, in his dispatch 'The Bravest Deed I Ever Saw', tells us that Beresford: 'bought his horses, requisitioned an Irish (very Irish) ex-trooper of the Royal Dragoons as groom, cook and body servant'; *Pearson's Magazine*, 1896.

Captain Lord William Leslie de la Poer Beresford, 9th (The Queen's Royal) Lancers.

Archibald Forbes – war correspondent for the *Daily News*; a canny Scot, with a whirling moustache.

Major General Frederick Marshall – commander of the Cavalry Brigade.

Beresford at Khambula, there was time for only a brief handshake before Beresford continued with his duty as staff officer – a duty which included keeping duty rosters of all units in the command, inspection of daily parades, briefing of reconnaissance detachments (and leading them, if necessary), restraining the foolhardy, heartening the funkers and being Buller's right-hand man on all occasions. Despite all of this, Archibald Forbes said: 'He was cheery; with his ready Irish wit, he had a vein of genial yet jibing badinage that kept queer-tempered fellows in good humour while it pricked them into obedience'.

As Buller's command, with Beresford in attendance, they crossed the river and came under sporadic rifle fire from the Zulu concealed on the bluff. At the same time, Chelmsford's artillery fired from the laager – the shells bursting on the same position. Buller sent Baker's Horse on a left-flanking move behind the bluff to take the Zulu snipers in the rear. The result of this was a brief and bloody skir-

mish. When the warriors realised what had happened, they broke from cover and ran for their lives; between 30 and 40 men took to their heels across the open plain. Baker's men calmly dismounted – and taking carefully-aimed shots, dropped the Zulu one after the other. Those that did manage to evade this fire were ridden down; there were few survivors.

As this was happening, Buller led the remaining units across the plain towards Ulundi. This was to be the swansong of the Frontier Light Horse, the Transvaal Rangers, Whalley's Natal Light Horse and the men of the Edendale Contingent. The area to be scouted was known as the 'Mahlabathini Plain' – described as a vast, gently-rolling basin of sandy soil and covered with long waving grass. The plain was encircled with seven or eight large villages – the largest of which was Ulundi.

A caricature of 'Ulundi Bill'.

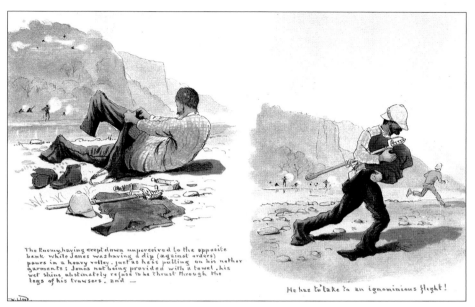

The watering parties under fire on 3 July. (From a sketch by Lieutenant William Whitelocke Lloyd, 1st Battalion, 24th Regiment. Lloyd, a talented artist, came from County Waterford)

'First Spear!'

While the patrol spotted many small bands of warriors, there was, as yet, no sign of a major *impi*. Buller forged ahead – searching for an ideal killing ground for the following day's battle. As the patrol advanced, they espied a large goatherd being driven by a party of Zulu warriors towards a grassy depression some distance ahead. Beresford quickly caught up with one of the warriors who had lagged behind the rest. As Beresford closed, the Zulu turned around and raised his shield above his head – a sign of surrender. Beresford – keen enough to come to Zululand, but not interested enough to learn anything about his intended enemy – killed the warrior with a mighty thrust of his sword that pierced both shield and man. He then turned and galloped back with the traditional cry of the pig-sticker: "First spear!" The Colonials were largely unimpressed.

As the patrol spread out to encircle the remaining Zulu and their herd of goats, Buller became suspicious. The 'herders' seemed in no hurry – and it appeared that they were leading the horsemen on. Sensing a trap, Buller at once gave the order to open fire from the saddle. Even as the troopers pulled their carbines from the saddle buckets, a tremendous volley of rifle fire erupted from the long grass approximately 150 yards to their front. As with most firing by untrained riflemen, most of the volley went high. Nevertheless, some horses were hit – and three men fell from their saddles. One of these was Trooper Pearce – killed by a Zulu bullet. Sergeant Fitzmaurice – a Mounted Infantryman from the 1st/24th – was wounded and his horse was bowled over by the volley; he was left stunned and bleeding. As the fallen man struggled into a sitting position, the Zulu closed in for the kill. Beresford, seeing the plight of a fellow Irishman, turned and rode back – arriving at the same time as the leading warriors. With him went Sergeant Edmund O'Toole, who kept the warriors at bay with shots from his carbine. Beresford offered his stirrup and ordered the Sergeant up behind him. Fitzmaurice – dazed by the fall and his wounds – either did not hear, or understand him. Beresford dismounted and attempted to lift him into the saddle, but Fitzmaurice was a well-built man and Beresford could not set him up on the horse. At this point, Fitzmaurice urged Beresford to save himself. Beresford's reply, although not exactly recorded, included a burst of broad Anglo-Saxon and the threat of a closed fist. As Beresford continued to try and hoist the wounded man into the saddle, he was also able to use his revolver to good effect on the encroaching enemy. Sergeant O'Toole, seeing the difficulty Beresford was having, dismounted – and between them, they managed to hoist Fitzmaurice onto the back of the horse. Beresford quickly followed – and with O'Toole covering the rear and helping to hold the wounded Fitzmaurice in the saddle, they rode after the patrol and the safety of the river just as the main body of enemy arrived.

Cecil D'Arcy was also making his way back towards the river when he saw Trooper Raubenheim tumble from the saddle. He immediately turned and raced back to the fallen man. Raubenheim was unable to stand, and D'Arcy was forced to dismount and assist him to his feet. As both men settled back on the horse, it suddenly shied and threw both men back onto the ground. The charging warriors were now very close – and with the noise of gunfire and the shouts of the warriors, D'Arcy's horse was going mad, bucking and kicking. Taking a few precious moments to calm the frightened animal, D'Arcy again attempted to get the injured Trooper into the saddle. In doing so, he strained his back to the extent that he was forced to drop the injured man. Scarcely able to hold onto the horse due to the severe pain in his back, D'Arcy struggled up into the saddle; and with a few scattered revolver shots, kept the enemy at bay until he could ride free – leaving the unfortunate Trooper Raubenheim to his fate.

Back at the drift, those Zulu that had escaped from Baker's attack had returned – and they were not alone! A force of several thousand Zulu had attacked and was being held off by a heavy fire from Baker's men – now ensconced on the reverse slope of the bluff. They were able to hold the drift open long enough to allow Buller's men to cross. Buller's men then, in turn, provided covering fire for Baker as he retreated across the river. A short sharp firefight developed, as both sides exchanged shots across the water before Buller ordered a withdrawal back to the camp.

Archibald Forbes would later write:

> It was one of Ireland's good days; if at home she is the "distressful country," wherever bold deed are to be done and military honour to be gained, no nation carries the head higher out of the dust. If originally Norman, the Waterford family have been Irish now for six centuries, and Bill Beresford is an Irishman in heart and blood. Sergeant Fitzmaurice, the wounded man who displayed a self-abnegation so fine was an Irishman also; and Sergeant O'Toole – well, I think one runs no risk in the assumption that an individual who bears that name, in spite of all temptation, remains an Irishman. So, in this brilliant little episode the Green Isle has it all to herself.

Later that afternoon, Forbes went into Beresford's tent and found him asleep. Rousing him with the news that Colonel Wood had recommended him for the Victoria Cross, he was greeted with a thrown boot and the phrase: "Get along with your nonsense, you impostor." With this, Beresford turned over and went back to sleep.[2] On returning home to County Waterford, Beresford was hailed in the papers as 'Ulundi Beresford'.[3]

2   Quoted in 'The Bravest Deed I Ever Saw' by Archibald Forbes, *Pearson's Magazine*, 1896.
3   *The Irish Times*, 1 September 1879.

21

Ulundi (Not so much a battle, as controlled slaughter)

Chelmsford was well aware that he must have the final victory before the arrival of Wolseley. On the morning of 4 July, the reconstructed 1st Battalion, 24th Regiment of Foot was detailed to remain on the south bank of the river to guard Chelmsford's camp. There was much bitterness and frustration among the surviving officers and men at being denied their chance for retribution, but perhaps not so much from those new recruits recently arrived from England.

One man thoroughly frustrated at not going was the battalion's commander, Major William Mathew Dunbar.

Born in Cork on 21 October 1833, Dunbar had seen action in the Crimea, including the attack on the Redan and siege of Sevastopol during the Indian Mutiny – being present at the relief of Lucknow. The previous January, Major Dunbar had been in command of four companies of the 2nd/24th along with a small contingent of native troops in the Ibashe Valley (about halfway between Rorke's Drift and Isandlwana). He and his men were charged with effecting repairs to the road and collecting a store of firewood. Major Dunbar was ordered to make his camp close to Sihayo's homestead in ground covered in thick scrub that offered little in the way of fields of fire. A result of this was that strong picquets had to be mounted each night – provided by men who had been working throughout the day.

On 16 January, Lord Chelmsford and his staff arrived to inspect the ongoing work. Major Dunbar expressed his view that the campsite was unsuitable and asked permission to move it to the far side of the stream. As this was discussed, Lieutenant

Major Matthew William Dunbar, 1st Battalion, 24th Regiment.

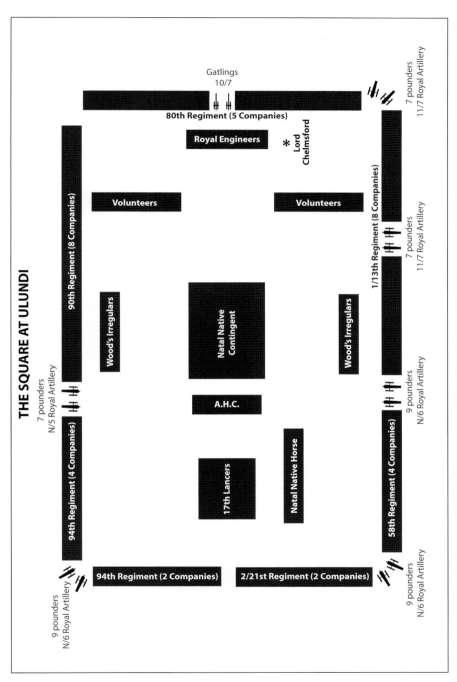

THE SQUARE AT ULUNDI

Gatlings
10/7

80th Regiment (5 Companies)

7 pounders
11/7 Royal Artillery

Royal Engineers

Lord Chelmsford

Volunteers

Volunteers

90th Regiment (8 Companies)

1/13th Regiment (8 Companies)

7 pounders
11/7 Royal Artillery

Wood's Irregulars

Natal Native Contingent

Wood's Irregulars

A.H.C.

7 pounders
N/5 Royal Artillery

9 pounders
N/6 Royal Artillery

94th Regiment (4 Companies)

17th Lancers

Natal Native Horse

58th Regiment (4 Companies)

9 pounders
N/6 Royal Artillery

94th Regiment (2 Companies)

2/21st Regiment (2 Companies)

9 pounders
N/6 Royal Artillery

Map 7 – The square at Ulundi.

Colonel Crealock was reported to have said: "If Major Dunbar is afraid to stay here, we could send someone who is not." As a result of this grievous insult, Major Dunbar immediately offered to resign his commission, but was persuaded not to by Chelmsford.

North of the White Umfolozi River,[1] Buller once again led his command of horsemen – the vanguard of Chelmsford's new army. Wood's Flying Column followed the cavalry, and Major General Edward Newdigate's 2nd Division followed this in turn. Newdigate was accompanied by his DAAG, Captain William Edward Montgomery, who was on secondment from the Scots Guards. Montgomery had been born in Grey Abbey, County Down and had received an education at Eton before purchasing a commission in the Guards. His leaving party was such an affair that an account of it was published in book form for distribution to friends and family.

Brevet Lieutenant Colonel John North Crealock, 95th (Derbyshire) Regiment, and Lord Chelmsford's Military Secretary.

The staff of Wood's 'Flying Column'.

1   Today known as the 'White Mfolozi River'.

Once across, the entire formation formed a hollow square – or, to be more precise, a rectangle. What followed was not so much a battle, as controlled slaughter. As Buller's cavalry galloped ahead – scouting for any sight of the enemy – Chelmsford began to organise his force. Wood's column drew up in formation and formed the 'front' of the square, while Newdigate's men formed the other three sides. Within this square were the 12 guns of the Royal Artillery, two Gatling guns, a company of Royal Engineers, a field hospital (including Surgeon Reynolds VC), a battalion of the Natal Native Contingent, a contingent of Wood's Irregulars and the ammunition wagons. To secure the 'rear' of the square, there were two squadrons of the 17th Lancers and a troop of the Natal Native Horse; a contingent of the 1st King's Dragoon Guards was also present. With the regimental band of the 13th Regiment beating out topical music, Chelmsford's army marched out across the veldt and Ulundi.

As the square marched across the Mahlabathini Plain, Chelmsford's horsemen ranged about – and as the rearguard passed the village of kwaBulawayo, the Natal Native Horse put it to the torch. Next in line for official arson was the village of kwaNodwengu, but Chelmsford suddenly realised that the palls of rolling smoke would provide cover for any advancing enemy – and those huts that had been set alight were quickly extinguished.

All around the square, the Zulu could be seen, but too far away (and in small numbers) to be any danger. Anxious to aggravate an attack and fight the battle he longed for, Chelmsford ordered the cavalry to attempt to provoke the enemy. Buller's men – covering the same ground as the previous day's reconnaissance – observed enemy all around, but they refused to close. In order to provoke an attack, Buller sent forward a detachment of Baker's Horse, who promptly became enmeshed with a strong party of Zulu, but managed to escape without suffering any casualties. The warriors, stung by these gestures, did as

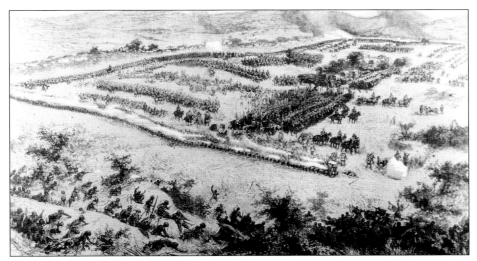

The British square on the Mahlabathini Plain near to the *ikhanda* of kwaNodwengu.

Chelmsford had hoped and charged the square from all sides! As they closed in, the cavalry retired inside – and the infantry and artillery prepared to do their bit.

The leading face of the square comprised of five companies of the 80th Regiment, with two Gatling guns of the 10th/7th, RA in the centre. There were two 7-pounder field guns on the right corner, with two 9-pounders on the left. On the left face were the 90th Light Infantry (eight companies strong) and four companies of the 94th Regiment, with two 7-pounders located between them. On the right face were the 1st Battalion of the 13th Light Infantry and four companies of the 58th Regiment, which were supported by two 7-pounders and two 9-pounders. The rear face was held by two companies of the 94th Regiment and two companies of the 2nd Battalion, 21st Regiment. Inside the square were two squadrons of the 17th Lancers, the 2nd Natal Native Contingent, a troop of Natal Native Horse, Wood's Irregulars and volunteers.

Within this living laager were a number of Irishmen and others who had previously shown their mettle: James Henry Reynolds VC, Surgeon John Anderson MD (he was attached to the Royal Artillery and Royal Engineers), Surgeon John Henry Hunt from County Limerick, Surgeon Major Patrick Stafford (in charge of the square's stretcher-bearers) and Walter Dunne (responsible as ever for the proficient distribution of ammunition), together with Jack Chard, with No.5 Company, RE. The infantry were formed up four deep, with the front two ranks kneeling and the remaining two standing in the 'Prepare to Receive Cavalry' position.

Inside the square at Ulundi.

The 90th (Perthshire Volunteers) Light Infantry under attack at the Battle of Ulundi.

The guns opened fire at 8.45am – recoiling on their carriages as they hurled shells into the approaching Zulu mass. As the warriors closed with the red square, the Gatling guns joined in – followed by the rifles of the infantry. No amount of bravery could stand up to the fire being delivered from the square, and warriors fell in their droves. Those few Zulu armed with rifles returned a desultory fire – and the defenders suffered few casualties. For many of the veterans in the ranks who had witnessed previous Zulu attacks, it seemed as if the assault lacked a certain ardour.

Only in one place did the Zulu come close to hand-to-hand combat: at the corner of the square – held by the 21st and the 58th Regiments – the kwaNodwengu (some 2,000 to 3,000 strong) made a determined rush, but even here, bullets beat bravery and the assault failed. The Zulu attacks faltered on all sides, and Chelmsford saw it was time for the cavalry. He ordered Colonel Drury Curzon Drury-Lowe to pursue, but not too far; the lessons had been learnt with regard to cavalry out-distancing their support in unfamiliar country. The 17th Lancers, commanded by Drury-Lowe, also rode out. He had been recalled from half pay to command the Lancers when their commanding officer had suffered an injury during a training exercise prior to departure.

While inside the square, a spent round had struck Drury-Lowe – knocking him from his horse. A brief examination showed no serious injury, and he quickly remounted. Drury-Lowe had served with his regiment in the Crimea, but unlike his brother, had not taken part in the Charge of the Light Brigade. This charge, while not to be compared with the action of 25 October 1855, would have to suffice – and he would have his moment of glory!

The attack from a Zulu perspective.

Colonel Drury Curzon
Drury-Lowe.

The charge of the 17th (Duke of Cambridge's Own) Lancers at Ulundi.

As Buller's cavalry were let slip from the front of the square, with them rode a troop of the 1st (King's) Dragoon Guards – and in the ranks was Trooper John Doogan from Aughrim, County Galway, who would later win the Victoria Cross at Laing's Nek in the First Boer War.

A bloody, relentless and murderous pursuit ensued, with no quarter being sought by the Zulu – and certainly none offered by the British. Scores were to be settled – Isandlwana and Ntombe River to be avenged. Wounded warriors were butchered where they lay by the men of the Natal Native Horse and the African infantry of the NNC and Wood's Irregulars. Any remaining Zulu buildings were put to the torch, while the British artillery shelled the retiring warriors.

Soon after 10.00am Chelmsford ordered Buller to take his command and burn Ulundi.

As the cavalry approached, a race developed to see who would be the first to enter Cetshwayo's capital. The victor was Captain Lord William Beresford, who not only won the race, but was also lucky enough to be able to leave again; Zulu warriors were still present. William Drummond, staff interpreter, lost his way in the jumble of huts (the site covered almost 90 acres) and his charred body was found several months later. Melton Prior narrowly escaped attack as he sketched the burning huts.

Brevet Lieutenant Colonel Redvers Buller
wearing his Victoria Cross.

Private John Doogan, 1st (King's)
Dragoon Guards.

The war artist Charles Fripp sketches the Zulu fallen at Ulundi – a sad testimony to the
ferocity of British firepower.

The Lancers rout the Zulu forces.

As the British artillery shells the retreating Zulu warriors in the distant hills, revenge is being extracted much closer, as can be seen on the left of this engraving.

Ulundi in flames.

Melton Prior – war correspondent and
illustrator for the *Illustrated London
News*; he rarely sketched himself
without a hat.

He noticed a Zulu approaching from the side – and quickly cramming his sketch-book into a pocket, he mounted his horse and fled to safety.

After all of this, the people of Britain were still hungry for more bloodshed – albeit of a 'pretend' kind. The following announcements appeared in the *Belfast News Letter* of 21 and 24 July 1879:

AMUSEMENTS
DELAY OF THE ZULUS.

VICTORIA HALL
COPY OF TELEGRAM.
"Chief taken ill. The others will not come without him."
The arrival of the Zulus will be duly announced. Probably they will be here on Tuesday.
AMUSEMENTS

VICTORIA HALL

THE FRIENDLY ZULUS

THE ZULUS WILL HOLD A FASHIONABLE
LEVEE
At 3.30 p.m. TO-DAY
POPULAR CONCERT AND LEVEE
At 8 o'clock p.m.
The ZULUS were received last night by a crowded audience with every mani-festation of wonder and delight.
There is no concert in the afternoon – only at Night.
WAR SONGS AND DANCES.
ASSAULT AT ARMS.
WRESTLING.
FIGHTING WITH THE ASSEGAI AND SHIELD
Admission, 2s 1s and 6d. Tickets at Cramer, Wood & Co's, Castle Place.

The Zulu must have proved hugely popular; by 25 July, they had been invited to the Whitehead Regatta. Whitehead is a small coastal village to the north of Belfast. The following report is taken from a Belfast newspaper, whose reporter seems to have had little, or no knowledge of the Zulu – but then again, did anyone in Britain?

THE ZULUS AND THE WHITEHEAD REGATTA
For the fourth annual regatta at Whitehead, which will take place on Saturday, unusual attractions are announced. Besides the regatta, the programme for which includes four sailing races, several rowing races, swimming races, & co,

the troupe of Zulus which arrived in Belfast on Wednesday will appear and go through various novel and interesting feats in the open air. They will exhibit the mode in which their countrymen hurl the assegai and use the shield in warfare. They will also engage in throwing the assegai at targets, and it is stated that they exhibit marvellous precision at this practice. After engaging in a wrestling contest, they will swim in the bay, and dive for various objects. We understand that they are most powerful swimmers and expert divers, and can with ease bring up a coin from great depths. The Zulu entertainment will conclude with a swimming match by the troupe. Whitehead is now admitted on all hands to be one of the most delightful watering places within easy access of Belfast. The surrounding land scenery could scarcely be surpassed for picturesqueness, while the view across the Lough on a fine summer day is magnificent. Should the weather prove fine, we doubt not that large numbers will avail themselves of this opportunity not alone to visit this charming spot, but also of judging of the physique, strength, quickness of motion, & co, of men belonging to a nationality which recent events have rendered unusually interesting to the British people. The Northern Counties Railway Company, who have [as] ever shown a desire to afford every facility to the travelling public, will run several trains during the day to Whitehead, one of which will be a special running direct from Belfast without stopping at any intermediate station, at 3.35 p.m. This train which will leave in

After the charge at Ulundi, a Lancer tends to his wounded horse.
(From a painting by Alphonse de Neuville)

time for some of the principle [sic] races, and for the entire of the Zulu performances, will start from the arrival platform of the Belfast terminus at Whitla Street, where tickets can be obtained. Tickets for all the trains will be issued at excursion fares.

Some men arrived too late for the war. The following letter is from Private George Williamson of Belfast, County Antrim. He transferred from his own regiment, the Inniskilling Dragoons, to the 17th Lancers in the hope of seeing some action. It was published in the *Belfast News Letter* on 20 September 1879:

LETTER FROM A SOLDIER AT THE CAPE

MAIN BARRACKS CAPE TOWN, August 18-

We had it very rough for four or five days after leaving Portsmouth, but it cleared up soon, and we had a very pleasant passage to Simon's Bay, where we stopped four days to coal. We then proceed to Natal, which took us four days, and arrived in time to hear that we were "too late" – news which disappointed us all I can assure you, after coming so far. We stopped in Natal port, which is a very dangerous place for a big ship like the 'Egypt', on account of the very heavy swell, which rolls in from the Indian Ocean. One night we thought we were going to the bottom, as the ship rolled till her yardarm actually touched the waves. We were in Natal three days, when we received an order to proceed back to Simon's Bay, and disembark there. We took on board about 150 of Lonsdale's Horse, and landed some at East London and Port Elizabeth, the remainder we brought on to Simon's Town.

When we arrived at Simon's Bay, the authorities there did not know what was up; they thought we had broken our engines. They had received no orders about us, so they had to telegraph to Cape Town for orders. An order came back, saying that we were to disembark at once, and I can tell you we were not sorry to hear it, after being kept on board ship for forty four days, and it was a good job, too, as we had only four days [sic] forage for the horses, of which we had three hundred on board. Our draft was the largest of any that came out, and we only lost three horses. When we landed, we saddled our horses and put our kits on, and then led them on foot for about three miles, to a place where we had to encamp. We could not ride them, as their legs and backs were tender after standing so long. We stopped about eight days at Simon's Town to exercise the horses and get them round a bit; of course we were under canvas all the time. We then marched to Cape Town, which is distant about twenty two miles. We halted at a place called Winberg, which is half way, and dismounted to water and feed the horses, and were treated very kindly by the English people, of whom there were a great many there. We arrived at Cape Town about seven p.m., and put up our horses, and as it was Saturday night we went out to have a look round the town, and if it were not for the natives, we would almost think we were at home. Fruit is cheap here, and vegetables dear; potatoes 3 1/2 per pound and butter is very dear. We sold all the horses on the 11th and 12th August, and they all brought a fair price – about £50 each; mares ran up to £80, and my own brought £75. There is a rumour that the 17th are going home, but we will not know for a week or two yet. Our pay is 1s 2d a day and free rations, of which we get plenty. It is now the middle of winter here, and just as hot as our own summer. If the regiment goes home it will only stop about 18 months, as it is for India then. I have not much more to say now, except that I am afraid we will not get the medal expected. – I am yours, & c.,

George Williamson.

The Zulu kingdom, founded in 1816 by Shaka, was in existence for some 63 years. Following the capture of King Cetshwayo, the country was destroyed on 1 September 1879 at the stroke of a pen wielded by an Irishman.

Sir Garnet Wolseley's action ensured that never again would a Zulu monarch hold absolute power over his people. They had become a divided nation, with Zulu pitted against Zulu – evoking old enmities that would eventually lead to a bloody civil war.

A print showing a detachment funeral. (Taken from W.W. Lloyd's publication *On Active Service*)

The capture of King Cetshwayo on 28 August 1879.

It seems somehow fitting that a King should be escorted by King's Dragoon Guards:
Cetshwayo under escort by members of the 1st (King's) Dragoon Guards and 60th Rifles.

With the stroke of a pen, Sir Garnet Joseph Wolseley seals the destiny of the sovereignty of the Zulu nation, 1 September 1879.

King Cetshwayo and four of his wives on board the transport ship *Natal* bound for captivity at the castle in Cape Town.

King Cetshwayo embarking at Port Durnford.

Zulu *izinduna* listen to the fate of their nation at Ulundi on 1 September 1879.

22

Aftermath

Our God and soldiers we like adore
E'er at the brink of danger; not before
After deliverance, both are requited, our God forgotten, and our
Soldiers slighted.[1]

When the war was over and the country no longer needed the redcoat, it was obvious that the officer fares much better that the ranker. An officer can continue to serve, or take the option of going on half pay. In many cases, he had an estate to go back to and a business to manage, or at least pay someone else to manage it for him.

For the ranker, things were a little different; few Irishmen seemed to have returned to their homes. Many married and settled close to their former barracks, while others stayed in South Africa to start a new life. As there was no provision for the posthumous award of the Victoria Cross at that time, no award was made to Melvill or Coghill for their actions at Isandlwana. Nevertheless, an announcement in the *London Gazette* of 2 May 1879 announced that both officers: '…would have been recommended to Her Majesty for the Victoria Cross had they survived'. Twenty-three Victoria Crosses were awarded for actions in the Zulu War of 1879. Of these, nine were awarded to Irishmen. Melvill left a widow, Sarah Elizabeth, and two small sons. She was placed on the Civil List, with a pension of £100 per year. Coghill's portrait hangs in the chapel of Haileybury College, while his Victoria Cross is held by the Regimental Museum. Sir John Jocelyn Coghill received a scrap of the colour – a fragment smaller than a postage stamp; this he had inserted into a gold and crystal locket. In 1907, the regulation regarding the award of posthumous VCs came into effect – and the first were issued to the families of the two officers. Coghill's Victoria Cross was sent to his brother, Sir Egerton Coghill. A memorial window was dedicated to Coghill in Cork

---

1   Francis Quarles (1592-1644).

Lieutenant Nevill Coghill VC. (From a painting by R.J. Marrion)

Cathedral. It carries the family coat of arms and the motto *Non Dormit Qui Custodit.*[2] There is also a memorial window to Melvill in St Finbarr's Cathedral in Cork.

When the 24th Regiment returned to England in 1880, Queen Victoria requested to see the famous colour – and it was taken to her at Osborne House in July. She placed a wreath of immortelles on the staff and a message was sent to the commanding officer of the regiment from the Adjutant General:

> As a lasting token of her act of placing a wreath on the Queen's Colour to commemorate the devotion displayed by Lieutenants Melvill and Coghill in their heroic endeavour to save the Colour on January 22nd, 1879, and of the noble defence of Rorke's Drift, Her Majesty has been graciously pleased to command that a silver wreath shall in future be borne on the peak of the staff of the Queen's Colour of the Twenty-Fourth Regiment.

The Rorke's Drift defenders did well for medals. On 2 May 1879, the *London Gazette* announced the award of the Victoria Cross to the following: Chard, Bromhead, Allan, Hitch, Hook, Robert Jones, William Jones and John Williams. Bromhead was promoted to Brevet Major, as was Chard.

2   'The sentinels sleep not'.

The Colour Party of the 1st Battalion, 24th Regiment, at Osborne House, 1880.

With the death of Captain Pope at Isandlwana, Bromhead had technically assumed the rank of Captain at that time – and therefore his promotion was not a double-jump. However, it took the authorisation of the Duke of Cambridge to allow Chard to rise from Lieutenant to Brevet Major – and he remains the only Royal Engineer officer to have skipped the rank of Captain.

Both men were invited to Balmoral together on their return home. Chard attended and was presented with a gold signet ring by the Queen. Bromhead had gone on a fishing trip to Ireland and did not receive the invitation in time. Despite tendering his apologies immediately, he did not receive a further invitation until the summer of 1880. The award of the Victoria Cross far outweighed any supposed handicap of Bromhead's hearing, and he continued to serve. However, he received no further promotion and died of typhoid at Allahabad, India on 9 February 1891 – being buried in the New Cantonment Cemetery; he was 46 years old. His fellow subaltern of Rorke's Drift, John Chard, rose to the rank of Colonel, but saw no further active service. He died of cancer of the tongue on 1 November 1897.

With the initial award of seven Victoria Crosses to the 24th and an award to Chard, the other units present felt they had played their part and clamoured for attention. It therefore became a matter of rationing several more VCs to the other Imperial units – not forgetting the Colonials, who had to be kept happy, as they would be needed for future campaigns. After discussion in the House of Commons, it was announced on 17 June that the Victoria Cross was to be awarded to Surgeon Major Reynolds, Army Hospital Corps for his actions at Rorke's Drift.

Brevet Major Gonville Bromhead VC,
1880.

Brevet Major John Rouse Merriott Chard VC,
1880.

As a result of a letter written to the magazine *Punch*, the Commissary General, Sir Edward Strickland, began a campaign to have the services of the Commissariat recognised. Both Dunne and Dalton were commended for their behaviour during the battle, although in written accounts, Dalton receives the most plaudits. Both men were recommended for the Victoria Cross, but only Dalton received the award – it being gazetted on 18 November 1879. It could not be understood by the press why Dunne did not receive the medal. *The Irish Times*, in particular, was most forceful:

> … the aid rendered to the defence by Assistant Commissary Dunne, and it is hard to see on what grounds the Cross has been

Surgeon Major James Henry Reynolds VC – a
later photograph.

withheld. Chard referred to the conduct of his young subordinate in assisting to
lay the last sod of the mealie bag defence work when exposed to heavy fire from
the enemy. There was certainly very little to choose in point of gallantry between
the conduct of the officers engaged in the fierce though brief fight. Each man did
his duty nobly and heroically and no one will grudge them the distinction. They
earned so well; but the military as well as the non military reader will, we think,
agree with us in saying that there was no reason that Dunne should have been
omitted from the list of those receiving the Cross.

Further pressure was brought to bear by the Colonial authorities in South Africa to
seek equal recognition for local troops. As a result of this, Corporal Schiess, Natal
Native Contingent was awarded the Victoria Cross. [3]
      While many critics say that the awarding of such a large number of medals for such
a small action smacks of propaganda – and the need to take the mind of the British
public away from the disaster that was Isandlwana – it must be remembered that in
1879, there were only two awards that could be made to other ranks: these were the
Victoria Cross and the Silver Medal for Distinguished Conduct. There were five of
these awarded to Rorke's Drift defenders: Colour Sergeant Bourne, Second Corporal
Attwood, Army Service Corps; Private Roy, 1st Battalion 24th Regiment; Second
Corporal McMahon, Army Hospital Corps and Wheeler John Cantwell, Royal
Artillery. Of these, two were Irishmen.
      John Cantwell, the Artilleryman, received his medal from Queen Victoria and was
later medically discharged at Woolwich on 19 July 1889 – being 'unfit for further
service'. He returned with his wife to South Africa and gave his intended place of residence at 8 Loop Street, Pietermaritzburg, Natal. He died in Durban, South Africa on
14 August 1900. The Army Hospital Corpsman, Michael McMahon, was the second
Irishman to be awarded the medal. Unfortunately, he had deserted by the time it was
announced, and it was subsequently withdrawn.
      Cecil D'Arcy – his recommendation for the award of a Victoria Cross at Hlobane
refused – received one for the unsuccessful attempt to rescue Trooper Raubenheim
during the reconnaissance prior to Ulundi. This mainly came about through newspaper

---

3   It has been stated in numerous publications, including the *Medal Yearbook* (2001 edition),
      that the 11 Victoria Crosses awarded for the defence of Rorke's Drift is the highest for
      a single engagement. While it remains the highest number for a single regiment in one
      action – seven to the 24th – the greatest number for a single 'engagement' are the 20
      VCs awarded for the attack on the Great Redan, Sebastopol, the Crimea, 18 June 1855.
      Eleven VCs were also awarded for the Zeebrugge Raid of April 1918; again, a degree of
      controversy is attached to these awards.
         Lucknow, 1857: the first siege had lasted 87 days; the second siege a further 61.
      Argument is also made for the largest number of Victoria Crosses awarded in a single day
      being the 24 earned on 16 November during the second relief – the bulk of these being for
      the assault on the Secundra Bagh.

'For Valour': five Victoria Cross deeds depicted in *The Penny Illustrated Paper*.

articles that appeared in which reporters had appended the letters 'VC' after his name – yet D'Arcy considered he was not the only one worthy of such a reward, and refused to accept the medal unless his comrade, Sergeant O'Toole, was also honoured.

Beresford received a VC for his rescue of Sergeant Fitzmaurice in the same action. When Beresford went to Windsor to receive his decoration from the Queen, he had been made aware of D'Arcy's position and stated he could not accept it unless Sergeant O'Toole, who had shared the danger, also shared the award.

The October issue of the *London Gazette* announced the award of the Victoria Cross to Captain Cecil D'Arcy and Sergeant Edmund O'Toole, Frontier Light Horse. Lord William de la Poer Beresford VC retired as a Lieutenant Colonel and died at Deepdene, Dorking, Surrey on 28 December 1900.

Sergeant O'Toole later enlisted with a regiment of native levies and was commissioned – rising to the rank of Captain; he subsequently served in the Basuto War.[4]

The death of Cecil D'Arcy must be one of the strangest events connected with any veteran of the Zulu War. After the 1879 campaign, he had fallen seriously ill – so much so that he was unable to make the journey to attend his father's funeral in King William's Town. He later recovered – and on 15 May 1880, he was commissioned as a Captain in the Cape Mounted Rifles. Prior to D'Arcy's appointment, the unit had fought at Morosi's Mountain in November 1879 and in the Basutoland Rebellion.[5]

The *Independent* newspaper in London reported that the Captain famously faked his own death:

> No longer is anyone likely to imitate Captain Henry Cecil Dudgeon D'Arcy of the Frontier Light Horse, who, having been awarded the VC in the Zulu wars, turned to drink.
>
> Later, a body wearing his clothes was found in a cave and, this being the pathology of a century ago, presumed to be his. Only many decades later was it learnt that D'Arcy had found a dead man lying in the snow, changed clothes with him, and gone to Natal, and lived out the rest of his life under an assumed name. He was once recognised in 1925, but swore his discoverer to the secret, which the man kept until D'Arcy died.

His story is told in the (out of print) book *What Happened to a V.C.* by Patricia D'Arcy. He is interred in the King William's Town Cemetery, Eastern Cape.

Percy Barrow became the Colonel of the 19th Prince of Wales's Own Hussars and was awarded a CB and a CMG. He died on 13 January 1886 in Cairo of wounds received at the Battle of El Teb, which were caused by over-exertion during a regimental sports day. The body was returned to England and he was buried in Saltwood

---

4   Today known as the 'BaSotho Gun War'.
5   BaSotho Rebellion.

Lieutenant Colonel
William Beresford VC.

Captain
Beresford's rescue
of Sergeant J.
Fitzmaurice of the
1st Battalion, 24th
Regiment.

Beresford escapes from the Zulu ambush, with Fitzmaurice clinging on behind him.

Beresford rides off with Fitzmaurice, as Sergeant Edmund O'Toole of the Frontier Light Horse covers their escape.

D'Arcy's attempted rescue of Trooper J.A. Raubenheim.

Captain Henry Cecil Dudgeon
D'Arcy, Frontier Light Horse.

Lieutenant Colonel Percy Barrow,
19th Hussars.

John Dartnell, circa 1899, as a Brigadier
General.

Sekhukhune of the Pedi.

Parish Church, Kent, where there is also a memorial plaque and window. Another memorial can be found at Cheltenham College, Gloucestershire.

John Dartnell later served with distinction in the Boer War (1899-1901) and retired as Major General John Dartnell KCB, CMG. He died in August 1913.

Shortly after the action at Rorke's Drift, Walter Dunne fell ill with fever. However, he had recovered in time to accompany Chelmsford's second invasion and was present in the square at Ulundi. Later, he was given command of the supply depot at St Paul's – and here he saw Cetshwayo being brought in as a captive. Despite preconceived ideas of him being a 'crazed black savage', Walter Dunne described the King in almost glowing terms – stating: "His demeanour was manly and dignified, and not unworthy of a captive King."

After his time at St Paul's, Dunne was dispatched to the north to accompany an expedition in the final campaign against Sekhukhune of the Pedi.[6]

Walter Dunne continued to serve after the Zulu War – and during the First Boer War, he found himself in the town of Potchefstroom in the Transvaal. Again, he performed his duties admirably – and while the garrison was forced to surrender after

6   Today known as the 'baPedi'.

Privates Thomas Flawn and Francis Fitzpatrick rescue Lieutenant Dewar of the 1st (King's) Dragoon Guards.

four months of siege, they were allowed to march out with full military honours. He returned to his home for a short time before going to Africa once again and taking part in the Battles of Tel-el-Kebir in 1882 and Suakim in 1885. In 1897, he was awarded the CB for distinguished service. Dunne retired with the rank of Colonel – and due to ill health, he retired to Italy for the remainder of his days. He died in a nursing home in Rome on 2 July 1908 and is buried in the Veterans' Cemetery.[7]

On 28 November, an assault was launched against the King's capital in the Transvaal. Among the units involved were the 94th Regiment and the 1st (King's) Dragoon Guards. The fighting was carried out in the face of determined resistance, with the British losing seven killed and 37 wounded, along with an estimated 300 to 1,000 natives being killed. Among the British wounded was Lieutenant Dewar of the 1st Dragoon Guards. He was in the process of being carried to the rear on a litter by a party of native bearers when they were attacked by approximately 30 of the enemy – causing the stretcher-bearers to flee. As the enemy closed with the severely-wounded Lieutenant, Privates Francis Fitzpatrick and Thomas Flawn of the 94th ran forward and picked up the wounded officer. Alternately carrying the Lieutenant and turning to fire at the pursuing enemy, they managed to get him to the safety of the main force; both men were awarded the Victoria Cross.

Francis Fitzpatrick was born in Tullycorbet, County Monaghan in 1859. He later served in the Boer War (1880-1881) – returning home in 1882 and being discharged in May 1888. For the South African War, he re-enlisted and served with the Argyll and Sutherland Highlanders. He returned home after his military service and died on 10 July 1933.[8] In June 1881, Fitzpatrick's VC was stolen by a fellow soldier – only to be found on that soldier's dead body the following August. Private Flawn VC died on 19 January 1925 – listed in *The Irish Times* as leaving the sum of £810. He was 69 years old and had been employed at the Woolwich Arsenal. He lived at 3 Olven Road, Plumstead, London.[9] The Victoria Cross had been presented to both men by their commanding officer, Lieutenant Colonel P.R. Anstruther, at Lydenburg in the Transvaal on 17 September 1880.

The army had granted Anthony Durnford a pension of £100 per annum for the injury he had suffered at Bushman's River Pass. When he died, it was discovered he had never drawn a penny of it. Natal society was less than charitable: in mid-1879, there was an extraordinary spiteful and, most probably, fraudulent attempt by Pietermaritzburg tradesmen to burden his estate with inflated bills and accounts. There was also an attempt to give credence to the rumour that Durnford had committed suicide towards the end of the battle.[10] During his time in Natal, Durnford had fallen in love with

7   Knight, Ian, *Nothing Remains but to Fight* (Greenhill Books: London, 1993); also, the website of the Keynsham Light Horse (now sadly defunct).
8   Doherty, Richard & Truesdale, David, *Irish Winners of the Victoria Cross* (Dublin, 2000).
9   *The Irish Times*, 21 March 1925.
10   Emery, Frank, *The Red Soldier* (London, 1977.)

Bishop Colenso's daughter. Frances Ellen Colenso was 25 years old to Durnford's 44, but it made no difference to their feelings. Durnford had not seen his wife or child for over 10 years, but this was Victoria's reign – and Natal was 'little England' in all its gossiping glory. The only way that Frances and Durnford could have enjoyed an open relationship was on the death of his wife – and she outlived them both. So complete did Durnford and Frances keep their love for each other that no hint of an affair ever arose – and Frances was one of the few who defended Durnford in the press during the years after the war. In the judgement of those most competent to decide, Durnford acted (under the circumstances) for the best. It was the opinion of Sir Lintorn Symons that Durnford had: '... fought and died as a true soldier, surrounded by natives, in whom he had inspired such love and devotion that they sold their lives by his side, covering the retreat of those who were flying...'[11] Sir Henry Bulwer stated: "Colonel Durnford was a soldier of soldiers, with all his heart in his profession: keen, active-minded, indefatigable, unsparing of himself, brave and utterly fearless, honourable, loyal, of great kindness and goodness of heart. I speak of him as I knew him." His brother officers of the Royal Engineers paid their own tribute by the placement of a stained-glass window to his memory in Rochester Cathedral.

Despite his wounds, Major Robert Henry Hackett survived Khambula and returned to the family home at Riverstown House, County Tipperary. Here he was cared for with great affection by his brother, Thomas, who had retired as a Lieutenant Colonel – having commanded the 23rd Regiment in the Indian Mutiny, where he had earned the Victoria Cross during the attack on the Secundra Bagh on 18 November 1857. Thomas was tragically killed in a shooting accident when the breech of his gun exploded during a shooting party at Arrabeg, King's County on 5 October 1880 – leaving his brother more dependent than ever.[12] Robert Hackett died on 30 December 1893, aged 54. He never married and is buried in Lockeen Churchyard near Riverstown, County Tipperary. A descendent of Robert's was General Sir John Hackett, who commanded 4 Parachute Brigade during Operation 'Market Garden' in September 1944.

Captain W.S. Hamilton of the 90th Light Infantry returned to the family home in County Wicklow. He died on 6 June 1893 and is buried in the Newcastle Church of Ireland Churchyard.

William Knox Leet received his Victoria Cross from Queen Victoria at Windsor on 9 December 1879. He went on to command the 1st Battalion, Somerset Light Infantry and then exchanged into the 2nd Battalion, which he commanded in the Burma War of 1885-87. He retired from the army as a General in July of the same year – having been awarded the CBE. He died on 27 June 1898 and is buried at Great Chart in Kent.

---

11   Quoted in *The Times*.
12   *The Irish Times*, 21 January 1898.

Surgeon James Henry Reynolds, Army Medical Department, not only cared for the wounded at Rorke's Drift, but was instrumental in passing out ammunition.

William Knox Leet VC.

Surgeon Reynolds was awarded the Victoria Cross for his actions at Rorke's Drift and was promoted to Surgeon Major. Lord Wolseley made the presentation at a special parade in St Paul's, Zululand on 16 July 1879. Reynolds died – holding the rank of Lieutenant Colonel – on 4 March 1932 and is buried in Kensal Green Roman Catholic Cemetery, Harrow Road, London. A full account of his life is told in *The Rorke's Drift Doctor* by Lee Stevenson (Brighton, 2001).

Robert Montressor Rogers VC retired as a Major General and was awarded a CB. He died at Maidenhead in Berkshire on 5 February 1895 and is buried there.

For Wolseley, the fates had prepared a tragic end. He won an easy victory

Robert Montressor Rogers VC, 90th Light Infantry – photographed in 1874.

against Arabi Pasha at Tel-el-Kebir in 1882, but failed to relieve Gordon in 1884 due to the incompetence of the British Government in its delay in authorising the expedition. In 1895, he achieved his ultimate goal in becoming Commander-in-Chief, but even as he took the position, the government stripped the post of much of its powers. During his remaining years, he was unable to implement the sweeping changes he had envisaged for the army. Added to this was the onset of illness, which robbed him of his brilliant intellect. He began to have lapses of memory – not significant at first, but soon too serious to be covered up, even by a loyal staff. He made mistakes: he selected Buller for command against the Boers – and when Buller failed, he was not approached with regard to his replacement. Wolseley retired in 1900 and died in 1913 aged 80. He is buried

Sir Garnet Joseph Wolseley.

in St Paul's Cathedral and there is a memorial in St Patrick's Cathedral in Dublin.

Warren Wynne died of typhoid fever and overwork on 9 April 1879. He is buried in the Euphorbia Redoubt Cemetery, Fort Pearson. He was posthumously promoted to Major for his distinguished service in South Africa.

In May 1882, Queen Victoria invited Private Edmund Fowler to Windsor, where she presented him with his Victoria Cross. Shortly after his discharge from the 90th, he returned to military service – enlisting in the Royal Irish Regiment and being quickly promoted to Sergeant in the 1st Battalion.

Private Henry Turner was called to a medical board at Pietermaritzburg on 9 September 1879. He was deemed as unfit for further military service and returned to England to spend time in the military hospital at Netley. He received a medical discharge on 9 February 1880 – the medical opinion being that he: '… may not be able to struggle for a precarious livelihood'.

Corporal John Graham died in 1899 and is buried in Aldershot Military Cemetery; it is no surprise that he is buried under his real name.

John Williams did not receive an invitation to Windsor. Major General Anderson presented him with his Victoria Cross on 1 March 1880 at Gibraltar.

The citation had appeared in the *London Gazette* on 2 May 1879. After service in India, he returned to England in October 1883 – and a short time later, transferred to the Army Reserve. He was discharged on 22 May 1893 and returned home

The Euphorbia Redoubt Cemetery, Fort Pearson – the final resting place of Captain Warren Wynne.

Private Edmund Fowler VC.

The presentation of the Victoria Cross to Private John Williams, 2nd Battalion, 24th Regiment on 1 March 1880.

– marrying Elizabeth Murphy. They had two daughters and three sons, with the eldest son enlisting in his father's old regiment. He was killed in action during the retreat from Mons in 1914. For many years, Williams served on the staff of the regimental depot at Brecon – from where he retired on 26 May 1920. In 1932, he was taken ill at the home of one of his daughters in Cwmbran – his wife having died some time previously. He died on 25 November 1932 and is buried at St Michael's Churchyard, Llantarnam. He was the last-surviving Rorke's Drift Victoria Cross holder to die. His Cross is held in the South Wales Borderers Museum. Fielding House – a home for the mentally handicapped – is named in his memory.

General Colley was sent from South Africa to Afghanistan as a result of the murder of Sir Pierre Louis Napoleon Cavagnari by mutinous Afghan troops in Kabul. Cavagnari, of Italian descent, had been born in France – his father being Count Louis Adolphus Cavagnari, while his mother was Caroline Lyons-Montgomery, of Anglo-Irish stock. Cavagnari had gained British citizenship, attended the Addiscombe Military Seminary and was employed by the East India Company. Having seen previous service during the Oudh campaign in 1858-59, he had been appointed as an Assistant Commissioner in the Punjab – and in 1877, he became Deputy Commissioner of Peshawar. Cavagnari negotiated and signed the Treaty of Gandamack, which allowed the admission of a British representative to Kabul – and he was granted the post in July 1879. On 3 September, the Residency was attacked and Cavagnari was killed, along with his escort: 75 men of the Corps of Guides, commanded by Lieutenant

Private John Williams
VC in later life.

The death of George Pomeroy
Colley at Majuba Hill on 27
February 1881.

Walter Pollock Hamilton VC. Hamilton, from Kilkenny, had been awarded his Cross for rescuing Sowar Dowlut Ram at Futterbad the previous April. The following year, Colley returned to Africa and succeeded Wolseley as High Commissioner. He commanded operations against the Boers in the First Boer War – being defeated at Laing's Nek and the Ingogo River. He was killed at the Battle of Majuba Hill on 27 February 1818 and is buried in Mount Prospect Cemetery, Natal.

Let the last word on this be from an 'old soldier'. The following letter appeared in *The Irish Times* in October 1919:

To The Editor Of *The Irish Times*

Sir; May I venture to encroach on your valuable space by asking you to print the following appeal? I am an old soldier. I served from the year 1870 to 1892, in which year I was discharged with a sergeant's pension of 2s *per diem*. I have two war medals – Perak 1876, and the Zulu War Medal for 1879.

I need not waste your time in stating how things have changed since then; but, while old age pensions and other Government allowances have been increased from 50 *per cent.*, we have been left out in the cold. I attribute this chiefly to the fact that, not being politicians, we have no political or any other influence. I hear that a Commettiee [sic] has for some time been sitting on the pension question generally, and it is in the hope that some influential person – be it Lord French or the member for Dublin University – may interest himself in our behalf that I make this appeal. For myself, were it not for the assistance I have received from members of my family, I would, perhaps have been living in one of the Unions for the past four or five years.

Yours etc., 'An Old Soldier', Dublin, October 2nd, 1919

23

A Report on Transportation (Courtesy of a serving officer of Engineers)

The permanent "scaling" of ordnance pattern wagons and carts to units had gone on over the decades but was something that really matured and became formalised over the last quarter of the 19th century, and was more apparent in UK garrisons, the Indian Army and artillery units than elsewhere. However, by the time of the "Great" Boer War units had a peacetime scaling of essential transport and would supplement it on deployment. Most UK-designed and procured carts were intended to be drawn by quite large horses or more often mules – on reasonable roads – and would therefore have had fairly limited utility in South Africa. They were usually also capable of being dismantled, repaired or (for the most part) even rebuilt by Royal Engineer and Royal Artillery wheelwrights and blacksmiths whenever suitable quality materials became available. However, this was an improvisation not usually resorted to.

There was some long established elementary standardisation for things like water carts, post carts, and tool carts which the unit might keep and move with them. Design drawings for these can still be found in museums and you can see surviving examples in the Army transport/logistic museums in Beverley and the Aldershot area. Generally, including on UK "home base" exercises, this very limited scaling would be supplemented according to need using a mixture of additional ordnance pattern wagons and locally hired/leased wagons – many of these being in the hands of contracting "carters" throughout. As the Army Service Corps developed and grew – and based on lessons learned in places like South Africa – unit scalings of horse/mule-drawn vehicles enlarged. This occurred mostly as a means of keeping a reserve of ammunition, water and rations well forward with the units, and to provide a small scaling of ambulances and cook wagons.

In the artillery, standardisation was much further advanced, with guns having carefully designed limbers for carrying ammunition and gun tools, and later the ammunition columns/trains of artillery units ingeniously used "double limbers" coupled together to form ammunition wagons for the lighter field guns. Engineers also had scalings of purpose built tool carts, and pontoon wagons etc.

A mule-drawn General Service wagon at Fort Pearson.

Mule-drawn General Service wagons hauling ammunition.

Locally-hired wagons at the halt during the advance of the Coastal Column.

The Pontoon Troop, Royal Engineers.

A six-gun battery of 9-pounder guns circa 1879; note the adapted limbers to the rear of the battery.

– viz. Lieutenant J.R.M. Chard's Royal Engineers tool cart just near the "well built kraal" at Rorke's Drift – which Driver Charles Robson RE did his best to defend during the many Zulu attacks because it contained "our things".

At Rorke's Drift we know what kind of wagons were hauled into the south rampart because we have Lieutenant Colonel Crealock's water colour sketch of one of them (there were two) in place when he arrived at Rorke's Drift just after the battle. We also have a series of drawings made by Royal Engineer Officers, to provide "procurement" models/specifications for those sent off to hire wagons from the local markets.

The appearance of the two Rorke's Drift wagons suggests that they were of the local type, commonly found throughout Colonial South Africa, and probably hired as part of the Commissariat arrangements. 'B' Company 2/24th would probably have had a water cart and might have had one or more small baggage carts to carry tents and *the mens' kit*. For the Centenary Commemorations of 1979, two wagons were again put in place as they might have been in 1879. They were later taken away, and at least one of them found a home at the Fort/Jail in nearby Vryheid. Other examples can still be seen in various places.[1]

1   The spelling and grammar in this report are as per the original.

24

The Grahamstown V.H. Artillery

While the war was in progress, actions were being fought elsewhere. The following letter from the *Belfast News Letter* of 18 June – the 54th anniversary of the Battle of Waterloo – tells of one such incident. Despite the references to 'Zulus', this was not part of the Anglo-Zulu War of 1879:

(With the Grahamstown V.H. Artillery)
Camp opposite Cabus

29 April 1879

You will think by the above that we are sticking at this place and doing nothing, but it is not so. This is our headquarters, from which we go out to attend to our friends the Korannas. We were out on several patrols, and ascertained where the enemy was posted. They were collected on an island which they had fortified opposite every available drift, and strongly posted they were. Our patrols could hear them at work busy building schanses. The smoke from their fires also showed where they were. It seems the island they were on is one which they considered it impossible for us to take.

Arrangements were made for a combined attack as follows; – A force under Captain W.A. Maclean to go down the middle island to one drift, Captain Dyason to guard the bottom of the island on the right, Lieutenant Breda on the Colonial side at the left, the artillery on the right. We were posted on a hill commanding the island. Corporal Marden with a rocket brigade, consisting of Privates Pitt, Allison, and Hawkens, accompanied Captain Maclean. We all took up our positions on the evening of the 25th. Next morning bright and early, everything was ready for action, only waiting for the signal – a rocket. Shortly after daylight the rocket went whizzing onto the island and fire was at once opened from both guns, shelling from left to right up and down the island. We then ceased fire and the other troops advanced. From our positions we could see by the fire of the rifles that the attack was centred in one place – the drift – and as no advance was made the natural conclusion was made that the enemy was too strongly posted and held our men in check. The rockets could be seen playing splendidly at low range tearing through the bush. The manner in which Corporal Marden and his men did their work is worthy of high praise. The firing flagged after a while, stray shots only being heard, and the commandant, who was with us, left to see how things were going on. Soon after an orderly came up with a message for Captain Nelson and one of his daughters (I told you we had christened our guns the Misses Nelson), so we limbered up and started. The detachment consisted of Sergeant Greenlees, Corporal Ware, Lance Corporal Jamison, Privates Mulholland, Minto, Emms, Mitton and Higgins. On arriving at the camp the limber was refilled and thence we went down to the boat. The gun was soon taken across and also the gun mules, but the horses were left behind, as they would not be required in the bush. On landing we started down the island, and it was a trip. I never went such a path on foot let alone with a gun, but good mules, strong arms and willing hands did the work. Over ledges of rocks, cutting down trees, removing bushes, hauling through sluits and sand-hills on we went. When the scene of action was reached it was dark, only a faint moonlight. The troops there welcomed us with a good cheer, and the Korannas with a heavy volley. I ought to have mentioned that during the morning attack Captain Maclean got a nasty shot in the stomach which fortunately did not penetrate, but it completely doubled him up for a time. He received the shot as he was standing by Corpl. Marden directing him where to send his rockets, and our men were in a pretty warm corner at the time. Well, to return to ourselves. We found it impossible to take the limber through the bush, so we unhooked and set to work to get the gun through. It was no joke; trees and bush had to be cut down to make a path. We always joke our Sergeant about his strength, but it was all needed then as he and Mitton held the trail, while we pushed or pulled along. Plenty of help was given us by other corps. At last we got into a position, at of [sic] clearance in front, and all was ready. Action commenced with case shot to clear the niggers out of the bush in front, and they replied to it with a smart fire, being well posted behind schanses and rocks, up trees &c. Their shots came thick round us. One struck the wheel of the gun, several passed between the gunners serving it. As Sergeant Greenlees held up his hand at the word "ready" his thumb was grazed by a bullet. Capt. Nelson congratulated us for the steady fire kept up, declaring that the gun was served as steadily as if on parade. Our fire soon began to tell on the enemy, who became fainter and fainter in replying. We then sent common shell into the schanses, and managed to tumble their fortifications about. Shortly after Capt. Nelson received a wound in the shoulder and splinters from a tree knocked of [sic] by a bullet out (hit?) his face. Fortunately the bullet struck him where there is a thick seam in his pilot jacket and glanced off lodging on the top of his shoulder. It was a Snider bullet showing that the Korannas are not without good arms. That it did no more damage we think is owing to the fact that the enemy's store of powder is very nearly bankrupt. We were quite joyed to find that we had escaped serious injury, but we could not help laughing at our captain when all was over. In a civilised country anyone seeing him would have thought he had been taking an active part in the felicities of dennublality [sic] – family jars, &c.

When daylight appeared the position of the gun was improved by digging down a bank and removing some trees. Sergeant Greenlees worked with a spade as coolly as if he had been digging a garden. The Korranas came to have a look at us, but did not fire. We think they were a party left behind by His Royal Highness Klaas Lucas to pick up the fragments of his men killed the previous day. Soon after we came into action again with guns and rockets and succeeded in clearing the stronghold. An advance was then made; Lieutenant Richards with the Zulus being the first over, closely followed by Southey's Rangers under Captain Crause. The Commandant, having the G.V.H.A. flag as a standard, took the other side of the drift. On the right a smart fire was opened by the enemy but it was soon silenced by a few rounds of shrapnel. One Zulu was slightly wounded, but a dose of "nervous stimulant" set him to rights again. Heavy firing to the front told us that our men were pushing the enemy. While it was going on Sergeant Greenlees and Private Emms went over to the fortification to inspect the effect of the shell and rockets. They reported that the place was riddled; some of the shells had demolished schanses. The gun did good work and cleared the way for our troops to go without losing a man where the day before anyone could not show his nose. One of the rockets struck a tree behind a schanse and firmly lodged there. The tree was as thick as a man, and the back fire from the rocket, jammed where it was, must have been far from enjoyable to those defending the schanse. In a few hours our men returned victorious, bringing prisoners – men, women, and children, cattle, goats, and general loot. The G.V.H.A. flag was torn and pierced with bullets, but it waved from the top of a tree which the night before was thick with the enemy's sharpshooters. Our forlaying [sic] parties shot the Korranas down as they tried to escape from the island. The enemy made a determined resistance to the capture of their cattle, but is was of no use. The women tried to cover the escape of the men, and it is believed one or two were shot, but it was impossible to help it. One man tried to conceal himself under some dead bodies, and when he was found had the cheek to declare he was a woman. But our men know cartwheels from balloons, and he was quickly "run in" with the other men prisoners. This has been the most successful affair we have had yet, and after the caution the niggers got it is thought the rest will surrender. A lot of Griquas have given themselves up with their guns to-day. We are having very hard and rough times, but are cheered by success, and the hope of bringing things to a speedy conclusion, and then – hurrah for home! I append an extract from general orders from yesterday:-

(Extract from General Orders, 28th April 1879.)

The commandant has much pleasure in thanking the officers, non commissioned officers, and men under his command for the admirable manner in which the principal islands were taken yesterday, more particularly Captain Nelson, Grahamstown Volunteer Horse Artillery, and the men of No.1 gun for their courage and bravery during the night of 26th inst., under a heavy fire from the enemy.

(Signed)

H. McTaggart, Commandant.

25

On the Health of the Soldier

___

The following extract was published in the *Belfast News Letter* of 19 September 1879:

ON THE HEALTH OF THE SOLDIER

To his Grace the Duke of Cambridge, Commander of Her Majesty's Forces.

My Lord – I request your Lordship's attention to the letters I herewith enclose on the health of the British soldier. The Secretary of State for India has already been good enough to lay them before the Indian Government, and I have further forwarded copies to the editor of the *Friend of India* in Calcutta. But India is not the only field of action of the soldier, and his health is of the moment wherever he may be stationed. Numbers of men, by birth and breeding gentlemen, forced by stress of circumstances, enlist yearly as private soldiers in the British Army. But every soldier is, ex-officio, a gentleman, and, I submit ought to be treated as one.

The mortality among soldiers, exposed as they are to every ordinary and extraordinary risk, is very great. It would be out of place in the course of a short communication to enter into statistics, but I may state out of seventy-five cases of Asiatic cholera, occurring among Europeans in Candahar, it is reported that up to the 6th inst. there were sixty deaths. In Scinde the disease has been most severe, whilst in the Muzapapore portion of the Tirhat district, there were actually ten thousand registered deaths; of deaths unregistered, it is not known how many. The English population in India may, I suppose, be roughly estimated at 100,000 persons. The yearly deaths per thousand I cannot to a fraction state, but the number is very considerable. Now, the half of this mortality I believe to be preventable. Each single private soldier, it has been said, costs the nation a hundred pounds before he can be made to handle a musket; but before he can be made efficiently serviceable in India this sum might doubtless, be doubled. The loss, were it of but a single soldier, the suffering of survivors, the closing of a promising career, is, in fact a public calamity; how much more so, then, when preventable deaths, amounting annually to hundreds, if not thousands?

The use of dilute acids, nitric, sulphuric, or muriatic, but especially sulphuric, as cheapest, and, on the whole, most effective, is not only extremely beneficial in the early treatment of cholera and dysentery, but, as I have shown, when taken as a prophylactic, tends to prevent cholera altogether. Each soldier, or at least the sergeants of companies, ought to be provided with a certain number of doses in a stoppered vial, enclosed in a wooden envelope, ready for instant use in case of emergency. The Romans used to supply every soldier with cruise vinegar, of which a portion was always mingled with the drinking water.

The much greater relative mortality among private soldiers than among commissioned officers shows that the moral and material conditions under which the former are placed are very far indeed from proving what they ought to be. The soldiers' barrack in every material, health-promoting respect ought to be as well appointed as the officers' bungalow, with chunam plastered ceilings, walls, and floors. The utmost attention ought to be paid to cleanliness and ventilation day and night, and always the punkah and the tattie, at least during the heats, should be kept going constantly. A well salaried, highly competent, regimental cook ought to be provided, and either the regimental colonel or the officer on duty should visit the soldiers' living and sleeping quarters daily. Barrack-rooms ought not to be on the ground level, but placed at a certain elevation, leaving a hollow space below. The barrack roofs should be constructed hollow, so as to mitigate the sun's rays. For the same reason the tents ought to be made double, with an India-rubber cloth on every tent floor. Parade should be held early in the morning; but before holding it, every man should have his chota hazaree, or little breakfast. The same rule must be observed before a march, which should not be too early, and a cup of coffee and biscuit served before going on night duty. Brandy or arrack should not, I think, be permitted in the canteen. But there might be a certain exception in favour of claret, which could be admitted free of duty. Native vendors of raki or raki sherbets ought to be sternly prohibited. Brandy, indeed I would place along with the medical stores, not to be issued or not in case of need, at the discretion of the medical officer. Officers and men ought to be cautioned against excess, as well as advised to drink at all between meals. Thirst, however, must be assuaged. I would recommend cold, weak tea, or cold, weak coffee, without sugar. Congee or rice water, flavoured with a little lime, or lemon juice, makes a very good drink. Cold water, at least water that has not been boiled and filtered, ought as a general rule, be prohibited. Brandy panee, or brandy and water, with unlimited smoking, I have known to produce enlargement of the liver and cirrhosis, or change of structure, in that organ, within a single year.

The following article appeared in the *Belfast News Letter* in September 1879:

AN INCIDENT OF THE ZULU WAR

An interesting correspondence has taken place with respect to one of the victims of the Zulu campaign, and it shows how even the memory of the humblest individual among the rank and file of the British army can be cherished and respected by his general when he happens to fall through the chances of war. Mr. William Henry Barry, J.P., of Carrigtwohill, writes to a Cork paper: –

Dear Sir – In the *Graphic* of last week you will observe the report of two young men who were killed by the Zulus last July. One is Mr. Scott Douglas, of the 21st Regiment, and the other is Corporal Cotter of the 17th Lancers. Cotter, before he joined the Lancers, was occasionally employed by me, together with his father, who is a carpenter, living in the parish of Carrigtwohill. He was a fine handsome young fellow, of about the average amount of intelligence. I am told he was a great favourite with his comrades. I enclose a communication received by the poor fellow's mother

The grave of Corporal William Cotter, 17th Lancers. (Courtesy of Paul Naish)

from General Evelyn Wood, together with a copy of the official report respecting the finding of the bodies of these young men. The father and mother have asked me to send them to you for publication, together with other papers from Colonel Lowe, commanding 17th Lancers, and Captain Belford, who commanded poor Cotter's troop, as they considered it the best way to thank Sir Evelyn Wood for the care he took in providing a proper resting place for their poor son, and the thoughtfulness and kindness of heart displayed in collecting, preserving, and causing to be forwarded the four articles referred to in the general's letter. While I write I have before me the three stripes denoting Cotter's rank, which were cut from the arm of his coat, the tinsel stained with the poor fellow's blood, also the flag carried at the end of his lance – sad memorials of this wretched war!

What a noble fellow General Wood must be to find [the] time to look after the humblest of his soldiers, even after death, and soothe the grief of her who must require it – the mother of the dead soldier. The Cotters also feel grateful to Colonel Lowe and Captain Belford for the kind expression contained in their reports respecting the death of their son. –

I am, dear sir, yours faithfully,

W.H. Barry.

Ballyadam, Carrigtwohill, Sept. 20.

Kapagsguess, Zululand, 7 July, 1879.

Mrs Cotter – I deeply regret to have to announce to you the death of your son. The accompanying copy of my official report will show you all I know of it. I saw by the 'Garden of the Soul' (Missal) found on your son's body, that he was a Catholic. I sent for Father Bardy, who buried him. I have had a cross erected over his grave, which was dug by soldiers of the 88th Light Infantry (my escort). I enclose herewith the corporal's stripes and good conduct badge, which I had cut off his coat. One of his comrades has some of the buttons. I enclose also the flag from his lance. I sympathise with your loss, and I am yours truly,

Evelyn Wood.

Colonel Drury-Lowe, commanding the 17th Lancers, writes a moving letter expressing his regret at the death of the young soldier – and Captain Belford (Captain of the regiment), writing to a niece of Cotter's, says:

To Miss Katie Horgan – I regret extremely to have to inform you of the death of your uncle, William Cotter, who was killed about a fortnight ago in company with Lieutenant Scott Douglas, 21st Regiment. He left Fort Evelyn to return to camp. They seem to have lost their way in a thick mist. As they did not return to camp every search was of course made, and the marks of their horses [sic] feet were traced some way, when the small party in search were driven back by about 500 Zulus. Of course after seeing so many of the enemy about no hope could be held out for their safety, and then, some days after, the sad news reached us that the bodies had been found by Colonel Wood's column. Although the 17th Lancers were too far away to have the honour of following your uncle's remains to their last resting place, yet I need hardly say everything was done by those who had that honour to pay him the respect he so richly deserved. As captain of his troop I feel his loss most deeply as he was an honour to the regiment, and an example to everyone of what a soldier should be. The only consolation is that he died as every soldier with his feelings must wish to die – in the discharge of his duty to his country. As he mentioned you only in his will, you will have merely to wait until the authorities in London write to you on the subject, and any little thing of his that may be found will be sent home to you. –

E.J. Belford, captain 17th Lancers, commanding B troop.

The official report of Brigadier General Wood – after referring to the finding of the bodies of Lieutenant Scott and Corporal Cotter – says:

Both soldiers had been killed by assegai wounds. Neither body had been muti-lated. There was no property on the body of Corporal Cotter except a notebook and a missal. Lieutenant Scott Douglas's tunic had been removed. In the trousers pocket was a small purse containing £10 10s (sovereigns), which had evidently been overlooked. I knew the deceased, and his name is on his linen. From his statement, and the opinion of Wood's Irregulars together, Lieutenant Scott Douglas and Corporal Cotter were dismounted, and when about a mile and a half N. N. E. of Kwamagwaso they met some Zulus and were killed. – (Signed)

Evelyn Wood, Brigadier General

Forwarded by Colonel Drury-Lowe, 17th Lancers.

26

A Dissenting Voice

While Victoria's harvest reaped men and support for the various Colonial wars and skirmishes, this being Ireland, the voice of opposition was never far from being heard. Alexander Martin Sullivan was born in Bantry, County Cork in 1830 and was a respected Irish nationalist politician, lawyer and journalist. As a result of his experiences during the famine of 1846-47, Sullivan became a supporter of the Young Irelanders – a revolutionary movement – before moving to Dublin in 1848 to look for work as an artist. After being employed in supplying sketches to the *Dublin Expositor*, he obtained a position as a draughtsman with the Irish Evaluation Office, prior to being employed by the *Liverpool Daily Post*. Sullivan was appointed as deputy editor of *The Nation* in 1855 – subsequently becoming editor and, eventually, owner. In his hands, the magazine became a potent weapon in the cause of Irish nationalism.

His views on the Zulu War were made obvious by a speech made in the House of Commons while he was serving as an MP. The circumstances in which this speech was delivered were described at the time as follows by the parliamentary correspondent of the *Liverpool Journal*:

> But the debate was not to be wholly and uninterruptedly dreary, for near the end of it there came a speech from Mr. Sullivan, the member for Louth, which drove away all dullness for the time, and lighted up the debate as a lightning flash illuminates the sky on a murky night. The speech was short, but the effect must have been startling. These people had been droning for several hours about mere money matters. Meanwhile Mr. Sullivan sat in his place on the second bench from the floor below the gangway. At last, when Sir Stafford had in his driest style delivered his winding-up speech, Sullivan's patience gave out, and up he sprang, and, kicking all precedent aside, and knocking old use and wont head over heels, he stormed into the debate like a tornado.
>
> I know there are honourable members round about me who will say: "We are as much opposed to this Zulu war as any man can be. We believe it to be an unjust war, but will vote for the money because the country is now engaged in the struggle." I can quite recognise that as a ground which some members

of this House may take up; far be it from me to quarrel with them; but, for myself, I say my conscience recoils from having act, hand, or part in voting a sixpence for this war. I challenge any man in or out of this House to defend it on the principles of public equity, if he will only suppose that it is Russia that is waging the war, and not England. I say no man in this House will dare to apply to such a war the principles which you apply elsewhere. If this dusky chief, spear in hand, set forth to defend his home against the Frank, the Russian, or the German, English pens would trace his record of glory, and English poets would sing his fame. We have had sympathetically dramatised for us the story of Pizarro, when men—savages perhaps, but patriots all the same—withstood the civilising tyrant that came upon their shores. And when we stand in Pizarro's place in South Africa to-day, is no voice to be raised in England better worthy of being heard than mine to say, as I say now, "This is an iniquitous and a wicked war; it is against all my convictions of right and wrong? And at what an hour do we find ourselves so far gone in this onward march of aggression, this lust of territory, this greed of annexation? It is at the very moment that you have been contesting the right of a Christian power to redress Christian wrongs in the east of Europe. You call Russia an aggressive power, and treat us to homilies on the iniquity of her pushing her frontiers forward. Was ever hypocrisy so gigantic as yours? To call Russia aggressive, when you are reaching out your hands to grasp more territory in every region of the globe, by every violation of right. It is incontestable that you led the Zulu king to conclude that you favoured his claims to this strip of land. But no sooner had you annexed the Transvaal than you turn round upon him in conduct which he calls, and I say, justly calls, something very like perfidy. Now that you are the rulers of the Transvaal, you say he shall not have what you notoriously led him to expect as his just and lawful right." Where slumbers the public morality of England? I look in vain in the public press of this country for that voice which ought to speak out, when we read the ultimatum—that impudent and insolent missive—of Sir Bartle Frere. I know of nothing more audacious than the document which was sent to provoke this war; yet now the land is agitated from end to end by the story of the terrible disaster at Isandlana, and money is being sought here to-night, not for defence of your South African possessions, but in order to wage a war of vengeance on Cetewayo [sic] and give up his people to sword and flame.

I pay my tribute to the gallantry and heroism of those British soldiers who fell beneath their flag. They served their queen and their colours well. But while I admire them, I more admire the men, savages tho they be, who fell with their feet on their native soil defending themselves against an invader. My morality is not cribbed, cabined, and confined by geographical lines. I mete out to the savage the same measure of justice which I extend to more civilised races. Altho a man be a savage, we ought not to deny him the degree of praise which is due to his patriotism, as praise is paid to Caractacus and

Kosciusko. This Zulu king stood within his own territories. He only did what Queen Elizabeth did in the case of the Spanish Armada when it threatened English soil. He called his forces around him, as she did hers, and said: "I will make the invader bite the dust."

And he did so. England, with the £1,500,000 you vote tonight, will doubtless succeed in a war of revenge upon this African prince. £1,500,000! Why, if the government had asked for £5,000,000 they would have got it. If I saw Cetewayo pushing his advantage so far as to invade the territories which do not belong to him, and to endanger the safety of peaceful settlers who are outside his own land, I could sympathise with your military movements. But in so far as he stands in the position of one who is resisting aggression, and is on his own soil, defending his own people and country, for my part I can not [sic] avoid confessing—whatever consequences may follow from my avowing it—that my sympathies are on his side. I say he ought to have from us the same admiration that the writers of history have taught us to pay to the men who resisted Spanish invaders in another clime.

I prize highly the advantages of civilisation, and the blessings of civil and religious liberty; but never shall a vote of mine be given to encourage unjust invasion and conquest on the pretext of pushing "civilisation," or to carry the Bible with the sword, so that rapacity may call its crimes "the diffusion of Christianity."

No, sir; I will give no vote to extend this already swollen empire at the cost of the liberty of these natives, howsoever dark their skin may be. I protest here to-night against further annexations. I believe if the representatives of Ireland, or the people of Ireland, had a voice in this question they would say that the British Empire is wide enough, great enough, grand enough, powerful enough, rich enough, without sending an ultimatum to take a rood of ground from Cetewayo. We might leave this dusky warrior to himself, and the British ensign would float as proudly from the turrets of Windsor Castle as it does now. Nay, much better and happier might we all be by giving up these aggressive enterprises and costly schemes of aggrandisement. It is while trade is languishing, and industries are perishing in our midst, and the cry of absolute destitution comes to us from the midland counties, £1,500,000 is being asked from us to carry out this most iniquitous business.

All vainly I speak. To-night this money will be voted. I know that well. But I know what verdict will yet be passed on this episode of British history. When the present feeling of resentment has passed away, when passion has cooled, and reason returned, there will arise some Allison, or some Macaulay, or some Lecky, to trace for our indignant posterity the story of this hour. They will say it was a reproach to the British Parliament that it had not patriotism enough or independence enough to resist and refuse this application for money to spend in a war which they will declare to be, as I declare it to be, as unjust, as wicked, and as wanton as that which George III. waged—thank God, he waged in vain!—against the liberty-loving people of the American Colonies.

27

'The Poems'

'Melvill's Ride': The attempt to save the Queen's colour at Isandlwana.

The following appeared in the *Belfast News Letter* of 26 June – and all spelling and grammar are as per the original:

Melville's [sic] Ride
(An Incident of the Zulu War)
Wave-worn cliffs, their snowy bosoms wear robes,
crystaline today;
Ah! Their story – Spain remembers, how along our
watery way,
Sprang as if from earth the dwellers of this island
of the sea,
Shouting with the winds, *We're God's breath, and
by God, we will be free!*
'Mid the chestnuts, red brick homesteads, porch
and lattice hung with vine;
Breezy uplands, vernal meadows, sleepy, lazy,
browsing kine;
County lanes, with lovers' trystings – love lies
bleeding by the side
Of that wild and swollen river, where brave English
Melville died!
Died? Not dead, O men, but sleeping! Valour
with her every breath,
Cries, "O grave, not thine the victory," cries, "not
thine the sting, O death!"
And the spirit of the hero mounts exulting to the
Spheres:
Look you! thus we wreath the glory of a thousand
English years.
Look you! thus we tell the nations that our banner
is unfurled,
And that God has given England His command
To rule the world!
On he sped, mid dead and dying, savage yells and
fiendish cries,
Bearing in his grasp our honour, our defiance in
his eyes.
Echoed Agincourt and Cressy, and his soul that
day a part.
Of our centuries, was companioned with our storied
lion heart.
By his side rode our dead heroes, they had come
they had come there from the sky:

Ay, to mingle in our triumph; longing once again
to die!
On he sped-the wrathful Zulu, full of hate and
vengeance dire,
Gathering, like clouds around him, meteor lights
their eyes of fire;
Christ love us! Melville's praying – "Not my
life, O Lord, I crave!
Poor and lowly as Thy servant, but the colours,
Jesu, save!"
Ah, that prayer was born to heaven, on the lightning
of the spheres;
Melville grasping still the triumph of a thousand
English years.
Look you! thus we tell the nations that our banner
is unfurled,
And that God has given England His command
to rule the world!
Like leaves when autumn's dying, fall around him
many a lance,
Like the lightening in the storm-time, murderous
fire and wrathful glance,
Meet his gaze as wildly onward with the spirit
of the free!
Dashed the bearer of the colours-then his heart
beat silently,
For he thought of home and England, and what
would her manhood day,
If by act of his her glorious name should sullied
be to-day.
And he prayed again to heaven, and he struck his
charger's side,
And he dashed him through the hell-hounds, yea,
a god in all his pride!
Dashed him through the conquering Zulu, royally,
kingly dashed him on:
Christ: I trow his soul was leavened by that God
that made the sun!
Leavened by the God whose utterance is the
thunder of the spheres,
And who minds him still the triumph of a thousand
English years.
Look you! thus we tell the nations that our banner

is unfurled,
And that God has given England His command
to rule the world:
Deep and wide's the yellow river – death before
him-death behind,
One wild leap, his chargers flying, God of Heaven,
like the wind;
"Has he gained the other bank yet, as you love me,
comrade say?"
"What, he falters torn and bleeding?
and his steed lies down to die?
And you fear that all is over?" *He is dead they
sadly cry.*
Bear the news unto the Old Land, till each Briton
thrills with pride!
Theme for song, and theme for story, English
Melville's famous ride!
Shout it out that hand of valour, down the grey old
aisles of time,
Shall place now the name of Melville 'mong the
names she calls sublime!
Sing it, hymn it, write it, shout it, till the radiance
of the spheres
Shall blend it with the triumph of a thousand
English years.
Look you! thus we tell the nations that our banner
is unfurled,
And that God has given England His command
to rule the world!
Charles P. O' Conor

'With downward spray where Ireland lies!': Alphonse de Neuville – 'The last Sleep of the Brave'.

IN MEMORIAM
Arthur Appleton Woods, M.D., M.R.C.S.E.,
Civil surgeon, No.1 Column, Zululand, who
Died of typhoid fever at Hirwin, Port Natal,
23dr May, 1879.

I.
Alas! My Lycidas! Too early gone
Art thou, thy nobler life work but begun,
Thy zealous worth half known, just as the sun
Gold tops Fame's mountain path with hope's bright
Dawn.

II.
Thy end was mournful, not inglorious; for
Earth's best crusaders ever fight 'gainst pain;
Beneath the red-cross ensign they must gain
Their highest conquests on the field of war,

III.
In olden times the fierce-souled Moslems found
Their fiercest foes when England's warriors
Swarmed;
Last year a band, thou not the last, went
Armed
With other weapons, to deal life around.

IV.
And later still, when death and danger sprung
From every yard of Southern Africa's soil,
Thou found'st a post of honour for thy toil,
In suffering mankind's cause, but died too young!

V.
Should highest purposes have highest powers?
Should noble missions aye have noble ends?
Alas! Thy grief struck mother, brother, friends,
See not as God sees, yet His will be ours!
W.H. Robinson
42 Fortingale Street, Belfast.

–Lancet.

The spelling of 'Melvill' is given as 'Melville' in this contemporary text and has been retained, as has the original spelling and grammar:

'THE RESCUED FLAG'
Streaming above the conflict dire,
O'er wounds and death, o'er blood and fire,
Now lost in smoke, now rising high,
While round it gather to fall and die
Hearts that with dauntless life blood bound
As the savage tore their camp surround –
That glorious banner waves in vain
O'er a ghastly ring of foemen slain.
While shoulder to shoulder the British stand
Why does horror spread through their gallant band?
When the combat is ever their heart's desire
Is this a moment to slacken fire?
Though worn with hunger and want of rest,
And by hurried marches sore distressed,
Not these the foes that o'ercome the brave
Seeking fame or the warrior's bloody grave.
Alas! The cause is too plainly read
In the swarthy Zulus' forward tread
Compact and close they come surging high,
Like the blackening wave when the tide runs high,
On the bayonet's point their dead they cast,
And those trusty weapons, borne down at last
By the weight of the ghastly forms, are bent,
And the shot is all gone and the powder spent.
A leader falls – and with dying eyes
Through blood and mist the flag descries,
"Mount Melville, mount! Ride, Coghill, ride!"
Preserve our honour whats'er betide.
From yonder staff the colours rend,
In their defence your life blood spend,
Nay! Linger not our fate to share
But the flag to a place of safety bear.
'Tis his last command, no more they need;
Each swiftly vaults on his foaming steed,
Like lions they plunge 'mid the startled foe,
Who fall right and left at every blow.
With Zulu blood their weapons gleam,
But the standard weeps a noble stream,
As wrapped round Melville's gallant breast

It drips with gore from his darkened vest.
At the desperate plunge the heroes make,
The ranks of the hostile legions break,
Beneath the chargers trampling hoofs
Lie writhing in heaps the dying proofs
Of the edge and might of British steel,
Which the savages now in earnest feel.
But hasten Melville! – Coghill ride
And gain the rivers friendly tide;
Ah, little they reck that glorious day
How their youthful lives are ebbing away.
Oh, haste! For both are wounded now,
And Death's cold dew's on either brow,
The path is out, one forward bound,
One race – the river – then British ground.
Their steeds they press, the spur they ply,
The foes on every side defy;
While these in clouds their arrows shoot,
And, yelling, join in hot pursuit.
Oh, haste! ye coursers, proud and fleet,
Your riders trust in your flying feet,
With faintness see their heads sink low,
And reeling bend o'er the saddle bow.
Oh! gallop, remember your regiment's glory,
Succeed in your gallant attempt, and in story
Of battle steed's efforts to succour his master
Your merit shall conquer – hie, faster and faster
They gain the river's bank so steep,
Where the stream is strong and the water deep,
They plunge in the current's foaming whirl,
Where the waves around them eddying curl,
Hence dashing onward, swollen with rains,
The snowy crests bear crimson stains;
Against them boils the raging flood,
Unused by aught to be withstood.
With toil and groan their course they take,
And the spray from ears and nostrils shake,
The baffled javelin whizzes by,
And many a well aimed assegai.
The darts and arrows harmless fall
And treason's base sold rifle ball
Into the rivers hissing breast,
Which shames to give such trophies rest.

Advancing slowly, side by side
'mid rocks and shoals and swelling tide,
Bearing their riders precious weight
And the rescued flag – a precious freight!
The noble steeds swam bravely o'er
And nearly gained the welcome shore.
Hugh was the wave with matchless force
Hurled Melville from his weary horse,
And bore him with resistless shock
Down mid-stream 'gainst a lofty rock
On this a comrade's form he spied,
"Save brother in arms, our flag," he cried,
They grasp, they strive. But still in vain,
The exulting waters once again
Engulf their struggling limbs and roll,
With all their prey, o'er rock and shoal.
Coghill had reached the bank, but turned,
And his last chance of safety spurned;
Observing Melville's fearful need,
In the surging wave replunged with speed.
Mark for a thousand foes, he guides
His steed down the swiftly flowing tides,
Till, by remorseless bullet sped,
The war-horse sinks in the river's bed.
The gallant rider now alone
Thro' leaden hail, o'er wave and stone,
For honour, friend, and life must strive
Wounded, immersed and scarce alive,
He saw where Melville floating lay
By current borne to deep still bay,
Hailed him – both toil one effort more
And again they reach the friendly shore.
The flag they brought to the British strand
Lay safely concealed in the stones and sand,
And soon by a comrades hand was found
And planted again on British ground.
Saved! For the desperate race is won,
In the far north west sinks the sun,
But lingers yet with parting glare
On drooping Melville's wavy hair,
And shows to Coghill's glazing eyes
With downward spray where Ireland lies!
As slowly to the earth he sank,

And, fainting, lay on the mossy bank.
Swift to his comrade Melville flies
To breath his name, to close his eyes,
For vain the attempt to staunch the tide
Which freshly wells from his wounded side-
His strife is o'er, and Melville now
To the stern summons next must bow,
He chokes, he falls – his noble breast
Is still – and from the burning West
Two glowing sunbeams upward roam,
And point to the heroes' final home.
The lifeless forms by friends are found
Stretched side by side on the dewy ground,
The wild flowers watching o'er their sleep
Bend round their early graves and weep.
Brave! now the Twenty-fourth may say,
And glorious borne away;
Though Britain mourns her champions true,
And Isandula long must rue.
Saved! and where'er the Twenty-fourth
Unfurls her flag and sallies fourth,
While banners float through wind and weather
While silk and bunting hold together
Till out and jagged, and rent and torn,
By time effaced, in ribbons worn,
That blood-stained, faded rag shall bear
The names of that young heroic pair.

                                    Emmeline R Canning
                                        April 1879

28

The Rorke's Drift Roll

Those deemed to have been present at Rorke's Drift on Wednesday, 22 January 1879 at approximately 4.00pm: this list has been compiled from various sources – the most important being the research carried out by Alan Baynam Jones; the authors are grateful for his assistance in this project.

Adams, Robert, Private, 'D' Company 25B/987: Place and date of birth are unknown, but he had previously served in the East Middlesex Militia and was posted to the 2/24th on 22 January 1877. He was a patient in the hospital and was killed during the action. Private Adams is buried at Rorke's Drift Cemetery and his name appears on the monument.

Allan, William Wilson, Corporal, 'B' Company 2/24th, No.1240: Born near Berwick-on-Tweed, Northumberland circa 1844 and attested at York on 27 October 1859 aged 15 years and eight months. During the action at Rorke's Drift, he was seriously wounded by a gunshot to the arm and shoulder – and despite this, he assisted the wounded as they emerged from the burning hospital. After having his wounds dressed, he continued to distribute ammunition to members of the garrison. He was subsequently awarded the Victoria Cross – the medal being presented by Queen Victoria at Windsor Castle. He retired as a Sergeant Instructor of Musketry and died on 12 March 1890 aged 46 at Monmouth, Monmouthshire.

Adendorff, Gert Wilhelm, Lieutenant, Natal Native Contingent: Brought the news to Rorke's Drift that the centre column had been destroyed at Isandlwana. According to an account left by Lieutenant Chard, he remained to assist with the defence, although this is debated by certain writers. He was born and died in South Africa; date and place not known.

Ashton, James, Private, 'B' Company 2/24th, No.913: Born in Ireland in June 1841; his real name was Anthony McHale. He lived at St Mary's, Liverpool and worked as a groom before attesting at Cork on 3 March 1859 aged 17 years and nine months. Described as being 5' 5" tall, of a fresh complexion, hazel eyes and dark brown hair, he had served in Mauritius, the East Indies and South

Africa. According to several sources, Private Ashton brought a Zulu prisoner to Lieutenant Bromhead, who told him to get rid of him. Ashton took this in a literal sense and promptly hanged the Zulu from a gallows that had been previously used to stretch cowhides. Ashton was discharged on 29 March 1881 on completion of 21 years' service. He died in Ireland; date unknown.

Attwood, Francis, Second Corporal, No.C–2469, Army Service Corps: Awarded the Distinguished Conduct Medal for his actions during the battle at Rorke's Drift. His place and date of birth are unknown, and he died in Plymouth, Devonshire on 20 February 1884.

Barry, Thomas, Private, 'B' Company 25B/1381: Attested at Newport on 6 April 1877 – being posted to the 2/24th on 11 May the same year. He served in South Africa and India –returning to England on 26 April 1883 and being discharged shortly after. Place of birth/death and relevant dates unknown.

Beckett, William, Private, 'A' Company 1/24th, 25B/135: Born in Manchester, Lancashire on 27 January 1856. He was a patient in the hospital and was mortally wounded during the action by an *assegai* piercing his abdomen. He died the following day.

Bennett, William, Private, 'B' Company 25B/918: Attested at Brecon on 22 November 1876 and was posted to the 2/24th as of 15 December. He deserted from the battalion on 21 December 1879 at Pinetown, Natal. Place and date of birth unknown; died in South Africa circa 1915.

Bessel, William, Corporal, 'B' Company 25B/1287: Born in Bethnal Green, London and served as a porter prior to attesting at Bow Street, London on 26 February 1877 aged 20 years and 11 months. Name sometimes spelt as 'Bissell'. He was discharged on 26 February 1889 and died in Bethnal Green circa 1903.

Bly, John, Private, 'B' Company 2/24th, No.2427: His date of attestation is not known, but he joined the 2/24th on 1 January 1873. He was sent to Netley Military Hospital on 1 February 1880 and from there, discharged to the Army Reserve (AGL 149). Place and date of birth/death unknown.

Bourne, Frank, Colour Sergeant, 'B' Company 2/24th, No.2459: Born in Balcombe, Sussex on 27 April 1854. He was awarded the Distinguished Conduct Medal for his actions during the battle. Possibly the last-surviving member of the garrison, he died in Dorking, Surrey on 8 May 1945 – holding the rank of Lieutenant Colonel.

Bromhead, Gonville, Lieutenant, 'B' Company 2/24th: Was the officer commanding 'B' Company at Rorke's Drift. Born in Versailles, Paris on 29 August 1845, his mother was Judith Christine Cahill of Woodville, County Sligo. He was awarded the Victoria Cross for his actions at Rorke's Drift. The Army List for 1878 lists Gonville Bromhead as having received his Lieutenancy on 28 October 1871. He died in Allahabad, India on 9 February 1891.

Bromwich, Joseph, Private, 'B' Company 25B/1524: Born at St Mary's, Warwick circa 1859 and worked as a porter prior to enlisting on 27 August 1877. As a result of his military service, he developed chronic hepatitis – resulting in a chronically-damaged liver. Following a medical examination at Netley Military Hospital on 1 July 1882, his disability was found to be permanent and 'will, for some 12 months, impair his power of earning a living'. He was invalided from the service on 25 July 1882 – dying at Warwick; date unknown.

Buckley, Thomas, Private, 'B' Company 25B/1184: Born in Liverpool, Lancashire circa 1859. He attested on 15 February 1877 and served in South Africa, India and Burma. He was promoted to Lance Corporal on 2 October 1882 and to Corporal on 1 August the following year. Reduced to the rank of Private in October, he returned to England on 12 January 1889. Date of discharge unknown; died in Liverpool on 31 December 1934.

Burke, Thomas, Private, 'B' Company 25B/1220: Born in Liverpool, Lancashire circa 1859 and worked as a labourer prior to enlisting. He attested at Liverpool on 14 February 1877 aged 18 years and had previously served in the Royal Lancashire Militia. He served in South Africa, the Mediterranean, India and Burma before transferring to the Army Reserve on 21 June 1883. He re-enlisted in the Liverpool Regiment and was discharged at his own request on 15 October 1897 – as a Sergeant – after 18 years' service. He died in Liverpool on 23 April 1925.

Bushe, James, Private, 'B' Company 2/24th, No. 2350: Born at St John's, Dublin circa 1852, he was an ex-tailor and enlisted on 14 September 1870. He was described as being 5'5" tall, with a fresh complexion, grey eyes and black hair; he was a Roman Catholic. He served in India, South Africa, the Mediterranean and Burma – being promoted to Corporal on 20 November 1875 and reduced to Private on 15 May 1877. At Rorke's Drift, the bullet that killed Private Thomas Cole wounded Bushe in the nose. He was again promoted – becoming a Lance Corporal on 10 February 1879 and transferring from 'B' Company to 'F' Company. Promoted to Corporal on 28 November 1879 and Lance Sergeant in November of the following year, he re-engaged at Secunderabad on 2 December 1880 and reverted to Private at his own request on 2 November 1881. Nevertheless, two years later he was again promoted to Lance Corporal on 1 June 1883 and to Corporal on 27 April 1887. He was discharged on 10 October 1891 – having served for 21 years. Place and date of death unknown.

Byrne, Louis, Acting Storekeeper, Commissariat and Transport Department: Born in Ireland in 1857. He was killed by a shot to the head fired by a Zulu on the afternoon of the action.

Caine, P., Private, 'B' Company, 25B/2420: Born in Ireland (date unknown) and died in Birr, County Offaly circa 1934.

Camp, William Henry, Private, 'B' Company 25B/1181: Born in Camberwell, Surrey circa November 1853 and served as a clerk before enlisting at Liverpool on 8 February 1877 aged 23 years. After the action at Rorke's Drift, his health decreased and he was shipped home aboard HM Troopship *Malabar* on 28 October 1881. Following a medical examination at Netley Military Hospital on 25 November 1888, he was diagnosed as suffering from melancholia – caused by an 'hereditary predisposition and aggravated self-abuse'. He was declared insane and discharged as unfit for further service on 27 December 1881. His intended place of residence was listed as c/o Union Authorities, Camberwell, Surrey. He died in Abbots Langley, Herefordshire on 15 April 1900.

Cantwell, John, Wheeler, Royal Artillery: Born at St James', Dublin circa May 1845. He enlisted in the 9th Foot in 1868 and transferred to the Royal Artillery in 1872. He joined 'N' Battery, 5th Brigade on 1 July 1877. During the action, he was responsible for his battery's supplies held at Rorke's Drift. He was awarded the Distinguished Conduct Medal for his actions during the battle and died in Durban, South Africa on 14 August 1900.

Chard, John Rouse Merriott, Lieutenant, 5th (Field) Company, Royal Engineers: Born in Boxhill, Devonshire on 21 November 1847. The senior rank present at Rorke's Drift, he was awarded the Victoria Cross for his actions during the battle. He died of cancer of the tongue at Hatch Beauchamp, Somerset on 1 November 1897.

Chester, Thomas, Private, 'B' Company 25B/1241: Born in Calthorpe, Leicester circa July 1852 and worked as a labourer prior to attesting at Bow Street Police Court on 19 February 1877. He saw action in South Africa, the Mediterranean and India before returning to England on 28 May 1883, where he married Miss Ellen Cave some seven months later. He was discharged to the Army Reserve on 21 June 1883 – having served for six years, 121 days. He died in Rhondda, Glamorganshire on 12 February 1908.

Chick, James, Private, 'D' Company 25B/1335: Date and place of birth are unknown, but he attested on 8 March 1877 – being posted to the 2nd Battalion on 11 May the same year. Despite being a patient in the hospital, he played a significant part in its defence. He was killed in action and received no award. Buried in the cemetery at Rorke's Drift; his name is listed on the monument.

Clayton, Thomas, Private, 'B' Company 25B/755: Born in Leominster, Herefordshire circa June 1855 and worked as a labourer prior to his military service. He attested at Monmouth on 9 February 1876 aged 20 years and eight months. He died of disease at Helpmekaar on 5 April 1879 – leaving the sum of £10-18s-3d in his will.

Cole, Robert, Private, 'F' Company 25B/1459: Born in Chatham, Kent circa 1858 and practised as a gun-maker prior to enlisting. He attested at Brecon on 29 October 1877 aged 19 years – having served in South Africa, Gibraltar and India. He served in 'F' Company and was a patient in the hospital during the attack. Posted from India to England on 1 December 1883, where he married Miss Elizabeth Gibelin at St Bartholomew's Church, Birmingham on 20 April 1884. He was discharged to the Army Reserve on 8 December 1883 and died in Birmingham, Warwickshire on 21 August 1898.

Cole, Thomas, Private, 'B' Company 25B/801: Killed during the action. He was born in Monmouthshire circa 1855 and had attested at Monmouth on 23 March 1876 aged 20 years and 10 months. He is buried in the cemetery at Rorke's Drift and his name is listed on the monument.

Collins, Thomas, Private, 'B' Company 25B/1396: Born in Camrose, Haverfordwest, Pembrokeshire circa 1855 and worked as a labourer prior to his enlistment. He was a member of the Church of England and attested on 22 May 1877 aged 22 years. He had previously served in the Monmouth Militia and went on to serve in South Africa, the Mediterranean, India and Burma. He was medically discharged on 16 June 1891 – being unfit for further military service due to chronic rheumatism. He died in Monmouthshire sometime between 1891 and 1918.

Connolly, John, Private, 'C' Company 25B/906: Born in Berehaven, County Cork sometime between December 1858 and February 1859. He worked at Trevethin, Monmouth as a labourer prior to enlisting on 20 November 1876. He was described as a Roman Catholic, aged 20 years and eight months; was 5'6" tall with a fresh complexion, blue eyes and light brown hair. He had previously served in the Monmouth Militia. Private Connolly had been injured while loading a wagon at the Lower Tugela River – partially dislocating his left knee – and this had resulted in synovitis. He was a patient in the hospital at the time of the attack and was successfully evacuated to the inner defences. Brought before a medical board in Natal, it was decided to return him to England. In an ensuing examination at Netley Military Hospital, he was found unfit for further military service and discharged on 25 August 1879. He died in Castletown, County Cork; date unknown.

Connors, Anthony, Private, 'B' Company 2/24th, No.2310: Born in County Cork circa 1852. He joined the 2/24th while it was stationed in India on 28 December 1871. In July 1873, he was sentenced to 168 days' hard labour at Millbank Prison. He was sent to Netley Military Hospital on 18 July 1880, but there is no trace of his date of discharge. He died in Ireland, but the date is unknown; name sometimes rendered as 'Connor'.

Connors, Timothy, Private, 'B' Company 2/24th, No.1323: Born in County Cork (date unknown) and worked as a labourer prior to enlisting on 15 March 1860. He was described as 5'4" tall, with a fair complexion, blue eyes and dark brown hair. He served in India, Mauritius, South Africa and Gibraltar. He was awarded the Long Service and Good Conduct Medal and discharged at Colchester on 2 February 1882 – having served for 21 years and seven months. His intended place of residence was given as Lough, near Bandon, County Cork. Date of death unknown – possibly a brother of Private Anthony Connors; name sometimes rendered as 'Connor'.

Cooper, William, Private, 'B' Company 2/24th, No.2453: Born in Liverpool, Lancashire circa 1856 and was posted to the 2/24th in January 1873 while it was stationed at Warley. He is listed as serving in 'F' Company at Rorke's Drift, so possibly he was a patient in the hospital. As a result of a medical examination at Netley Military Hospital held on 1 February 1880, he was discharged to the Army Reserve. He died in Worthing, Sussex on 19 February 1942 and is believed to have committed suicide.

Dalton, James Langley, Acting Assistant Commissary, Commissariat and Transport Department: Along with Walter Dunne, was the most responsible for the successful defence of Rorke's Drift. He was born in Holborn, London on 20 November 1832 and died in Port Elizabeth, South Africa on 7 January 1897. He was awarded the Victoria Cross for his actions at Rorke's Drift.

Daniells, Mr A.: A civilian, he was the 'pontsman' in charge of the ferry at Rorke's Drift. Place and date of birth are unknown, but he died in South Africa (date and place are not known).

Davis, George, Private, 'B' Company 25B/470: Born in Glamorganshire circa 1853 and attested at Wrexham on 15 October 1874 aged 21 years. He was posted to the 2nd Battalion on 4 December 1874. His name disappears from the regimental records after 4 March 1881 and it is presumed he was discharged on or around this date. His place and date of death is presently unknown.

Davis, William Henry, Private, 'B' Company 25B/1363: Born at St Bartholomew's, London circa 1853 and was employed as a porter. He attested at Bow Street Police Court on 26 February 1877 aged 24 years. He served in South Africa, the Mediterranean and India before being transferred to the Army Reserve on 21 January 1883. He was finally discharged on 10 August 1889 and died in Radnorshire (date, as yet, not known).

Daw, Thomas, Private, 'B' Company 25B/1178: Born in Merriott, Somerset on 8 July 1858 and worked as a labourer. He attested at Crewkerne on 5 February 1877 aged 18 years and six months. He served in South Africa, India and the Mediterranean before being discharged to the Army Reserve on 31 May 1883. He died in Taunton, Somerset on 20 April 1912; name sometimes rendered as 'Dawe'.

Deacon, George, Private, 'B' Company 25B/1467: Born in Bank, Yorkshire circa 1853 and worked as a clerk prior to attesting at Chatham on 10 November 1877 aged 24 years. The records show him confined to cells on two occasions – the second time from 11 to 24 February 1879 for 'failing to obey an order'. He deserted at Pietermaritzburg on 9 September 1879. He died in Romford, Essex on 6 February 1934; real name George Deacon Power.

Deane, Michael, Private, 'B' Company 2/24th, No.1357: Attested on 10 March 1877 and was posted to the 2nd Battalion on 26 January 1878. Deserted at Gibraltar on 22 July 1880 and to date, his place and date of birth or death are unknown.

Desmond, Patrick, Private, 25B/568: Suffered a gunshot wound to the fleshy part of the thumb during the action at Rorke's Drift. He is believed to have been born in Pembrokeshire circa 1857 of Irish parents, who had fled from Ireland to Wales during the potato famine of the 1840s. He attested on 27 March 1875 aged 18 years, but did not state any next of kin. Throughout his military career, he was constantly in trouble. Between July and October 1878, he received 20 fines for drunkenness from the Civil Powers and received a gaol sentence from 31 July to 21 August 1880 for a total of 22 days. Desmond was discharged from the army on 15 November 1880 at Pembroke Dock, Pembrokeshire as a 'worthless character'. He had served for a total of four years, 362 days; not transferred to the reserve. He was awarded the South Africa Medal 25 September 1877–2 December 1879, with clasp 1877–8–9. The medal was forfeit as of 19 June 1906 under Order 68/24/263. No reason was given and there is no record of it being returned to the Woolwich Mint. Place and date of death are unknown.

Dick, James, Private, 'B' Company 2/24th, No.1697: Born in Island Magee, County Antrim circa 1847, he attested at Belfast on 3 February 1862 aged 15 years.[1] Described as being 5'7" tall, with a fresh complexion, grey eyes and curly brown hair, he served in India, South Africa and the Mediterranean. He is believed to have served at Rorke's Drift and re-engaged at Secunderabad on 18 November 1881. He was discharged at his own request on 20 February 1889 – having completed 24 years and 15 days' service. He was awarded the Long Service and Good Conduct Medal and died in Secunderabad.

Dicks, William, Private, 'B' Company 2/24th, No.1634: Born in Islington, London circa 1847 and was working as a labourer prior to attesting at Westminster Police Court on 26 November 1864. Dicks transferred from the 1st to 2nd Battalion on 31 January 1865 – serving in India, South Africa and the Mediterranean. He re-engaged at Secunderabad on 6 August 1882 and was appointed Lance Corporal on 17 September 1877 – rising to Corporal two months later. Although appointed to Lance Sergeant on 3 May 1878, he was reduced to Private in September of the same year. He may have served in 'B' Company in the defence of Rorke's Drift, but there is confusion between him and James Dick (No.1697). He was discharged on 9 February 1886 – having served for 21 years and 65 days – and died in Chelsea, London on 19 October 1925; name sometimes rendered as 'Dickes'.

Dougherty, Michael, Corporal, Natal Native Contingent: Was a patient in the hospital during the action. His date and place of birth/death are unknown; name sometimes rendered as 'Doughty', 'Docherty', 'Doherty' etc. (there are 14 known ways of spelling this surname).

Driscoll, Thomas, Private, 'B' Company 25B/971: Born in Dowlais, Glamorganshire circa 1863/64. This would have made him 16 at the time of the battle, which is not impossible. He attested on 15 December 1876 and was posted to the 2nd Battalion on 22 January 1877. He served in South Africa and India (date of discharge unknown) and he died as a bachelor at Ebbw Vale, Monmouthshire on 16 June 1931.

Dunbar, James, Private, 'B' Company 25B/1421: Born in Scotland; date unknown. He attested at Newport on 20 June 1877 and was posted to the 2nd Battalion on 13 December of the same year. Appointed Lance Corporal on 1 February 1878 – and further promotion to Corporal followed on 15 March. This was followed by a demotion to Private and the award of 28 days' hard labour as of 22 July 1878. He

---

1   Dick told recruiters that he was 18 years old.

served in India – returning to England on 11 April 1883 and being discharged to the Army Reserve on 9 October the same year. At some later time, he returned to South Africa and died in Pinetown on 29 January 1940.

Dunne, Walter, Alphonsus, Assistant Commissary, Commissariat and Transport Department: Held a rank equal to that of Lieutenant. Dunne was the officer in charge of the stores held at Rorke's Drift. Described as 'a tall, pleasant-looking man', he was 26 years old and had been born in County Cork on 10 February 1853. His contribution to the defence of Rorke's Drift on 22 January was considerable, and he was recommended for the Victoria Cross, but received no official recognition. Dunne was present at the Battle of Ulundi to see the final defeat of the Zulu nation. He was awarded the CB in 1897 for distinguished service, and also the Egypt Medal with bars for Tel-el-Kebir and Suakim. Dunne ended his career with the rank of Colonel – and due to ill health, retired to Italy for the remainder of his days. He died in a nursing home on 2 July 1908 and is buried in the Veterans' Cemetery, Rome.

Edwards, George, Private, 'B' Company 25B/922: Real name George Edward Orchard, he was born at Charles Street, St James', Bristol on 25 August 1855. He was employed as a shoemaker's apprentice and in the building trade prior to enlisting on 24 November 1876, aged 21 years. He was posted to the 2nd Battalion as of 15 December 1876. Confined to the cells for 10 days in June 1880, the reason was not recorded. He then served in India – returning to England on 29 January 1883 and being discharged in 1889. He lived at New Pit, Paulton, Somerset, where he worked in a boat factory and was married to Rena Elizabeth; they had 10 children. He died in Paulton on 14 February 1940.

Evans, Abraham, Gunner, Royal Artillery, No.1643, 'N' Battery, 5 Brigade: Was a patient in the hospital. He was born in Trevethin, Monmouthshire on 3 February 1855 and died in Abersychan, Monmouthshire in March 1920.

Evans, Frederick, Private 25B/954: Date and place of birth/death are not known.

Fagan, John, Private, 'B' Company 25B/969: Attested on 13 December 1876 and was posted to the 2nd Battalion on 22 January the following year. Fagan was convicted by the Civil Powers to five days' imprisonment on 7 November 1878. He was killed in action at Rorke's Drift and is buried there – his name appearing on the memorial; place and date of birth are unknown.

French, George, Corporal, 'B' Company 2/24th, No.582: Born in Kensington, London circa 1841 and was employed as a groom before enlisting on 16 December 1859. During his military career, he gained extra pay as a fencing and gymnastics instructor. He was discharged on 3 January 1882 on completion of 22 years and 11 days' service; date and place of death are unknown.

Galgey, Patrick, Drummer, 'D' Company 2/24th, No.1713: Born in Ireland and attested at Cork on 12 March 1865, aged 14 years. He was appointed as a Drummer on 1 February 1866 – joining the battalion in India on 5 April 1869. He was discharged (date unknown) under AGL 89. His medal for South Africa – with clasp 1877–8–9 – was issued on 17 June 1881. On the 1901 census, he was living in St Marylebone, London, aged 49 years as a tailor and packer; date and place of death are, as yet, not known.

Gallagher, Henry, Sergeant, 'B' Company 25B/81: Born in Killenaule, Thurles, County Tipperary, he enlisted at Liverpool on 23 March 1874 – aged 19 years – and was described as 5'6" tall, with a fresh complexion, amber eyes and dark brown hair; his religion was Roman Catholic. He served in South Africa, Gibraltar, India and Burma. He married Caroline Maria Stanley at Dover on 7 April 1877; they had six children. He was discharged on 12 May 1897 after serving for 23 years and died in Drayton, Hampshire on 17 December 1931.

Gee, Edward, Private, 'B' Company 2/24th, No.2429: Attested in November 1872 and initially served in the 1st Battalion. He transferred to the 2nd Battalion on 1 January 1873. His transfer to the Army Reserve, under AGL 120, is not recorded; place and date of birth/death are, as yet, not known.

Graham, J., Corporal, No.1123, 90th (Perthshire Volunteers) Light Infantry: The only member of this regiment to serve at Rorke's Drift, he also served as Private 2202 Daniel Sheehan – a deserter from the 2nd Battalion, 6th (*Royal Warwickshire*) Regiment of Foot. Daniel Sheehan was born near the city of Cork in July 1851. He gained a second class certificate of education and became a clerk. On 5 December 1870, he enlisted in the 2nd/6th – and by January 1876, he was a Sergeant. In June of the same year, he went absent without leave for a week. He was apprehended, tried and sentenced to be reduced to the rank of Private. On 15 December 1876 – having served six years in the army – he passed to the reserve to serve a period of six years as a Reservist in the Liverpool District. Instead, he returned to Ireland and enlisted at Bin under the guise of 'James Graham' – stating he was born at 'St Mary's, near Dublin' and that he was a 'labourer' with no prior military service. He joined the 90th Light Infantry, with the regimental number 1123. However, someone must have recognised him as Sheehan, for he was arrested on 26 February 1877 and confined whilst awaiting trial. On 2 May 1877, he was tried and convicted of Fraudulent Enlistment. He lost his 29 days' pensionable service and good conduct pay gained whilst with the 90th, and was confined in a military prison until 26 June 1877. On 11 January 1878 (possibly aboard *The Nubian*), he arrived in South Africa, where the 90th were deployed against the amaXhosa in the Transkei. On 2 April 1878 he was tried by local court martial and his rights and privileges gained in the 2nd/6th were forfeited. He died in Farnborough, Hampshire in February 1899.

Green, Robert, Trooper, Natal Mounted Police: Place and date of birth are not known. He was a patient in the hospital at Rorke's Drift and died in Mossel Bay, South Africa on 21 January 1925.

Hagan, James, Private, 'B' Company 25B/798: Born in Neenagh, County Tipperary circa 1857/58, he worked as a labourer prior to enlisting at Monmouth on 23 March 1876, aged 18 years and seven months. He is described as being 5'6" tall, with grey eyes, brown hair and a fresh complexion. His religion was listed as Roman Catholic. He had previously served in the Royal Monmouth Militia and his next of kin was listed as his sister, Mary Ann Martland. He served in South Africa, Gibraltar and India before being transferred to the Army Reserve on 24 March 1882, but was recalled to army service at Salford, Lancashire on 3 August 1882. He re-transferred to the Army Reserve on 8 February 1883. He was married to Catherine Barry at Treforrest, Glamorgan on 8 July 1872 and was discharged from the Army Reserve on 23 March 1888. His date and place of death are, as yet, not known.

Halley, William, Lance Corporal, 'B' Company 25B/1282: Attested on 3 March 1877 and served in South Africa, India and Burma, where he died on 30 April 1887 at Thayetmyo.

Harris, John, Private, 'B' Company 25B/1062: Born in Crickhowell, Breconshire circa 1858 and worked as a labourer prior to his enlistment on 15 January 1877, aged 19 years. He served in India, South Africa and Gibraltar. He was brought before a medical board at Gibraltar on 16 July 1880 and was medically discharged as a result of suffering from chronic osteoarthritis – the discharge taking effect from 14 February 1881. His place and date of death are, as yet, not known.

Hayden, Garret, Private, 'D' Company 2/24th, No.1769: Date and place of birth are not known, but he attested at Dublin on 9 December 1865 – aged 18 years – and was posted to the battalion at Port Blair on 11 July 1867. He was appointed as a Drummer on 1 October 1868, but reduced to Private on 10 September 1875. He was a patient in the hospital during the attack on Rorke's Drift and died as a result of multiple stab wounds. After his death, his father claimed his effects; the family home was in John Street, Brecon. He is buried in the cemetery at Rorke's Drift.

Hayes, Patrick, Drummer, 'B' Company 2/24th, No.2067: Born in Newmarket, County Clare on 9 September 1854, he attested at Ennis on 8 September 1868, aged 14 years – his previous employment being as a labourer. He served in India, South Africa, the Mediterranean and Burma. He re-engaged on 22 November 1879 and was permitted to continue in service beyond 21 years by authority dated '29 October 1889'. He was discharged on 30 November 1892 – becoming a civilian worker at the barracks at Brecon and remaining here until well past 60 years of age. Upon his eventual retirement, he moved to Riverhall Street, Wandsworth Road, London. He died here on 4 October 1940.

Hitch, Frederick, Private, 'B' Company 25B/1362: Born in Edmonton, London on 29 November 1856, he attested at Westminster Police Court on 7 March 1877, with his trade listed as 'bricklayer's labourer'. He was seriously wounded by a gunshot to the shoulder; nevertheless, he continued to pass out ammunition to the defenders during the battle and was subsequently awarded the Victoria Cross for his actions. He was medically discharged on 25 August 1879 and died in Chiswick, London on 7 January 1917.

Hook, Alfred Henry, Private, 'B' Company 25B/1373: Born in Churcham, Gloucestershire on 6 August 1850, he was slightly wounded by a contusion to the forehead when a Zulu spear struck his helmet plate. Hook was awarded the

Victoria Cross for his actions during the battle – and his character was grossly misrepresented in the film '*Zulu*'. He died in Gloucester on 12 March 1905.

Horrigan, William, Private, 1/24th, No.1861: A member of 'G' Company, he was killed whilst a patient in helping to defend the hospital. He was born in Cork, Ireland in April 1849 and had attested on 12 November 1863 at the age of 14 years and seven months.

Howard, Arthur, Gunner, No.2077, 'N' Battery: Born in Eynsford, Kent circa 1853 and died in London on 15 July 1935. He was a patient in the hospital at the time of the action.

Hunter, Sydney, Trooper, Natal Mounted Police: Born in Barnet, Hertfordshire circa September 1856. He was a patient in the hospital and was killed as he attempted to escape.

Jenkins, David, Private 25B/295, 1/24th.2

Jenkins, James, Private, 25B/841: Born in Littledean, Gloucestershire circa March 1850, he was a patient in the hospital and was killed while assisting with the defence. According to the family grave at Littledean, he was killed at 'Isandula'; this is incorrect.

Jobbins, John, Private, 'B' Company 25/1061: Born in Newport, Monmouthshire on 18 July 1856 and attested at Pontypool on 12 January 1876 – having previously served in the Monmouth Militia. Jobbins described the battle in a letter to his father and returned to England from India on 29 January 1883; discharge, as yet, not traced. He died in Pontnewynydd, Monmouthshire on 22 September 1934, aged 79 years.

Jones, Evan, Private, 'B' Company 25B/1428: Real name John Cosgrove, he was born in Ebbw Vale, Monmouthshire of Irish parents circa April 1853 and attested at Brecon on 20 July 1877, aged 18 years and four months – having previously worked as a labourer – and served in the Royal Monmouth Engineers. He had changed his name before enlisting – taking the name of his landlady. Described as 5'4" tall, with a fresh complexion, grey eyes, brown hair and Roman Catholic, he was posted to the 2nd Battalion on 26 January 1878 and served in South Africa, the Mediterranean, India and Burma. Jones transferred to the Gloucester Regiment on 30 September 1889 – and to the unattached list as of 10 October 1889 – before transferring to the South Wales Borderers (SWB No.2835) as of 31 December 1892. Attached to the permanent staff of the 4th Battalion at Brecon, on 27 May 1896, he was allowed to continue in service beyond 21 years. He married Alice Evans, a widow, at Welshpool Registry Office on 15 October 1898. He attested at Welshpool on 17 March 1900 for service with the Royal Northern Reserve Battalion as a musician and was discharged on 16 March 1901. He then served in the Montgomery Yeomanry, but dates are, as yet, not known. He attested at Aberystwyth on 15 April 1915 for the 2nd/7th Royal

---

2   This is all of the information available on Pte David Jenkins.

Welsh Fusiliers (No.291067) and was discharged on 15 February 1919. Jones again attested at Wrexham on 12 August 1919 for service as a Private in the Northumberland Fusiliers (No.99052). He was discharged on 10 February 1920 – and his intended place of residence was 18 Union Street, Welshpool. By the end of his service, Evan Jones had completed 43 years in uniform. He died in Welshpool, Montgomeryshire on 29 July 1931, aged 72 years; he is buried in Welshpool.

Jones, John, Private, 25B/970: Served in 'B' Company 2/24th and attested on 13 December 1876. He was posted to the 2nd Battalion as of 22 January 1877; date of discharge not traced as yet – and date and place of birth/death are, as yet, not known.

Jones, John, Private, 25B/1179 'B' Company 2/24th: Born in Merthyr Tydfil, Glamorgan circa 1852/53 and worked as a labourer prior to attesting at Tredgar on 2 February 1877, aged 24 years. He had previously served in the Cardiff Militia and was posted to the 2nd Battalion on 23 February 1877 – going on to serve in South Africa, Gibraltar and India. He was transferred to the Army Reserve as of 28 June 1883 and was discharged on 6 February 1889; date and place of death not known.

Jones, Robert, Private, 'B' Company 25B/716: Born in Tynewydd, Monmouthshire on 19 August 1857. He was slightly wounded by a contusion to the abdomen and was awarded the Victoria Cross for his actions during the battle. He died in Peterchurch, Herefordshire on 6 September 1898.

Jones, William, Private, 'B' Company 2/24th, No.593: Born in Birmingham, Warwickshire circa 1839/40, he was awarded the Victoria Cross for his actions during the battle. He died in Manchester, Lancashire on 15 April 1913.

Judge, Peter, Private, 'B' Company 2/24th, No.2437: Was posted to the 2nd Battalion in January 1873; his date of attestation has not, as yet, been traced. He was awarded a good shooting prize in 1878 and was discharged to the Army Reserve (AGL105) – the date of which is presently unknown; place and date of birth/death are not known.

Kears, Patrick, Private, 'B' Company 2/24th, No.972: Listed as being born in Liverpool, Lancashire, but more likely Ireland, and worked as a labourer before enlisting on 6 December 1876. He was 19 years old and had previously served in the 2nd Royal Lancashire Militia. He was described as being 5'4" tall, with a fresh complexion, blue eyes and brown hair; he was a Roman Catholic. He was examined by a medical board at Pietermaritzburg on 23 July 1879 as a result of debility and recommended for a 'change of climate'. He was sent to Netley on 3 October 1879 and was posted to the depot at Brecon two weeks later. He married Annie Lewis at Brecon on 16 November 1880 and transferred to the Army Reserve on 1 February 1883. He was discharged on 8 December 1888 and died at the family home in Roscommon on 16 March 1932; name sometimes rendered as 'Kear'.

Keffe, James, Drummer, 'B' Company 2/24th, No.2381: Born at St Andrew's, London on 4 May 1856. No previous trade is listed, but he attested at Marlborough Police Court on 3 March 1871, aged 14 years and 10 months. He served in South Africa, the Mediterranean, India and Burma. He re-engaged at Secunderabad on 18 December 1879 to complete 21 years' service. He was wounded in the action at Rorke's Drift and died in Ebbw Vale, Monmouthshire on 18 September 1893.

Key, John, Corporal, 'B' Company 2/24th, No.2389: Both born in and attested at Secunderabad, India. His date of birth is not recorded, but he attested on 28 August 1871. He was appointed as a Drummer in 1873 and reduced to Private in 1877. He took his discharge in Secunderabad on 1 March 1884 – and it is assumed he had family there; date and place of death unknown, but possibly also in Secunderabad.

Kiley, Michael, Private, 'B' Company 25B/1386: Attested at Brecon on 24 April 1877 and was posted to the 2nd Battalion on 11 May of the same year. On 7 October 1878, he was confined by the Civil Powers and sentenced to five days' hard labour. Two months after the action at Rorke's Drift – on 11 March – he was again in prison and was tried by court martial on 17 March for insubordination. He was sentenced to receive 50 lashes and to be fined £1. He was once again confined by the Civil Powers on 26 September – the duration of which is presently unknown. On release, he was sent to the general depot on 1 January 1880 and would appear to have been struck of the regimental strength. He made a remittance from his pay to two women: Helen Kiley and Mary Sullivan; date and place of birth/death are, as yet, not known.

Lewis, David, Private, 'B' Company 25B/963: Born in Gorsgoch, Carmarthenshire on 25 May 1852 – his real name being James Owen. He died in Swansea, Glamorganshire on 27 July 1938.

Lewis, Thomas, Bombardier, No.458, 'N' Battery: Born in Brecon, Brecknockshire circa 1854 and died here circa 1920.

Lines, Henry, Private, 'B' Company 2/24th, No.1528: Born in Northampton, Northamptonshire circa 1846. He died in Lower Boddington, Oxfordshire circa 1902/20.

Lloyd, David, Private, 'B' Company 25B/1409: Born in Llanfair, Glamorganshire circa 1855 and died in Merthyr Tydfil, Glamorganshire on 16 September 1917.

Lockhart, Thomas, Private, 'B' Company 25B/1176: Born in Manchester, Lancashire on 15 April 1857. He died in Krugersdorp, South Africa on 25 June 1943.

Lodge, Joshua, Private, 'B' Company 25B/1304: Born in Manchester, Lancashire; date unknown. He died in Manchester on 26 July 1906.

Luddington, Thomas, No.3037, Private, Army Hospital Corps: Born in Lavendon, Buckinghamshire circa December 1855 and died in Plymouth, Devonshire on 22 March 1934.

Lugg, Henry (Harry), Trooper, Natal Mounted Police: Born in Clovelly, Devonshire on 9 September 1859 and died in Port Shepstone, South Africa on 12 October 1927.

Lynch, Thomas Michael, Private, 'B' Company 2/24th, No.942: Born in Limerick, County Limerick circa 1852. He enlisted on 10 November 1876, aged 18 years. He was discharged on 17 April 1888.

Lyons, John, Corporal, 'B' Company 25B/1112: Born in Trevethin, Monmouthshire on 23 August 1844. He was dangerously wounded by a gunshot to the neck (?) – fracturing his spine. The bullet lodged in the wound, but was later removed and mounted on a silver watch chain. Both bullet and watch chain are on display in the Regimental Museum. He died in Newport, Monmouthshire on 1 May 1923.

Lyons, John, Private, 'A' Company 2/24th, No.1441: Born in Killaloe, O'Briens Bridge, County Clare circa 1837. He enlisted in the 87th Foot on 31 March 1859 and transferred to the 2/24th on 1 July 1861. He was a patient in the hospital at the time of the attack. He was discharged on 4 August 1879; date and place of death are, as yet, not known.

Mabin, George W., Colour Sergeant, No.1566: Attached to the General Staff and was born in Bristol, Gloucestershire on 5 October 1848. He died in Rondebosch, South Africa on 23 October 1938.

McMahon, Michael, No.3359, Second Corporal, Army Hospital Corps: Came from Rathkeale, County Limerick and was awarded the Distinguished Conduct Medal for his actions at Rorke's Drift when he rescued Private Cole (No.1459) from the Zulu. The award was later rescinded when he was found guilty of theft.

Manley, John, Private, 'A' Company 2/24th, No.1731: Born in Cork, Ireland in January 1850. He enlisted at Cork on 17 April 1865, aged 15 years. He was a patient in the hospital at the time of the action; place and date of death are unknown.

Marshall, James, Private, 'B' Company 25B/964: Born in Hitchin, Hertfordshire circa January 1858. His place and date of death is unrecorded.

Martin, Henry, Private, 'B' Company 25B/876: Born in West Lydford, Somerset circa January 1858; date and place of death are unknown.

Mason, Charles, Private, 'B' Company 25B/1284: Born in Shoreditch, London on 13 August 1855; date and place of death are unknown.

Maxfield, Robert, Sergeant, 'G' Company 25B/623: Born in Llangarron, Herefordshire circa June 1855 and attested on 30 July 1875, aged 18 years. He was a patient in the hospital at Rorke's Drift and was killed during the evacuation.

Mayor, Jessy H., Corporal, Natal Mounted Police: Was a patient in the hospital – having been wounded at Sihayo's stronghold. Apart from 'Ireland', his place and date of birth/death are not known. He went on to serve with Robert's Horse in the Second Boer War; name sometimes rendered as 'Mayer'.

Meehan, John, Drummer, 'A' Company 2/24th, No.2383: Born in Limerick, Ireland; date unknown. He was appointed as a Drummer on 7 August 1876 and was discharged on 29 January 1883; name sometimes rendered as 'Meeham', with varying initials ('P' or 'T'). The date and place of his death are, as yet, not known.

Miller, Robert, No.3169, Corporal, Army Hospital Corps: Born in Wellington, New Zealand circa May/June 1855 and died in Bouet, Guernsey, the Channel Islands circa 1896/1946.

Millne, Frederick, Sergeant, 3rd East Kent Regiment (The Buffs): A patient in the hospital, he was born circa 1854 at a place unknown. He died in Manchester, Lancashire on 5 June 1924.

Minehan, Michael, Private, 'B' Company 2/24th, No.1527: Born in Castlehaven, County Cork circa 1855 and enlisted on 14 October 1864, aged 19 years. He died on 26 May 1891 and is buried in the Castlehaven Churchyard, Cork.

Moffatt, Thomas, Private, 'B' Company 25B/968: Born in Runcorn, Cheshire on 15 December 1855. He died here on 18 November 1936.

Morris, Augustus, Private, 'B' Company 25B/1342: Born in Dublin circa 1857 and enlisted on 3 March 1877, aged 20 years. He was discharged on 5 March 1889 and died in Liverpool in November 1914.

Morris, Frederick, Private, 'B' Company 25B/525: Born in Dublin circa 1855 and died in Secunderabad on 26 September 1883. He was the brother of Private Augustus Morris.

Morrison, Thomas, Private, 'B' Company 25B/No.1371: Born in Armagh, County Armagh, Ireland circa 1858/59; date and place of death are not known.

Murphy, John, Private, 'B' Company 25B/662: Born in Tredgar, Glamorganshire circa 1856/57. He died in Newport, Monmouthshire on 28 July 1927.

Neville, William, Private, 'B' Company 25B/1279: Born in Wigan, Lancashire circa 1858; date and place of death are not known.

Nicholas, Edward, Private 25B/625: Born in 1857; place unknown. He was killed by a gunshot to the head while a patient in the hospital on 22 January 1879.

Norris, Robert, Private, 'B' Company 25B/1257: Born in Liverpool, Lancashire circa December 1857 to January 1858; date and place of death are unknown.

Orchard, George (see Edwards, George).

Osborne, William, Private, 'B' Company 25B/1480: Born in Blaenavon, Monmouthshire circa 1858/59 and died here on 19 February 1931.

Parry, Samuel, Private, 25B/1399: Born in Sirhowy, Glamorganshire circa 1857; date and place of death are, as yet, not known.

Parry, Thomas, Private, 'D' Company 25B/572: Born in Stretton Sugwas, Herefordshire; place and date of death unknown.

Partridge, William, Private, 'G' Company 25B/1410: Born in Ross-on-Wye, Herefordshire circa June 1855, he was possibly a patient in the hospital at Rorke's Drift. He died in Blaina, Monmouthshire on 16 April 1930.

Payton, Thomas, Private, 'G' Company 25B/372: Place of birth unknown, but attested at Manchester on 13 July 1874, aged 21 years. He was discharged at Gosport on 2 January 1880 and transferred to the Army Reserve. His intended place of residence was 7 Planet Street (off Cross Street), Stafford; place of death unknown, but possibly his last known address.

Pearce, William: Surgeon's servant; date and place of birth/death are not known.

Pitt, Samuel, 'B' Company 25B/1186: Born in Caerau, Glamorganshire; date unknown. He died here on 21 November 1926.

Reynolds, James, Surgeon, Army Medical Department: Born on 3 February 1844 at Dun Laoghaire (Kingstown), County Dublin. He was the son of Lawrence Reynolds JP of Dalyston House, Granard, County Longford and was educated at Castle Knock and Trinity College, Dublin, where he graduated BA, MB, ChB in 1867. He joined the Medical Staff Corps on 24 March 1868 and was attached to the 36th (Hereford) Regiment on 24 March 1869 as medical officer. While serving with the regiment in India, he earned a commendation from Lord Sandhurst for his work during a cholera outbreak. He was promoted to Surgeon in 1873 and was mentioned in despatches and awarded the Victoria Cross for his actions at Rorke's Drift. He then went on to be promoted to Surgeon Major. Lord Wolseley presented Reynolds with his Victoria Cross at a parade in St Paul's, Zululand on 16 July 1879. He died – holding the rank of Lieutenant Colonel – on 4 March 1932 and is buried in Kensal Green Roman Catholic Cemetery, Harrow Road, London.

Robinson, Thomas, Private, 'B' Company 2/24th, No.1286: Born at St Patrick's, Dublin circa 1853 and enlisted on 23 February 1877. He died in Bristol, Gloucestershire circa 1883.

Robson, E., Driver, No.1204–6, 5th (Field) Company Royal Engineers: Born in Victoria, London on 7 January 1855 and died in Plumstead, London on 19 July 1933.

Roy, William, Private, 1/24th, No.1542: Was awarded the Distinguished Conduct Medal for his actions during the battle. Born in Edinburgh, his trade is given as 'baker' – and he originally attested for the 32nd Light Infantry on 8 August 1870, aged 17 years. He transferred to the 1/24th as of 4 December 1877. Following an examination by a medical board on 2 October 1879, he was found unfit for further service and was discharged on 7 December 1880 – having served for eight years, 303 days. He died in Parramatta, Australia on 30 May 1890.

Ruck, James, Private, 'B' Company 25B/1065: Place and date of birth/death are, as yet, not known.

Savage, Edward, Private, 'B' Company 25B/1185: Born in Newport, Monmouthshire on 19 April 1858 and died in Bridgend, Glamorganshire on 30 January 1893.

Sawyer, Peter (see Thomas, John).

Saxty, Alfred, Corporal, 'B' Company 2/24th, No.849: Born in Buckland, Dinham, Somerset circa 1857. He worked as a labourer prior to enlisting on 18 September 1876, aged 19 years. He was promoted to Sergeant on the day after the battle at Rorke's Drift, and was reduced to Private on 18 May 1881. He re-engaged at Wellington, Madras on 1 January 1888 into the 2nd Battalion, Bedfordshire Regiment to complete 21 years' service. On 30 November 1891, he transferred to the 2nd Battalion, Royal Inniskilling Fusiliers in the rank of Sergeant. He was discharged at his own request at Thayetmyo, Burma on 28 February 1895 as a Corporal, with 18 years and 107 days' service. Admitted as an In-Pensioner to the Royal Military Hospital, Chelsea on 12 June 1930, he died of myocarditis and senility on 11 July 1936 at Woolaston House Infirmary, Newport, Monmouthshire.

Scammell, C., Corporal, Natal Native Contingent: Was a patient in the hospital during the battle and received a further wound.

Scanlon, John, Private, 'A' Company 2/24th, No.1051: Place and date of birth are unknown, but he attested on 16 January 1877, although where is unknown. He was posted to the 2nd Battalion of the 24th on 31 January 1877 and saw service in the 9th Cape Frontier War of 1878. He was a patient in the hospital and was killed during the battle.

Schiess, Christian Ferdinand (also known as 'Friedrich'), Corporal, Natal Native Contingent: Born in Berdorf, Switzerland on 7 April 1856. He was a patient in the hospital during the battle and received the Victoria Cross for his actions. He died on the voyage from South Africa to England while aboard HMS *Serapis* on 14 December 1884.

Sears, Arthur, Private, 'A' Company 2/24th, No.2404: Born in Kingston, Middlesex in March 1854. He died in Fulham, London on 15 December 1906.

Shearman, George, Private, 'B' Company 2/24th, No.1618: Born in Hayes, Middlesex on 5 November 1847. His place and date of death are not known.

Shergold, John, Private, 'B' Company 2/24th, No.914: Born in London circa March 1840 and died here on 18 January 1884.

Smith, George, Sergeant, 2/24th, No.1387: Born in Islington, London circa 1842. He was an ex-labourer and attested at Finsbury on 29 May 1860, aged 18 years. He served in 'B' Company at Rorke's Drift and was discharged on 31 July 1883 – having served for 23 years; place and date of death are unknown.

Smith, The Rev George, Weenen Yeomanry: Born in Norfolk on 8 January 1845. He was the Volunteer Chaplain to the centre column – and despite being wounded, performed excellent service during the battle in giving out ammunition and raising the spirits of the men. He died in Fulwood, Lancashire on the night of 26/27 November 1918.

Smith, John, Private, 'B' Company 25B/1005: Born in Wigan, Lancashire circa 1851. He was slightly wounded during the action at Rorke's Drift; place and date of death are unknown.

Stevens, Thomas, Private, 'B' Company 25B/777: Born in Tiverton, Devon circa 1854 and died in Bristol, Gloucestershire circa 1902.

Tasker, William, Private, 'B' Company 2/24th, No.1812: Born in Birmingham, Warwickshire on 22 March 1846. He was slightly wounded when a splinter from a bullet broke the skin on his forehead during the action at Rorke's Drift.

Taylor, Frederick, Private, 'B' Company 25B/973: Born in Newport, Monmouthshire circa 1858 and died in Pinetown, South Africa on 30 November 1879.

Taylor, James, L/Sergeant, 'E' Company 25B/82: Born in Meltham, Halifax, Yorkshire circa 1855 and was employed as a clerk prior to enlisting on 13 March 1874 at Manchester. Presumed discharged after 8 March 1894, his next of kin is listed as 'Mrs. S Taylor, 33 Parkfield Road, Rusholme, Manchester'. He died in Trefnant, Denbighshire on 15 November 1919.

Taylor, Thomas, Private, 'B' Company 25B/889: Born in Hatton, Cheshire on 9 September 1856 and died in Runcorn, Cheshire on 17 April 1926.

Thomas, John, Private, 'B' Company 25B/1280: Real name Peter Sawyer, he was born in Liverpool, Lancashire circa 1853 and died in Canada circa 1940/45.

Thompson, John, Private, 'B' Company 25B/1394: Place and date of birth/death are unknown.

Tobin, Michael, Private, 'B' Company 25B/879: Born in Windgap, County Kilkenny circa 1856 and enlisted on 6 November 1876, aged 20 years. He was discharged on 9 February 1880; place and date of death are, as yet, not known.

Tobin, Patrick, Private, 'B' Company 25B/641: Born in Eire circa 1857; place and date of death unknown – and was possibly related to the previous Tobin.

Todd, William John, Private, 'B' Company 25B/1281: Place and date of birth/death are unknown.

Tongue, Robert, Private, 'B' Company 25B/1315: Born in Ruddington, Nottinghamshire on 3 June 1857 and died here on 29 January 1918.

Turner, Henry, Private, 25B/104: Born in Ballsbridge, Dublin – but alternative places mentioned are Bassbridge and Killeaty, Wexford – in either February or June 1851. He enlisted at Aldershot on 27 March 1874 – and his previous trade was given as 'bricklayer'. He was described as 23 years old, 6'1" tall, with a fresh complexion and light hazel eyes; his religion was Church of England. As a result of being struck on the head by a bottle while on picquet duty, he suffered (on occasions) from epilepsy. Following a medical board held at Pietermaritzburg on 9 September 1879, he was deemed as unfit for further military service. He returned to England and spent time in the military hospital at Netley. He received a medical discharge on 9 February 1880, with the medical opinion being that he 'may not be able to struggle for a precarious livelihood'.

Unknown, Private, Natal Native Contingent: Born in South Africa, he was a member of the Prince Mkhungo's iziGqoza – a group of disaffected Zulu. He was killed while a patient in the hospital at Rorke's Drift.

Wall, John, Private, 'B' Company 2/24th, No.1497: Believed to have come from a County Waterford family. He was born in Deptford, London circa 1859.

Waters, John, Private, 1/24th, No.447: Born in Lichfield, Staffordshire in January 1840. He attested at Westminster on 8 March 1858, aged 18 years and two months. He suffered a severe gunshot wound to his arm and shoulder during the action. A medical board found that 'from length of service and wound, his capacity to earn a living will be considerably impaired'. He was found unfit for further military service and was discharged on 27 October 1879. He died in London on 17 November 1883.

Whetton, Alfred, Private, 'B' Company 2/24th, No.977: Born in Chelsea, London on 24 May 1841 and died in Shoreditch, London circa 1891.

Wilcox, William, Private, 'B' Company 25B/1187: Place of birth and death are, as yet, not known.

Williams, John, Private, 'B' Company 25B/1395: Real name John Fielding, he was awarded the Victoria Cross for his actions during the battle. He was the son of Michael Fielding, who was born in Ireland, and Margaret Godsil, who was also of Irish descent. Michael arrived in Monmouthshire in the early 1850s and married Margaret at St Michael's Roman Catholic Church, Abergavenny on 21 January 1855. His son, John, was born in Abergavenny on 24 May 1857 and joined the army 20 years later – leaving his previous employment as a labourer. He attested at Monmouth on 22 May 1877 and was posted to the 2nd Battalion of the 24th on 3 August 1877. (He had run away from home and changed his name to avoid being traced.) He served in South Africa and India, and Major General Anderson at Gibraltar presented him with his VC on 1 March 1880; the citation had appeared in the London Gazette of 2 May 1879. After service in India, he returned to England in October 1883 – and a short time later, he transferred to the Army Reserve; he was discharged from the reserve on 22 May 183. He married and had two daughters and three sons – the eldest of whom was killed during the retreat from Mons during the First World War. For many years, he served on the civilian staff of the regimental depot at Brecon, from where he retired on 26 May 1920. In 1932, he was taken ill at the home of one of his daughters in Cwmbran – his wife having died some time previously. He died on 25 November 1932 and is buried at St Michael's Churchyard, Llantarnam; he was the last Rorke's Drift VC holder to die. His Victoria Cross is held in the Regimental Museum at Brecon. Fielding House, a home for the mentally handicapped, is named in his honour.

Williams, John, Private, 'E' Company 2/24th, No.934: Born in Barristown, Glamorganshire (date unknown); died at Rorke's Drift on 5 February 1879.

Williams, John, Private, 25B/1374: Place and date of birth/death are unknown.

Williams, Joseph, Private, 'B' Company 25B/1398: Born in Newport, Monmouthshire; date unknown. He was killed in action while defending the hospital at Rorke's Drift.

Williams, Thomas, Lance Sergeant, 'B' Company 25B/1328: Place and date of birth are unknown, but he enlisted at Brecon on 6 March 1877. During the action, he received a gunshot wound to the left side of his chest – fracturing several ribs. The bullet did not lodge in the body and he died on 25 January. He is buried in the cemetery at Rorke's Drift and his name appears on the monument.

Williams, Thomas, Private, 25B/1060: Born in Cardiff, Glamorganshire (date unknown); date and place of death are also unknown.

Wilson, Edward, Sergeant, 25B/56: Born in Peshawar, India, his trade is given as 'labourer' and his religion as Church of England. He died of a heart attack in Aldershot, Hampshire on 19 February 1891.

Wilson, John, Corporal, Natal Native Contingent: Real name John Wilton, he was a patient in the hospital; place and date of birth/death are unknown.

Windridge, Joseph, Sergeant, 'B' Company 2/24th, No.735: Born in St Saviour, Surrey on 14 May 1842. He worked as a carpenter before enlisting on 26 January 1859, aged 18 years and four months. Sergeant Windridge suffered from dyspepsia and was promoted and demoted on several occasions. He was discharged at Gosport – holding the rank of Corporal –on 7 August 1883 and died in Birmingham, Warwickshire on 30 August 1902.

Wood, Caleb, Private, 'B' Company 25B/1316: Born in Ruddington, Nottinghamshire on 24 April 1858 and died there on 20 February 1935.

Appendix I

A selection of brief biographical sketches relating to some of the men who served in South Africa during 1879[1]

The Zulu War
Memorial.

1 Ranks given are those believed to have been held during the campaign, but may not
necessarily be so!

The Zulu War Memorial in Pietermaritzburg garlanded with wreaths and flowers –
photographed on Isandlwana Day, 1904.

Adair, John, Colour Sergeant, No.779. Born in the townland of Mullaglass, County Armagh, he originally enlisted in the 42nd (The Black Watch) Royal Highlanders in Edinburgh on 13 September 1860, aged 20 years. He transferred to the 57th Regiment and served in New Zealand in the fighting against the Maoris between 1864 and 1866. In 1879, while serving in Ceylon, the regiment was ordered to South Africa – and Adair was awarded the 1879 Medal with clasp. In 1881, he joined the 1st Battalion, Middlesex Regiment and was promoted to Paymaster and Quartermaster Sergeant. He received the Long Service and Good Conduct Medal prior to being discharged on 15 October 1889 – having served for 29 years and 33 days. Of these, nine years and 300 days were served abroad. He was discharged at Buttevant Camp, County Cork and died in that city on 17 January 1931.

Adrian, William James was born in Belfast, County Antrim and served with the 1st Battalion, 13th Regiment in the Zulu War. He returned to Belfast on his discharge.

Colour Sergeant John Adair,
57th (West Middlesex) Regiment
– photographed as a Paymaster
Sergeant, circa 1882.

Alcock, Nathaniel, Surgeon Major, Army Medical Department was born in New Ross, County Wexford on 25 May 1839 – serving from 8 February 1878 until 11 April 1879. He served on the Eastern Frontier and was congratulated for his excellent service in the Cape – being awarded the South Africa Medal 1878. He died in Dublin on 4 April 1904 and is buried in Dunmore East Cemetery.

Anderson MD, John Albert, Surgeon, Army Medical Department was born in Ireland on 24 June 1844. He was in command of the Bearer Company of the Flying Column and was mentioned in despatches. Anderson was present at Ulundi, where he was the officer in charge of the medical detachments attached to the Royal Artillery and Royal Engineers. He was awarded the South Africa Medal 1879, Egypt Medal with clasp for Tel-el-Kebir and the Khedive's Star. He died on 9 November 1910.

Andrews, William Henry was born in Newry, County Down and served in the 13th Regiment. His intended place of residence was stated to be Market Hill, Armagh, County Armagh.

Appelbe, Edward Benjamin was the second son of the late Edward Alexander Appelbe of Kildarra House, Bandon, County Cork. He served in the Zulu campaign of 1879 with the Ordnance Store Department – gaining the medal and clasp. He went on to serve in the Boer War of 1881, the Sudan campaign and, during the Second Boer War, was present at the relief of Ladysmith – being mentioned in despatches three times and gaining the Queen's Medal with three clasps. He retired as a Brigadier General.

A LESSON.

'John Bull' is taught a lesson.

Ardies, David was born in Belfast, County Antrim and served with the 1st Battalion, 13th Regiment. He returned home after his discharge.

Ashton MB, Gough, Surgeon Major, Army Medical Department was born in Doneraile, County Cork on 1 September 1839. He served from 18 April 1879 until 7 February 1880 and was awarded the Afghanistan Campaign Medal 1878-80 and the South Africa Medal 1879. He died on 20 January 1905 at Oxmanstown, Birr, County Cork.

Babington, George, Natal Mounted Police was the first man to enlist in this unit on its formation on 12 March 1874; he survived the war. The *Londonderry Sentinel* published a letter from Babington to his mother, dated 3 February 1879.

Barton, Nathaniel Albert Delap was the youngest son of the late Lieutenant Colonel H.W. Barton of Waterfoot, County Fermanagh. He was commissioned into the 88th (Connaught Rangers) Regiment in 1878 – and a year later, was on service in South Africa; he gained the medal and clasp for the Zulu campaign. He again served in South Africa from 1889-1902 and was present at the relief of Ladysmith. He retired in 1905, but joined the army once more upon the outbreak of the Great War, In 1917, he was awarded a DSO – and two years later, he was promoted to Lieutenant Colonel. He died at Dinard, France aged 80.

Barton, Robert Johnston, Lieutenant and Captain, Coldstream Guards was the fourth son of T.J. Barton DL of Glendalough, County Wicklow. He was born in Dublin on 20 February 1849 and initially trained for a career in the Royal Navy at the training ship *Britannia.* However, he did not pursue an appointment in that service, and instead continued his education at Blackheath Proprietary School before attending the Royal Military College at Sandhurst. He obtained a commission as a Cornet in the 9th Lancers on 14 September 1866 and joined them at their quarters at Island Bridge Barracks, Dublin. In 1874, Barton exchanged to the Coldstream Guards – and in 1878, he volunteered as a Special Service officer in the 9th Cape Frontier War. He was appointed as second-in-command of the locally-raised Frontier Light Horse, which was commanded by Redvers Buller.

Lieutenant and Captain Robert Johnson Barton, 1st Battalion, Coldstream Guards.

Bayly, John Cave, Lieutenant was born in 1852 and was commissioned into the Ceylon Rifles. He went on half pay in 1871 – returning to the colours in 1873 with the 56th (West Essex) Regiment before transferring to the 27th (Inniskilling) Regiment. He served with the 27th in the Zulu War – initially with the Transport Service and subsequently with the Remount Establishment. He died suddenly in London in 1891. His Zulu War medal is held in the Royal Inniskilling Fusiliers Museum, Enniskillen, County Fermanagh.

Blood, Bindon, Captain, 30th Company, Royal Engineers was a descendant of the notorious Colonel Thomas Blood – an adventurer who had obtained estates in Ireland, which were forfeited at the Restoration. He was instrumental in an attempt to take Dublin Castle from the Royalists in 1663 – fleeing the country and taking refuge in Holland. He made an unsuccessful assassination attempt on the Duke of Ormond and planned an elaborate operation to steal the Crown Jewels in 1673. He, along with an accomplice, actually managed to remove the Crown and Globe, but was quickly arrested. Despite all of this, he gained the favour of Charles II and had his Irish estates returned.

Bindon Blood was born in Jedburg, Scotland in 1842 and was educated at Eton and Addiscombe College. He received a commission in the Royal Engineers in 1860 and continued in military service for the next 80 years. He joined the Bengal Sappers and Miners in 1873 and served in India. He was at home on leave when news of the debacle of Isandlwana reached England, and he immediately volunteered for service in South Africa. He was appointed to the 1st Division as Senior Engineer.

After the cessation of hostilities in Zululand, he returned to India and went on to serve in the Second Afghan War. By 1882, he was in Egypt and took part in the Battle of Tel-el-Kebir. From 1895 to 1897, he was involved in a number of expeditions on the North-West Frontier – including the Chitral Relief Expedition, for which he was appointed KCB. He acted as commander of the Malakand Field Force in 1897 and, after a successful expedition, he went on to form the Buner Field Force – again scoring a success in an operation which lasted from 2-17 January 1898. During the Boer War, he was involved in operations in the Eastern Transvaal. He returned to India after the war and was

Captain Bindon Blood, Royal Engineers – a later engraving.

appointed as military commander in the Punjab. He finally retired in 1907, with the rank of full General. On the outbreak of the Great War in 1914, despite being 72 years old, he was recalled to the colours and made Colonel Commandant of the Royal Engineers. With the onslaught of Hitler's *blitzkrieg* in 1940, even Blood conceded he was getting on a bit.

Sir Bindon Blood died in 1940, aged 97. His ashes are interred in the family tomb at Cranaher, County Clare.

Bolton, Archer Clive, Second Lieutenant, 58th Regiment was the son of Richard Bolton JP of Castlering, Dundalk, County Louth. He later served in the 7th Battalion, (The King's Own) Lancaster Regiment with the British Expeditionary Force in the Great War – earning the Military Cross.

Bothwell, Thomas, Private, 36B/142 was born in County Armagh. He served in the 13th Regiment and resided in Belfast, County Antrim after his discharge.

Bradfield, Samuel, Private, 36B/464 served with the 1st Battalion, 13th Regiment. He returned to Ireland after his discharge and lived at 13 Carlisle Terrace, Dublin.

Brady, James, Private was born in Belfast, County Antrim and served with the 13th Regiment. He returned home after his discharge.

Brook, Edmund Smith, Captain, 94th Regiment died as a Major General CB on 18 April 1910 and is buried in Castlehyde Cemetery, Fermoy, County Cork.

Brown, John, Captain and Paymaster, 17th (Duke of Cambridge's Own) Lancers was born on 28 March 1834 and enlisted aged 14 years as a Bandsman. He took part in the Charge of the Light Brigade on 25 October 1854 as a Trumpeter and was brought to the ground close to the Russian battery – his horse's off hind leg being carried away by a cannon shot and his own thigh being pierced by a rifle bullet. He was commissioned as Cornet and Adjutant as of 23 March 1867 and Lieutenant from 30 October 1869. He served at Ulundi and held campaign medals for the Crimea, the Indian Mutiny, the Zulu War and Egypt. He retired as (Hon.) Lieutenant Colonel on 28 March 1894 and died on 26 February 1905. He is buried in Mount Jerome Cemetery, Harold's Cross, Dublin.

Brown, Thomas Philip, Colour Sergeant, No.1118, 1st Battalion, 24th (2nd Warwickshire) Regiment was from County Cork. He was killed at Isandlwana.

Brownlow, William Vesey, Captain (subsequently Brevet Major) was the son of William and Charlotte Brownlow of Knapton House, Queen's County. He was born on 14 June 1841 and received a private education before being commissioned into the 1st Dragoon Guards and serving with them in the Zulu War, where he was promoted to Brevet Major. He served as assistant transport officer to the 2nd Division and as an extra aide-de-camp to Colonel Drury-Lowe at the Battle of Ulundi.

During the Boer War, he commanded a mounted force as a Brevet Lieutenant Colonel. At the Battle of Laing's Nek on 28 January 1881, Brownlow's horse was shot and he was saved by the actions of his soldier-servant, Private John Doogan – a native of County Galway, who received the Victoria Cross for doing so. Brownlow retired as a Major General and died at his home in Henley, Hampshire.

Butcher, Robert, Colour Sergeant, No.1264 served with the 1st Battalion, 13th Regiment during the Zulu War. Born in Gibraltar in 1841, he survived the war – and on his discharge, gave his intended place of residence as Birr, County Offaly. He died in 1900 in Manchester.

Butler, William, Major was born in Ballyslatten, County Tipperary on 31 October 1838. He was commissioned in the army in September 1858 – and in May 1859, was appointed as an Ensign in the 69th (South Lincolnshire) Regiment. Shortly after, he found himself deployed on the streets of Limerick after the Riot Act had been read to quell civil unrest. Despite holding several overseas postings, did not see action until the Fenian raids in Canada in 1870. It was here that he first came into contact with Sir

Major Sir William Butler, 69th
(South Lincolnshire) Regiment.

Lady Elizabeth Butler – renowned
artist...

Garnet Wolseley – eventually becoming one of the celebrated 'Wolseley Ring', who were a number of young and forward-thinking officers each destined to leave their mark in military history. Butler served with Wolseley in the Ashanti campaign of 1874 and again in Natal in 1875, when Wolseley served (for a short time) as Lieutenant Governor. In 1877, Butler married Elizabeth Thompson, who as Lady Butler became the leading painter of military scenes in Victoria's reign. (Her painting of Rorke's Drift is considered one of the more accurate renderings of the action.) During the Zulu War of 1879, Butler served mainly on the lines of communication, in which he excelled. He was in Egypt in 1882 and, like fellow Irishman Sir Bindon Blood, took part in the Battle of Tel-el-Kebir. Two years later, he was part of the unsuccessful expedition to relieve Gordon at Khartoum. He then went on to command a brigade at Ginnis on 30 December 1885, where the British troops changed from their khaki jackets back into red tunics to lower the morale of the enemy. This may well have been the case, as General Stephenson's Anglo-Egyptian Field Force defeated the Madhist Army effectively – ending the First Sudan War. During 1888, he became very closely acquainted with Charles Stewart Parnell MP. After this, his career consisted of a series of peacetime appointments – ending with that of Governor of the Cape Colony. He resigned this appointment on 29 June 1899 on principle – having discovered the Home Government's involvement in acquiring Boer lands without consent. He left South Africa on 29 August 1899 just before the commencement of hostilities to take up the Aldershot Command. Despite a number of requests, he refused an active command in South Africa. In 1906, he was appointed to the role of Commissioner of the Board of National Education in Ireland.

He died at Bansha Castle in 1910 and is buried in Killardrigh Cemetery, County Tipperary.

Byrne, Michael, Corporal, 61B/989, 2nd Battalion, 21st Regiment (Royal Scots Fusiliers) served in the Zulu War and is buried in the Military Cemetery, Crinkill, Birr, County Offaly.

Cardwell, William, Private, 36B/336 served in the 1st Battalion, 13th Regiment. He returned to Ireland after his discharge and resided at Market Hill, County Armagh.

Carroll, Frederick Harry, Second Lieutenant, 94th Regiment served at Greytown in Natal on the lines of communication, from where he was invalided home. He is buried in Ashford Anglican Church, County Wicklow.

Carroll, William, Private, 36B/299 served with the 1st Battalion, 13th Regiment and returned to Belfast, County Antrim after his discharge.

Chapman, John, Sergeant, 36B/119 served with the 1st Battalion, 13th Regiment. His intended place of residence after discharge was to be Bishopscourt, Straffan, County Kildare.

Clarke, Peter, Private, 36B/203 served with the 1st Battalion, 13th Regiment and had as his intended place of residence Belfast, County Antrim.

Collier, C., Sergeant, No.1126, 1st Battalion, 13th Regiment is buried in the Military Cemetery, Crinkill, Birr, County Offaly.

Condon, Sergeant Major, Natal Native Contingent was the son of a Royal Irish Constabulary officer from County Cork.

Connolly, Benjamin Bloomfield, Surgeon, Army Medical Department was born in Ireland on 16 September 1845 and served aboard the SS *Russia* from 4 April 1879 until 17 March 1880. He was secretary and statistical officer of the lines of communication and base of operations, Durban. In his service, he was awarded the CB, the Indian General Service Medal with clasp for Jowaki, the South Africa Medal without clasp, the Egyptian War Medal with clasp for Tel-el-Kebir, El Teb, Tam and Nile 1884; the Order of Osmanié and the Khedive's Star. He died on 20 June 1924 in Brighton, England.

Corcoran, Patrick served with the 1st Battalion, 13th Regiment. Upon his discharge, his intended place of residence was Ballyhone, County Galway.

Corkan, Francis, Private, 36B/329 served with the 1st Battalion, 13th Regiment. His intended place of residence was listed as Bow Street, Lisburn, County Antrim.

Cotter, William, Corporal, 17th (Duke of Cambridge's Own) Lancers came from Carrigtwohill, County Cork. He was ambushed and killed by Zulu on 30 June 1879 whilst on signalling duties – in company with Lieutenant James Henry Scott Douglas of the 21st (Royal Scots Fusiliers) Regiment – near to the kwaMagwaza mission station.

Courtney, David Charles, Captain, 2nd Company, Royal Engineers was the son of Henry Courtney of 24 Fitzwilliam Square, Dublin, where he was born on 27 January 1845. Present at the Battle of Nyezane and the investment of Eshowe, he died holding the rank of Major on 28 November 1909. He is buried in Deans Grange Cemetery, Dun Laoghaire, Dublin.

Creagh, Arthur Gethin, Lieutenant, Royal Artillery was the son of John Bagwell Creagh and Matilda Emily Victoria Wolseley. He was born on 12 February 1855 in County Cork and attended the Royal Military College, Woolwich. He was commissioned as a Lieutenant in the Royal Artillery on 12 February 1874. From January to May 1879, he acted as aide-de-camp to his uncle, Sir Garnet Wolseley – the High Commissioner and C-in-C, Cyprus. When Wolseley was sent to South Africa, Creagh accompanied him. In the latter phase of the 1879 campaign, Creagh accompanied

Captain Lord Gifford's command in the pursuit of King Cetshwayo. In this chase, lasting 17 days, there had been little rest or comfort. Creagh was also present at the capture of the stronghold of Chief Sekhukhune of the Pedi, where he earned a mention in despatches for his actions. Creagh continued to serve – seeing action in the Egyptian campaign of 1882, the Nile Expedition of 1884-85 and the Suakim campaign of 1885. By his retirement, he had reached the rank of Major General.

On leaving the army, he settled in Creagh House, Doneraile, County Cork, which he inherited from Mrs Arthur Creagh (he being her great-grand-nephew). He died on 21 February 1941.

Lieutenant Arthur Gethin Creagh,
Royal Artillery.

Cuffe, Charles McDonagh, Surgeon, Army Medical Department was born in Ireland on 15 April 1842 and served from 27 October 1877 to 14 December 1879. He served on the Eastern Frontier in 1877-78 in the campaign against the Gcaleka, and was the senior medical officer with Wood's column. Cuffe was awarded the KCB, the South Africa Medal 1877-78-79 and the Indian General Service Medal 1887-89; he was a very good friend of Surgeon James Henry Reynolds. His award of the KCB was received from Queen Victoria in September 1879 at a reception (lasting approximately one hour) in Windsor Castle, with luncheon taken afterwards in the Waterloo Chamber. Cuffe died in London on 14 October 1914 and is buried in St Mary's Cemetery, Kensal Green, London.

Surgeon Major Charles McDonagh Cuffe,
Army Medical Department.

Cumberland, James, Private, 36B/106 served in the 1st Battalion, 13th Regiment and resided in Coalisland, County Tyrone after his discharge.

Cunningham, Robert, Private, 36B/87 served with the 1st Battalion, 13th Regiment and resided in Belfast, County Antrim after his discharge.

Cunningham, Thomas, Drummer, 80th Regiment (Staffordshire Volunteers) was born in the parish of Shankill, Belfast, County Antrim. He enlisted on 19 September 1871, aged 14 years – being 4'7" in height, with blue eyes and a fair complexion. A Roman Catholic, his trade was given as 'labourer' – his army number being 1769. Cunningham joined his regiment on 22 September 1871 and transferred to the 3rd Battalion, South Staffordshire Regiment on 16 October 1887, with the new army number of 521. His date of discharge is unknown, but he was awarded the campaign medal of 1878-79 with clasp.

Curran, John Philpot, 88th (Connaught Rangers) Regiment was a grandson of the famous Irish judge, John Philpot Curran (1750-1817). He was also a relative of Robert Emmet – an Irish nationalist and Republican orator, who was executed for high treason.

Daley, Patrick was born in Ennis, County Clare and served in the 13th Regiment. He was discharged in 1891 and returned to his home.

Daly, Martin was born in Clonmel, County Tipperary and served in the 13th Regiment. After his discharge in 1882, he was to reside at 10 Rum Street, Clonmel.

D'Arcy, William Irvine – from Castle Irvine, County Fermanagh – previously served in the Fermanagh Light Infantry Militia. He died of disease following the campaign of 1879 and is buried in the Old Military Cemetery, Durban, South Africa.

Lieutenant William Irvine D'Arcy, 99th Duke of Edinburgh's (Lanarkshire) Regiment.

Darragh, John, Private, 36B/83 was born in Belfast, County Antrim and served in the 1st Battalion, 13th Regiment. He was discharged in 1886 with the intention of returning to his home.

Dawson, Charles Todd, Paymaster, HMS Boadicea**, Royal Navy** is buried in Southsea. There is a memorial plaque in St Anne's Church, Dungannon.

Delahunty, Robert, Private, No.1014 served in the 1st Battalion, 13th Regiment. He was discharged in 1884 and intended to reside in Bohola, County Mayo.

Dillon, Mark, Private, 36B/226 was born in Belfast, County Antrim and served in the 13th Regiment. He was discharged in 1886; no place of residence is listed.

Dobson MB, George Edward, Surgeon, Army Hospital Department was born in Ireland on 7 September 1844. He attended Trinity College, Dublin and was seconded for service in the Zulu War from duties in Ceylon. He served in South Africa from 9 January 1879 to 11 June the same year and was awarded the South Africa Medal without clasp. He died at West Malling, Kent.

Donaldson, Robert, Lance Corporal, 36B/377 was born in Newry, County Down and served in the 1st Battalion, 13th Regiment. His intended place of residence was Lisnaree, Banbridge, County Down.

HMS *Boadicea* – on which Paymaster Charles Todd Dawson served.

Donnelly, Joseph, Private, 36B/154 served in the 1st Battalion, 13th Regiment and was discharged in 1886. His intended place of residence was given as Belfast, County Antrim.

Dougal, Arthur, Private, 36B/69 was born in Belfast, County Antrim and he served in the 1st Battalion, 13th Regiment – being discharged in 1886. His intended place of residence was Belfast.

Dowman, John Frederick, Surgeon, Army Medical Department was born in Cork on 15 May 1849 and served in South Africa from 28 July 1879 until 4 September 1882. He resigned his commission on 17 June 1883 and returned to Ireland, where he continued to practise medicine. His date of death is unknown, but he was awarded the South Africa Medal without clasp.

Driscoll, (Driskill) Michael, Private, 36/376 served in the 1st Battalion, 13th Regiment and was discharged in 1880. He returned to Ireland – residing in Cherry Grove, Croom, County Limerick.

Drury MD, Robert, Surgeon, Army Medical Department was born in Ireland on 1 October 1847 and served in South Africa from 1 May 1879 until 9 May 1880. He served in the Zulu and Sekhukhune campaigns – being awarded the South Africa Medal 1879 – and later served in the First Boer War. He died on 23 January 1928.

Duff, James, Private, 36/307 served in the 1st Battalion, 13th Regiment and was discharged in 1886. He intended to reside in Belfast, County Antrim.

Duncan, J., Private, No.168, 1st Battalion, 13th Regiment came from Belfast, County Antrim and was killed in action at Khambula on 29 March 1879.

Dunne, Robert, Private, No.1077 served in the 1st Battalion, 13th Regiment and was discharged in 1888. He intended to reside in Dublin.

Dunne, Thomas, Private served in the 1st Battalion, 13th Regiment and was discharged in 1884. He intended to reside at 6 Harbour Street, Mountinellick, Queen's County, Ireland.

Edge MD, John Dallas, Surgeon Major, Army Medical Department was born in Timahoe, Queen's County, Ireland on 9 March 1838 – the son of the late Joseph Edge. Edge joined the army in 1871 – and a year later, was promoted to Staff Surgeon in recognition of his gallant services against Indians at Orange Walk, British Honduras. He served in South Africa from 13 March 1879 until 7 February 1880 – being present at Gingindlovu and the relief of Eshowe. He was awarded the CB, the South Africa Medal 1879, the Afghanistan Campaign Medal 1878-80, the

Egyptian Medal with clasp for Tel-el-Kebir, the Indian General Service Medal with clasp for Burma 1887-89, the South Africa Medal 1899-1902, the 4th Class Order of Osmanié and the Khedive's Star. He served in the Great War and died at his home in Raglan Road, Dublin on 30 April 1937, aged 90 – being buried in Mount Jerome Cemetery, Dublin.

Edmonds, James, Private, 36B/441 served in the 1st Battalion, 13th Regiment and was discharged in 1887. He intended to reside in Newtownards, County Down.

English, William, Lance Sergeant, No.2002 served in the 1st Battalion, 13th Regiment and was discharged in 1890. He intended to reside in Dublin.

Evry, Thomas, Private, No.518, 1st Battalion, 24th Regiment had attested at Cork on 1 December 1874, aged 19 years. He was killed at Isandlwana on 22 January 1879.

Falvey, John Joseph, Surgeon, Army Medical Department was born in Tralee on 16 April 1852. He served in South Africa from 28 July 1879 until 22 April 1882 – during which he took part in the campaign against Sekhukhune and in the First Boer War. He was awarded the South Africa Medal 1879, the Egyptian Medal with clasp for Abu Klea, Nile 1884; the Queen's South Africa Medal with clasp and the Khedive's Star. He died on 21 May 1922 and is buried in an unmarked grave at Glasnevin Cemetery, Dublin.

Fee, James, Private, 36B/94 served in the 1st Battalion, 13th Regiment and was discharged in 1886 – intending to reside in Belfast, County Antrim.

Fitzgibbon, Charles, Private, No.1246 served in the1st Battalion, 13th Regiment and was discharged in 1886. He intended to reside at 26 Buckingham Street, Dublin.

Flanaghan, John, Private, No.2032 was born in County Wicklow. He served in the 1st Battalion, 13th Regiment and was discharged in 1884 – returning home.

French-Brewster, Robert Abraham Brewster, Lieutenant of Merrion Square, Dublin served with the 1st (King's) Dragoon Guards in the Zulu War. He performed the role of Deputy Provost-Marshal for the 2nd Division and, as such, was present at the Battle of Ulundi. He was MP for Portarlington from 1883 until 1885.

Furlong, James, Private, No.1482 served in the 1st Battalion, 13th Regiment and was discharged in 1882. He intended to reside in County Waterford.

Gasteen MB, William Charles, Surgeon attended Trinity College, Dublin and served in the Zulu War 1879 – being mentioned in despatches. He died in Rathmines, Dublin on 2 January 1918.

Gastion, Robert, Private, 36B/41 served in the 1st Battalion, 13th Regiment and was discharged in 1886. He intended to reside in Belfast, County Antrim.

Gelston, Arthur William Hill, Captain and Paymaster, 3rd (East Kent) Regiment (the Buffs) was the youngest son of John Gelston, Commissariat Department, Dublin Castle. He died on 4 October 1923 and is buried in Deans Grange Cemetery, Dun Laoghaire, Dublin.

Glenfield, James C., Private, 36B/75 served in the 1st Battalion, 13th Regiment and was discharged in 1886. He intended to reside in Lisburn, County Antrim.

Glover, Benjamin Lucas, Veterinary Surgeon was attached to 'N' Battery, 5 Brigade, Royal Artillery and accompanied Lord Chelmsford's reconnaissance on 22 January 1879. He was subsequently involved in acquiring remounts in the Transvaal. He retired as a Colonel and died on 18 April 1904, aged 55. He is buried in Mount Jerome Cemetery, Dublin.

Gough, Hugh Rudolph was the son of Viscount Gough of Cutra Castle, County Galway. Lieutenant and Captain, Coldstream Guards, he held a Captain's commission in Commandant William John Nettleton's 5th Battalion, Natal Native Contingent. Despite suffering from dysentery, he fell in and commanded his company during the Battle of Gingindlovu. He died at Herwen on 19 April 1879.

Captain Hugh Rudolph Gough, 5th Battalion, Natal Native Contingent, formerly of the Coldstream Guards.

Greer, Carlile, Captain, Royal Artillery was the son of Edward Greer of Ivy Lodge, Newry, County Down and was born on 1 May 1841 – being educated at the Royal School, Dungannon. Commissioned into the Royal Artillery in June 1862, he served throughout the New Zealand War of 1863-64 and was present during the attack against the Great Pah. He was appointed to the Royal Horse Artillery in 1873 and was promoted to Captain in 1875. In the autumn of 1880, he was posted to the Cape of Good Hope as ADC to Sir George Strahan, the Acting Governor. Here, he volunteered for service against the insurgent Boers in the Transvaal and commanded the artillery at the Battle of Ingogo on 8 February 1881, where he was killed. Greer – a member of the Masonic Order – is buried at Mount Prospect in the Transvaal. Despite contemporary newspaper accounts claiming he was actively involved in the Zulu War, no evidence can be found to substantiate this.

Captain Carlile Greer, Royal Artillery.

Gribben, Joseph, Private, 36B/165 served in the 1st Battalion, 13th Regiment and was discharged in 1882. His intended place of residence was Ballyhannis, County Mayo.

Gubbins MB ChB, Charles O'Grady, Army Medical Department was born in County Limerick in 1855. He attended Trinity College, Dublin, where after taking first class honours in History and Literature, he entered the medical facility and gained his MB ChB in 1878. Answering the call for reinforcements in 1879 for the Zulu War, he accompanied the Royal Artillery Ammunition Column to South Africa – serving as a civilian surgeon during the campaign. He settled in Newcastle, Natal – and during the Boer War of 1881, he held the office of District Surgeon and was in charge of the base hospital; he performed a similar role in the war of 1900. Gubbins went on to have a successful career in politics and was elected as a senator in the new South African Parliament – joining its first Cabinet as Minister without Portfolio. He was a younger brother of Sir William Launcelot Gubbins, Director General of the Army Medical Staff, and received the honour of a knighthood in 1911; he died the following year.

Gunn MD Mch LM, Christopher attended Queen's University, Belfast, County Antrim. He resided in Talbot Street, Dublin and is buried in Glasnevin Cemetery, Dublin.

Hagan, John served as Private No.1453 in the 1st Battalion, 13th Regiment. He was discharged in 1886 and gave as his intended place of residence: 44 Capel Street, Dublin.

Hamilton, William Stewart, Captain, 90th (Perthshire Volunteers) Light Infantry was present at the Battle of Khambula and Ulundi. He survived the Zulu War and returned to Ireland. He is buried in the Newcastle Church of Ireland Churchyard, County Wicklow.

Hanlon, William served as Private 36B/1883 in the 13th Regiment. He was discharged in 1885 and returned to his home in Belfast, County Antrim.

Captain William Stewart Hamilton, 90th Light Infantry.

Hanna, James, Private, 36B/71 served in the 1st Battalion, 13th Regiment. He was discharged in 1886 and returned to his home in Belfast, County Antrim.

Hardy, Thomas, Private, 36B/195 served in the 1st Battalion, 13th Regiment. He was discharged in 1886 and returned to his home in Belfast, County Antrim.

Hart, Arthur Fitzroy, Captain was from County Clare. He was a 'Special Service officer' on detached service from the 31st (Huntingtonshire) Regiment – having been commissioned in December 1864. He saw action during the Ashanti Expedition, where he was wounded, and received a mention in despatches. He proceeded to South Africa in November 1878 and served throughout the war – firstly as a staff officer of the 2nd Regiment, NNC (taking part with Pearson's

Arthur Fitzroy Hart circa 1899.

column at the Battle of Nyezane, where he was mentioned in the after-action report). He was mentioned in despatches for his actions at Gingindlovu and later served as Brigade Major of the 2nd Brigade, 1st Division – ending his service in South Africa as principal staff officer of Clarke's column, with the rank of Brevet Major. During the Second Boer War as a Major General, he commanded the 5th (Irish) Brigade – performing badly at Colenso on 15 December 1899 (during what became known as 'Black Week').

Hayes, J., Private, No.277, 1st Battalion, 13th Regiment was from Belfast, County Antrim. He was killed in action at Khambula on 29 March 1879.

Head, Bob S., 2/24th: According to a letter in *The Irish Times*, this man was actually John Williams VC of Rorke's Drift fame, who enlisted under the name of 'Bob S. Head'. This has, as yet, to be proved.

Headley, George, Sergeant Major, No.368, 13th Regiment is buried in the Military Cemetery, Crinkill, Birr, County Cork.

Henderson, Hugh, Private, 36B/1924 served in the 1st Battalion, 13th Regiment. He was discharged in 1882 and returned to his home at 42 Agnes Street, Belfast, County Antrim.

Hendley, James Francis, Private, 88th Regiment (Connaught Rangers) was born in Boyle, County Roscommon and died in South Africa. This service cannot be confirmed.

Henry, John F., Private, 36B/146 served in the 1st Battalion, 13th Regiment. He had been born in Belfast, County Antrim circa 1852 and enlisted at Belfast on 6 July 1874. He was the author of a letter that was published in the *Belfast News Letter* of 19 May 1879. He was discharged in 1886 and returned to his home in Belfast.

Hickson MB, Richard Charles Coleman, Surgeon Major, Army Medical Department was born in Cashel, County Tipperary on 13 August 1841 and served in South Africa from 11 January 1875 until 7 December 1879. He took part in the campaigns on the Eastern Frontier 1877-78 and Zululand 1879. He served as senior medical officer in Cape Town and the Ciskie District in 1877-78 and held a similar position in Utrecht and Newcastle for the duration of the Zulu War. Hickson was awarded the Indian General Service Medal with clasp for Hazara 1868, the South Africa Medal 1877-78, the Egyptian Medal 1882 and the Khedive's Star. He died on 13 August 1887 while at sea.

Higgins, James, Private, 36B/99 served in the 1st Battalion, 13th Regiment. He was discharged in 1886 and returned to his home in Drumkeeran, County Leitrim.

Hillas, Robert William Goodwin, Lieutenant was from Dublin and served in the 1st Battalion, 13th Light Infantry. He was present at the Battle of Ulundi and retired as a Major. In 1896, he was appointed as High Sheriff of Sligo. He died on 5 February 1937 at Donneycoy House, Templeboy, County Sligo.

Hughes, John, Private, No.1732 served in the 1st Battalion, 13th Regiment. He was discharged in 1881 and returned to his home in Glasslough, County Monaghan.

Hulton, Samuel, Private, 36B/136 was born in Comber, County Down. He served in the 1st Battalion, 13th Regiment and was discharged in 1886. He returned home to Comber.

Lieutenant Robert William Goodwin Hillas, 1st Battalion, 13th Light Infantry.

Hunt, John Henry, Surgeon Major, Army Medical Department was born in Askeaton, County Limerick on 16 January 1834 and served in the Zulu War from 2 April 1879 until 25 January 1880. He served as a sanitary officer and was present at Ulundi. He was awarded the South Africa Medal 1879 and died at Aldershot, England on 23 February 1887.

Hunter, Charles, Private, 36B/227 served in the 1st Battalion, 13th Regiment. He was discharged in 1887 and returned to his home in Belfast, County Antrim.

Hutchinson, Samuel, Corporal, 36B/145 was born in County Monaghan. He served in the 1st Battalion, 13th Regiment and was discharged in 1886. His intended place of residence was Belfast, County Antrim.

Hutchinson, Samuel, Private, 36B/209 served in the 1st Battalion, 13th Regiment. He was discharged in 1886 and returned to Belfast, County Antrim.

Hutton, Howard, Captain, Frontier Light Horse was born on 18 July 1832 and was the youngest son of Thomas Hutton JP DL, who lived at Eden Park, Dublin – a family that could trace its roots back to the time of Cromwell. Educated in Switzerland, Hutton was proficient in French and German and had a working knowledge of both carpentry and saddlery. When he was 19, he emigrated to New Zealand – arriving in

1852 – and here, he took up farming, as well as acquiring a working knowledge of Maori. During the time known as 'the fire in the fern', Hutton served in the Otahuhu Cavalry under Colonel Nixon of the Colonial Defence Force, and was elected Lieutenant. Upon the death of Colonel Nixon, he was promoted to the command of a troop and served till the end of the war in 1866. In 1878, Hutton arrived in South Africa and offered his services to Colonel Redvers Buller – then commanding the Frontier Light Horse – and was appointed as Paymaster and Adjutant. Upon the outbreak of the Zulu War, the Frontier Light Horse marched to the border at Khambula, where they joined the column under Sir Evelyn Wood VC; he was present with Buller at the finding of the Prince Imperial's body.

Captain and Paymaster Howard Hutton, Frontier Light Horse.

Hutton was at Hlobane, where, after storming the mountain, Buller's men were caught on its summit by the sudden appearance of a Zulu *impi*, and they lost heavily – having to retreat down an almost precipitous path. The next day, the Battle of Khambula was fought, when the Zulu *impi* – 20,000 strong – made repeated and desperate assaults on the camp from early morning until 4.00pm. Captain Hutton was one of the mounted men who were sent out to draw the enemy onto the British guns and, as a consequence, was mentioned in despatches; he also accompanied his regiment on the advance to Ulundi.

Captain Hutton returned to England in September 1879. Already possessing the New Zealand Medal, he also received the South Africa Medal with clasp. He was married with two children and died on 1 January 1891.

Ingham, William James, Surgeon Major, Army Medical Department was born in Belturbet, County Cavan on 24 May 1827 and served in South Africa from 20 August 1877 to 9 July 1879. He was the Senior Surgeon in command of the field hospital in Pietermaritzburg, base of operations Natal, Lower Tugela and the lines of communication Greystown. He was awarded the Indian Mutiny Medal 1856-59 and the South Africa Medal without clasp. Ingham was invalided home circa June 1879 and died on 23 May 1884.

Jackson, Sir Robert William, Surgeon Major, Army Medical Department was born on 11 August 1827 at Bank House, Edenderry, King's County and served in Zululand from 25 August 1879 until 24 May 1880. He served in the campaign against Sekhukhune in December of 1879 and during his military career was awarded the CB, the Crimean War Medal 1854-56, the Indian Mutiny Medal 1856-59, the Ashantee Medal 1873-74, the South Africa Medal 1879, the Egyptian Medal with clasp for Tel-el-Kebir, the Order of Medijie (Turkey) 3rd Class and the Khedive's Star. He died on 12 May 1911 in Sandymount, Dublin. There is a memorial to him in St Patrick's Cathedral, Dublin.

Jagoe MB, Henry, Surgeon, Army Medical Department was born in County Cork on 8 November 1844. He served aboard the hospital ship *City of Paris* from 31 March 1879 until 26 October the same year. He died on 5 October 1932 and is buried in Kensal Green Cemetery, London – having been awarded the Afghanistan Medal 1878-80 and the South Africa Medal 1879.

Jennings, Charles Barremeo came from Ireland and served in South Africa with the Army Medical Department from 3 February 1878 to 3 March 1882 – being awarded the South Africa Medal 1878. He died on 30 May 1926 and is buried in Deans Grange Cemetery, Dun Laoghaire, Dublin.

Jennings MD, Ulick Albert, Surgeon Major, Army Medical Department was born in Dublin on 27 January 1842 and served in South Africa from 28 July 1879 until 31 May 1881. He retired as a Lieutenant Colonel and lived at Ironpool, Kilconly, County Galway. He died in Dublin on 23 December 1920 and is buried in Deans Grange Cemetery, Dun Laoghaire, Dublin – having been awarded the South Africa Medal 1879.

Johnson, Joshua William, Private, No.1814 served in the 1st Battalion, 13th Regiment. He was discharged in 1882 and returned to his home in Dublin.

Keane, James, Private, No.1061 served in the 1st Battalion, 13th Regiment. He was discharged in 1883 and returned to his home in Tralee, County Kerry.

Kearns, John, Private, 36B/201 served in the 13th Regiment and was discharged in 1886. He gave his intended place of residence as Belfast, County Antrim.

Kelly, Edward, Private, No.1602 served in the 13th Regiment. His discharge date is unknown, but his intended place of residence was given as Monkstown, County Cork.

Kelly, John, Private, 36B/420 served in the 13th Regiment and was discharged in 1886. His intended place of residence was Belfast, County Antrim.

Kelly, John, Private, No.2400 served in 'A' Company, 2nd Battalion, 24th Regiment and was born in Drung, County Cavan. He worked as a labourer prior to enlisting in January 1873 and was killed at Isandlwana.

Kennedy, Thomas, Private, No.1707, 'A' Company, 2nd Battalion, 24th Regiment attested at Clonmel, County Tipperary on 27 February 1865, aged 19 years. He was killed at Isandlwana.

Kerr, John, Private, 36B/82 served in the 1st Battalion, 13th Regiment and was discharged in 1886. He gave his intended place of residence as Belfast, County Antrim.

Lamb, Henry, Surgeon Major, Army Medical Department was born in Youghal, County Cork on 16 January 1838 and served in South Africa from 31 March until 8 September 1879. He was stationed at Pietermaritzburg and was awarded the New Zealand Campaign Medal 1863-65 and the South Africa Medal without clasp. He died on 2 August 1902.

Lane, Thomas, Sergeant was born in County Cork in May 1836 and had been awarded the Victoria Cross for his actions at the Taku Forts, China on 21 August 1860 – being gazetted on 13 August 1861 while serving with the 67th (South Hampshire) Regiment. He possibly served in the Zulu War as a member of the 3rd Regiment, Natal Native Contingent and may have survived Isandlwana. He did serve in Captain J.W. Cooke's No.2 Troop, Natal Horse, which was formed in February 1879 from the former NCOs of the 3rd Regiment; this troop was present at Gingindlovu on 2 April 1879. Lane received the Zulu War Medal with clasp for 1879; however, this was later returned.

During the Boer War, he served with Landry's Light Horse and deserted on active service on 7 April 1881. Captured, he received four months in prison with hard labour. His Victoria Cross was forfeited and his VC pension cancelled on 30 September 1881. He

Sergeant Thomas Lane VC, No.2 Troop, Natal Horse.

died in Kimberley, South Africa on 13 April 1889 and his Victoria Cross is today held by the Royal Hampshire Regiment Museum.

Leake, George Dalton Nugent, Surgeon, Army Medical Department was born in Camberwell – the son of Dr Jonas Leake of County Clare – and served in the latter stages of the campaign; he later became a Surgeon-Colonel. His son, Lieutenant Eric Larkin Wheedon Leake, 1st Lancashire Fusiliers, was killed at Gallipoli on 4 June 1915, aged 19 years.

Lee, James, Private, 36B/1938 served in the 1st Battalion, 13th Regiment and died in service at Londonderry on 3 May 1885.

Leslie, Armand, Doctor was born in 1845 – a son of the late Dr David Leslie of Leslie Hill, County Armagh and Wandsworth, London. In 1868, he held the post of medical officer on the staff of the Poti and Tiflis Railway Company in the Caucasus – a position he held for almost four years, and during which he gained much experience in local diseases and other ailments. In 1876, he was sent to Serbia by the British National Aid Society for the Sick and Wounded, but after a short stay with the Serbian Army, he proceeded (via Widdin) to Nisch to take charge of the Turkish ambulances. At the end of the First Turkish-Serbian War, he returned to England for a short time – only to return to Europe upon the outbreak of war between Russia and Turkey. For his services during this arduous campaign he was awarded the Orders of the Osmanié and Medjidié.

In 1879 – after the Battle of Isandlwana – Leslie was sent out by the British

Surgeon George Dalton Nugent Leake, Army Medical Department – photographed in 1873.

Dr Armand Leslie.

Government to Zululand and was present at the Battle of Ulundi. He was awarded the Zulu War Medal and was only back in England a short time when he was dispatched to assist the Egyptian authorities during a cholera epidemic. On the eve of his return to England, he was offered the post of Chief of the Medical Department by Baker Pasha. He then accompanied the column to Souakim and met his death in the fatal conflict at El Teb on 2 February 1885.

A contemporary report states: 'When last seen, Dr. Leslie, Morice Bey and Captain Forestier Walker, with drawn swords and pistols, were standing in a group surrounded by the enemy, close to the guns, encouraging the troops, but scarcely one escaped'.

Linden, Henry Cooke, Civilian Surgeon, Army Medical Department (attached) came from Corn Market, Belfast, County Antrim, where his parents owned a confectioner's shop. He served in the Eshowe relief column and in Durban. Stationed in Pietermaritzburg circa May 1879, he was awarded the South Africa Medal 1879.

Linnane, John, Private, 1/24th, 25B/531 attested at Ennis on 7 December 1874, aged 20 years and three months. He was killed at Isandlwana.

Lion the dog was owned by Lieutenant James Patrick Daly of the 1st Battalion, 24th (Warwickshire) Regiment. Lieutenant Daly was apparently killed in one of the last desperate rallies at Isandlwana to the east of the camp. Despite receiving several spear cuts, Lion survived the battle and was adopted as the regimental dog of the 1st Battalion, 24th Regiment. He died in October 1884 and is buried in Kilkenny Barracks, Kilkenny. His gravestone bears the inscription: 'Here lies 'Lion' the Regimental dog 1s Btn. 24th Regiment who died Oct. 1884. This faithful creature followed the fortunes of the Battalion through the Kaffir and Zulu wars of 1877-78-79 and was severely wounded at the battle of Isandlwana'.

Lion the dog.

Little, Robert, Private, 36B/246 served in the 1st Battalion, 13th Regiment and was discharged in 1886 – giving his intended place of residence as County Londonderry.

Lloyd, Henry Craven Jesse, Lieutenant served in the 47th (Lancashire) Regiment and as a Trooper in the Natal Mounted Police. He was the only son of Lieutenant Colonel Jesse Lloyd of Ballyleck, County Monaghan. Lieutenant Lloyd was killed on 22 January 1879 at Isandlwana; he was 23 years old. A monument to his life and service was erected in St Patrick's Church, Monaghan Town, County Monaghan. He is also mentioned on the Natal Mounted Police Memorial on the battlefield.

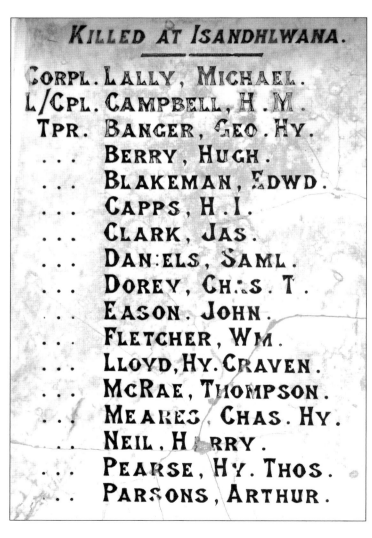

The Natal Mounted Police Memorial at Isandlwana, including Trooper Henry Craven Lloyd.

Lloyd VC KCB, General Sir Owen Edward Pennefather was born at Bridestown House, County Roscommon on 1 January 1854 and was commissioned into the Army Medical Service on 4 August 1878. He served in South Africa from 13 July 1879 until 21 January 1882 – and during this time, he was involved in the latter part of the Zulu War and the subsequent campaign against the Pedi of Sekhukhune in November 1879 (under Wolseley). During the Boer War 1880-81, he served during the siege of Standerton, along with members of the 94th Regiment.

During service in Burma, he was awarded the Victoria Cross for his actions on 6 January 1893. He died in St Leonards-on-Sea on 5 July 1941 and is buried in Kensal Green Cemetery, London.

Surgeon Owen Edward Pennefather Lloyd VC KCB – photographed after 1893 when he was awarded the Victoria Cross.

Lloyd, Thomas, Private, 36B/148 served in the 1st Battalion, 13th Regiment. He was discharged in 1886 and gave his intended place of residence as Belfast, County Antrim.

Lonsdale, James Faunce, Captain was a cousin of Rupert de la Trobe Lonsdale. In the Zulu War, James served as a Captain in No.9 Company, 1/3rd Natal Native Contingent. He was 21 years and 11 months old when he died on 22 January at Isandlwana – one of the first to be engaged, as he was on picquet duty at the time. His father was Mayor of King William's Town in the Eastern Cape, and had previously served with the 27th Regiment.

Macartney MD, James, Surgeon, Army Medical Department was born in Dublin on 28 January 1842 and served in South Africa from 24 October 1877 until 10 January 1879. He was present at

Captain James Faunce Lonsdale, 1st Battalion, 3rd Regiment, Natal Native Contingent.

the engagement near Draaibosch in 1877 and was mentioned in despatches on 26 February 1878 'for zealously attending the wounded under fire'; his later promotion was withheld due to 'Unsatisfactory conduct'. He died on 27 January 1930 – having been awarded the South Africa Medal 1877-78.

McCalmont, Hugh was born on 9 February 1845 and served as a Brevet Major on detached service from the 7th (Queen's Own) Hussars. He was a protégé of Sir Garnet Wolseley – having served under him on the Red River Expedition against the Metis in Canada in 1870. Here, he was employed to convey despatches from Fort Garry to Her Majesty's Government. Serving in the Ashanti War, he was awarded the 1873 Medal – and during the Russo-Turkish War of 1877-79, he served as the military attaché at the headquarters of the Turkish Army in Armenia. He served in the latter stages of the Zulu War as an aide-de-camp to Sir Garnet Wolseley (and subsequently against Sekhukhune's Pedi), and was mentioned in Wolseley's after-action report of 1 December 1879.

Brevet Major Hugh McCalmont, 7th (Queen's Own) Hussars.

McCalmont went on to serve in the Marri Expedition of 1880 on the North West Frontier of India, as well as receiving a mention in despatches for his role in the 'Midnight Charge' at the Battle of Kassassin in Egypt on 28 August 1882. In 1884-85, he served in the attempt to relieve General Gordon at Khartoum – and during the latter stages of the campaign, he commanded the Light Camel Regiment.

McCalmont was a Member of Parliament for North Antrim from 1895 until 1899, but resigned from the House of Commons by way of the Crown Steward and Bailiff of the Manor of Northstead. He then assumed command of the Cork Military District – and in 1902, took command of the 8th Division, Third Army Corps.

With the onset of the Home Rule crisis in Ulster, McCalmont became involved in the formation of the Ulster Volunteer Force (UVF) – and, after allowing his home to be used for UVF drilling, his home (Abbeylands, in Whiteabbey, County Antrim) was burned by suffragettes in protest. He died as Major General Sir Hugh McCalmont KCB CVO DL on 2 May 1924; there is a memorial plaque in St Patrick's Cathedral, Dublin.

McRoberts, R., Private, No.503, 2nd Battalion, 21st (Royal Scots) Fusiliers was from County Down. He was awarded the medal for the 1879 campaign and later served against Sekhukhune and in the First Anglo-Boer War. He died while on active service.

Mally, Robert Nelson, Surgeon Major, Army Medical Department was born in Ballina, County Mayo on 20 June 1844 and served in South Africa from 15 May 1879 until 14 May 1880. During the Zulu War, he was medical officer to the 3rd and 60th Regiments and was present at the Black Mfolozi; he was awarded the South Africa Medal 1879. He died on 7 July 1895 in County Sligo, Ireland.

Manley, John, Private, No.1731 served in 'A' Company, 2/24th. He was born in Cork in January 1850. He enlisted at Cork on 17 April 1865, aged 15 years. He was a patient in the hospital at Rorke's Drift at the time of the action; place and date of death are unknown.

Markham, Patrick, Corporal, No.524, 1st Battalion, 24th Regiment was killed at Isandlwana.

Martin MB, Joseph Walter O'Malley, Surgeon, Army Medical Department was born in Ireland on 3 June 1846 and served in South Africa from 28 July 1879 until 6 July 1882. He died in Dublin on 16 September 1895 – having been awarded the South Africa Medal 1879, the Egyptian Medal 1885 and the Khedive's Star.

Montgomery, S., Private, No.163, 1st Battalion, 13th Regiment came from Belfast, County Antrim. He was killed in action at Khambula on 29 March 1879.

Montgomery, William Edward, Lieutenant, Scots Guards was born in Grey Abbey, County Down on 18 July 1847. He was educated at Eton and purchased a commission into the Scots Guards on 27 June 1866. He served in the Zulu War as Deputy Assistant Adjutant General, 2nd Division under Sir E. Newdigate and was mentioned in despatches. He was Lieutenant

William Edward Montgomery, Scots Guards – photographed as a general officer, post-1895.

Colonel of the 1st Battalion between 1885-94 – becoming Major General in 1895. He retired in 1900 and died on 11 June 1927.

Montagu, George Victor Drogo, Viscount Mandeville (later the 8th Duke of Manchester) was born in London on 17 June 1855. He was educated at Eton and served as a Lieutenant in the Huntington Militia, as well as being a Member of Parliament for Huntingdonshire from 1877 to 1880. Montagu was Worshipful Master of Union Lodge No.105 – and in 1879, he served in South Africa as an ADC to Sir Garnet Wolseley. In a report carried in the *Belfast News Letter* it is told: '... on one occasion Captain Montague [sic] was assegaied by a Zulu running amok and shot him'. He was appointed as a Captain in the Armagh Militia, which was later to become the 3rd Battalion, Royal Irish Fusiliers – a post he held for two years. He died at Tandragee Castle on 18 August 1892, aged 39 years.[2]

Moore, Maurice George – a Lieutenant in the 88th Regiment – was one of the Moore family from Moore Hall in County Mayo. He was the brother of the famous writer and went on to command the 1st Battalion of the regiment. He was a founder member of the Irish Volunteers and a senator in the Dáil; his only son was killed in the Great War. Lieutenant Moore is buried in Kiltoon Graveyard, which is located in a wood behind Moore Hall.

Morris, Edward was the son of Robert Morris of Rosbercon House, County Kilkenny. He was born in 1833 and married firstly Elizabeth Dorcas in 1858 (she died in 1875) and secondly Helen Converse. He served in the Crimea during 1854-55 and in the Zulu War from April 1879 – being appointed DCG of the lines of communication and base. He subsequently served as Commissary-General to the northern columns with Lord Chelmsford, and was present during the march to Ulundi (and operations there). Afterwards, he proceeded to Pretoria in charge of the department in the Transvaal. Upon the departure of Sir Edward Strickland to England, he assumed charge in the South African Command. He was awarded a CB in 1879 and went on to serve in Egypt in 1882, where he was twice mentioned in despatches – being awarded the KCB that same year and the 2nd Class Order of the Medjidie. He was Commissary-General from 1881-86 and later JP in the City and County of Dublin.[3]

Murphy OBE DL, James Fraser, Major, Royal Artillery was educated at Dr Stackpool's School, Kingstown and Foyle College, Londonderry. He served in the

---

2   Despite various internet website and newspaper reports, we can find no actual evidence of this officer's presence in the Zulu War of 1879, either in the *London Gazette*, or on the Medal Roll.

3   At the time of writing, the authors had checked various website and newspaper sources, but could not find any reference to Edward Morris' death.

Cape Frontier War, the Sekhukhune War and the Zulu War – receiving the relevant medals and clasps. The son of the late Mr Edmund Murphy – Chief Receiver of the Court of Chancery – he retired from the army in 1891, but was appointed as Area Commander and Area Organiser of the Sligo District (1914-18). Murphy was awarded the OBE in 1919 and died 1 November 1924. Despite the claims, there is no evidence to substantiate he served in Southern Africa.

Murray, James, Private 65B/2253, 94th Regiment was later awarded the Victoria Cross while serving as a Lance Corporal in the 2nd Battalion, Connaught Rangers at Elandsfontein, Pretoria on 16 January 1881. He died on 18 July 1942 and is buried in Glasnevin Cemetery, Dublin.

Mussen, R., Private, No.2843, 24th (2nd Warwickshire) Regiment died in Belfast and was given a full military funeral – complete with gun carriage. He was awarded the South Africa Medal without clasp.

Private James Murray VC, 94th Regiment.

Norris, Alexander, Private, 36B/160 served in the 1st Battalion, 13th Regiment. His intended place of residence after his discharge in 1886 was Belfast, County Antrim.

Nugent, James, Private, 36B/1813 served in the 1st Battalion, 13th Regiment. He died in Belfast, County Antrim while in service with the Royal Irish Fusiliers on 28 September 1885.

Nugent, Nicholas, Private, 36B/229 served in the 1st Battalion, 13th Regiment. He was discharged in 1879 and returned to his home in Belfast, County Antrim.

Nuthall, Henry Metcalf, Lieutenant, 58th (Rutlandshire) Regiment left the regular forces and joined the militia in 1880. He died on 20 January 1935 and is buried in Mount Prospect Cemetery, Dublin.

O'Brien, Bartholomew, Corporal, 36B/1894 served in the 1st Battalion, 13th Regiment. He died while in service at Enniskillen on 3 May 1885.

O'Callaghan, George Henry Kenneth McDonald, Civilian Surgeon, Army Medical Department was born in Cork on 3 July 1852. He served in the campaign against the Zulu in 1879 and was later attached to Newdigate's division – and later still, to Wood's field hospital. He joined the AMD on 6 March 1880 and was awarded the South Africa Medal 1879 and the Indian General Service Medal with clasp for Burma 1885-87. He retired from the army on 16 April 1890, but continued to serve while on the retired list. He died in Birkenhead, Cheshire, aged 60 and was buried on 14 December 1911 in Flaybrick Cemetery, Birkenhead.

O'Connell, Maurice, Lieutenant, 60th Rifles was the eldest son of Sir Maurice James O'Connell, Bart of Lake View, Killarney, County Kerry. He entered the army from the Kerry Militia on 22 January 1879 and served with the 3rd Battalion of the Rifles throughout the Zulu War – obtaining both medal and clasp. In December 1879, Lieutenant O'Connell was in Durban – under orders to embark for England in charge of invalids – when intelligence reached the station of the outbreak of hostilities in the Transvaal. He applied for, and was granted, permission to proceed to the front – and was present at Laing's Nek on 28

Lieutenant Maurice O'Connell, 3rd Battalion, 60th Rifles.

January 1880. The high popularity which this officer had gained in the militia corps of his native county followed him into the Rifles, where he speedily won the esteem of both officers and men by his warm-hearted and generous disposition. He was killed in action on 8 February 1881 at the Battle of Ingogo (also known as the 'Battle of Schuinshoogte'). Previously, Lieutenant O'Connell had been mentioned in 'Hansard' for his efforts in burying the bones of the dead at Isandlwana.

O'Connor, Eugene, Private, No.1509 served in the 1st Battalion, 13th Regiment. He was discharged in 1887 and returned to his home at 48 Charlemont Street, Dublin.

O'Flanagan, Thomas, Private, No.787 served in the 1st Battalion, 13th Regiment. He was discharged in 1879 and returned to his home in Dublin.

Ogilvy, Robert Alexander of Ardnargle and Pellipar House, Dungiven, County Londonderry was born in 1850. He married Helen Sarah – daughter of The Rev George Bomford Wheeler, Rector of Ballysax, County Kildare – in 1875. He served as a Lieutenant in the 4th (King's Own) Regiment on the lines of communication

– initially at Helpmekaar and then at Luneberg – and is buried in the churchyard at Dungiven.

O'Hare, Daniel served with the 13th Regiment and was discharged in 1886. He returned to his home in County Limerick.

O'Neill, John, Private, 36B/135 served in the 1st Battalion, 13th Regiment and was discharged in 1886. His intended place of residence was Belfast, County Antrim.

O'Reilly MB, James, Surgeon, Army Hospital Department was the senior medical officer with Wood's column. He was born in County Longford on 18 February 1845 and qualified as a doctor in Dublin in 1866. He served in South Africa from 4 November 1877 until 6 May 1879 – being present at Khambula and Ulundi. He received a mention in despatches for Khambula and the operation against Sekhukhune. He died on 5 January 1928 – having been awarded the South Africa Medal 1877-78-79.

Parry, Robert, Private, No.471, 1st Battalion, 24th Regiment attested at Cork on 6 November 1874, aged 21 years. He was killed at Isandlwana.

Peacock, James, Private, 36B/224 served in the 1st Battalion, 13th Regiment. He was discharged in 1886 and returned to his home in Ballymena, County Antrim.

Persse, Dudley Thomas, Brevet Major, 1st Battalion, 13th Regiment was from Mayode, County Galway and the fifth son of Burton Persse Esq. He served in the Zulu War with the 13th Regiment and was later wounded in action during the fighting in Burma. He retired as a Lieutenant Colonel and was killed while out with the Galway Hounds on 6 November 1894, aged 55. The Persse family had come to Ireland from Northumberland in 1602 and had contributed several generations to the British Army.

Phillips, Charles, Veterinary Surgeon, Veterinary Department was on attachment to the Royal Artillery. He died in Ireland on 14 June 1895.

Pyne, William, Private, No.1866 was born in Clonmel, County Cork and served in the 1st Battalion, 13th Regiment. He was discharged in 1883 – returning home to Clonmel.

Quail, James, Corporal, 36B/184 served in the 1st Battalion 13th Regiment. He was discharged in 1898 – returning to his home in Peters Hill, Belfast, County Antrim.

Quinn, Hugh, Private, 36B/55 served in the 1st Battalion, 13th Regiment. He was discharged in 1886 and returned to Belfast, County Antrim.

Quirk, James, Private, No.513, 1st Battalion, 24th Regiment attested at Clonmel, County Cork on 7 December 1874. He was killed at Isandlwana on 22 January 1879.

Raye LK QCPI, John Joseph Ardavon was the Late Surgeon on HMB *Transport*, No.14 during the Zulu campaign and a Surgeon in the East India Government Rifles. The author of the *Ambulance Handbook for Volunteers and Others* (circa 1884), he is not listed on the Medal Roll for South Africa – and it is possible his claim to have served in the campaign was restricted to service aboard a troopship. He graduated from the Royal College of Surgeons in Ireland (RCSI) circa 1870 as 'J.J.A. Ray' – changing his name in 1894. No reason for this has been found, but one would suspect an inheritance might have been involved. The medical registers list a different address for him for each year – information that was supplied by the doctors themselves. Some time after 1879, the initials 'VC' appeared after his name; these letters have no medical meaning. As well as claiming to service in Egypt, his last recorded position was with the West African Field Force in Nigeria – and by this time, he had dropped the letters 'VC'.

Reavey, Hugh, Private, 36B/207 served in the 1st Battalion, 13th Regiment and was discharged in 1886. He returned to his home in Belfast, County Antrim.

Redpath, Samuel, Private, No.1145, 1st Battalion, 13th Regiment came from Tandragee, County Armagh and was mortally wounded at Khambula on 29 March 1879.

Reed, John, Private, No.1469 was born in County Cork and served in the 13th Regiment. He was discharged in 1882 and his intended place of residence was given as Cork.

Reeves, Edward Hoare, Captain and Acting Adjutant, Lonsdale's Horse (Lonsdale's Mounted Rifles) was from Castle Kevin, County Cork. He was born on 6 December 1840 and had been commissioned as a Lieutenant in the 1st (King's) Dragoon Guards. He married Katherine – the eldest daughter of William Wrixon Leycester Esq of Ennismore, County Cork. Lonsdale died on 19 September 1888, aged 47.

Reilly, James, Private, 57th (West Middlesex) Regiment died in Belfast, County Antrim on 17 October 1922. There were two other men of this name serving in the 57th: **Reilly, D., 50B/1795** and **Reilly, P., 50B/284**.

Reilly, Patrick, Private, 36B/184 served in the 1st Battalion, 13th Regiment. He was discharged in 1882 and returned to his home in Ballyalton, County Down.

Ring MD, James, Surgeon, Army Medical Department was born in Templemore, County Tipperary on 5 March 1850 and served in South Africa from 13 July 1879 until 28 February 1882. He died on 16 October 1898 at Rawalpindi, India – having been awarded the South Africa Medal without clasp and the Indian General Service Medal with clasp for the North West Frontier 1897-98.

Ritchie, Brian, Lance Sergeant, 36B/158 served in the 1st Battalion, 13th Regiment and was discharged in 1886. He returned to his home in Belfast, County Antrim.

Roche, Ulick de Rupe Burke, Lieutenant The Hon, 1st/24th (2nd Warwickshire) Regiment was born on 16 February 1856 at Trabalgan, County Cork. He was the fourth son of the Baron Fermoy and had served in the North Cork Militia prior to being appointed as a Lieutenant in the 1/24th on 6 September 1876. Roche was on detached service during the Zulu War on the Natal/Pondoland border and later saw service in the Burma campaign of 1885-89 and the Second South African War – during which he was mentioned in despatches. He retired from the South Wales Borderers – holding the rank of Lieutenant Colonel – on 29 November 1903 and died in 1919.

Robinson, Thomas, Private, 'B' Company, 2/24th, No.1286 was born at St Patrick's, Dublin circa 1853 and enlisted on 23 February 1877. He died in Bristol, Gloucestershire circa 1883.

Rogers, Robert Montresor, Major (Brevet Lieutenant Colonel) was born in Dublin and served with the 44th (East Essex) Regiment in China – being awarded the Victoria Cross for his actions at the Taku Forts in August 1860. In the Zulu War, he served with the 90th Light Infantry and was later awarded a CB. He died at Maidenhead, Berkshire on 5 February 1895.

Rourke, John, Private, No.1674 served in the 1st Battalion, 13th Regiment and was discharged in 1884. He returned to his home at 11 Irwin Street, Dublin.

Russell, Edward, Private, No.922 served in the 1st Battalion, 13th Regiment and was discharged in 1880. He returned to his home at 2 Clare Street, Limerick.

Ryan, Thomas, Private, No.1998 served in the 13th Regiment and was discharged in 1880. He gave his intended place of residence as Waterford, Ireland.

Salter, Frederick George, Private, 36B/256 served in the 1st Battalion, 13th Regiment and was discharged in 1885. His address was given as 2 Royal Avenue Belfast, Ireland, which, at that time, was the Provincial Bank of Ireland Ltd.

Scully, Michael, Private No.1551 served in the 1st Battalion, 13th Regiment and was discharged in 1889. He returned to his home in Goldenbridge, Inchicore, Dublin.

Sharp, Thomas, Sergeant Major, 'S' Company, 1/1st Natal Native Contingent survived Isandlwana.[4]

Shea, Daniel, Private, 25B/497, 1st Battalion, 24th Regiment attested at Tralee on 27 November 1874, aged 18 years. He was killed at Isandlwana on 22 January 1879.

Shea, Michael, Private, No.1950 served in the 1st Battalion, 13th Regiment and was discharged in 1884. His intended place of residence was given as Enniskillen, County Fermanagh.

Shelvin, Robert served in the 13th Regiment and was discharged in 1886.

Shervington, Charles Robert St Leger, Captain, 2nd Battalion, 3rd Regiment, Natal Native Contingent was one of three brothers to serve in the Zulu War of 1879. Upon the outbreak of the Cape Frontier War, Charles sailed from Britain in company with his younger brother, Tom, to search for 'adventure'. Both served throughout the war, with Charles joining up with 'Pulleine's Rangers'. With the onset of the Zulu War, they were attached to the Natal Native Contingent and served with Pearson's column. Charles was present throughout the siege – and his audacity on patrol brought him to the attention of Pearson on more than one occasion. After the relief of Eshowe, Charles went on to serve with the First Division – and it was at about this time that a third brother, William, joined them to serve in the closing stages of the war. Tom died of disease in February 1880, aged 21, and Charles went on to serve with the Cape Mounted Rifles during the Basuto War. Later still, he travelled to Madagascar, where he became a Colonel of Malagasy troops and led them against the French. His later career was not a success and he returned home in poor health – dying in April 1898.

Captain Charles Robert St Leger Shervington, 2nd Battalion, 3rd Regiment, Natal Native Contingent – photographed in later life.

4   Account: *The Irish Times*, 5 May 1879.

Shelvin, Robert, Private, 36B/216 served in the 1st Battalion, 13th Regiment and was discharged in 1886.

Stafford, Patrick Walter, Surgeon Major, Army Medical Department was born in Wexford on 10 April 1838 and served in South Africa from 1 May 1879 until 29 December 1881. He received a mention in despatches and was present at Ulundi, where he commanded the stretcher-bearers. He was awarded the Ashantee Medal 1873-74 with clasp for Coomassie and the South Africa Medal 1879. He died on 14 April 1925.

The signature of Surgeon Major Patrick Walter Stafford, Army Medical Department, from a document dating from 1879.

Stevens, Robert, Private, 36B/180 served in the 13th Regiment during the Zulu War and died in service at Dublin on 8 March 1883.

Stewart, John, Private, 36B/ 310 served in the 13th Regiment and was discharged in 1882. He returned to his home in Ballymena, County Antrim.

Stoker MD, George was the youngest brother of Dublin-born Bram Stoker – the author of *Dracula*. He was sent to South Africa by the Stafford House South African Aid Society in the role of Assistant Commissioner. He died on the Isle of Wight on 23 March 1920.

Stokes MB Mch, Alexander Haldane, Surgeon, Army Medical Department was born in Ireland on 9 October 1843 and served in South Africa from 5 July 1879 until 18 February 1880. He was awarded the South Africa Medal 1879 and the Indian General Service Medal with clasp for Hazara 1891. He died on 6 July 1929.

Dr George Stoker, Stafford House South African Aid Society.

Stokes MB, Henry Haldane, Surgeon, Army Medical Department was born in Ireland on 11 September 1846 and served in South Africa from 28 July 1879 until 11 January 1880. He is believed to be the brother of Surgeon Alexander Haldane Stokes MB Mch and was awarded the South Africa Medal 1879 without clasp, the Egyptian Medal with clasp for Suakin 1885 and the Khedive's Star. He died on 13 November 1930.

Sullivan, Alexander Martin: While not a soldier, A.M. Sullivan's impact on the Zulu War was considerable. His speech to the House of Commons in the vote on the war subsidy of £1.5 million on 27 February 1879 remains a powerful piece of rhetoric. Sullivan had been born in Bantry, County Cork in 1830 and was later editor and owner of the *Dublin Nation*. In 1874, he was elected as Member of Parliament for Louth, but did not take his seat. He was re-elected in April 1880 and again (in a by-election) the following May – serving until he resigned due to ill health in February 1882. He died on 17 October 1884 and is buried in Glasnevin Cemetery, Dublin.

Swain, Thomas, Private, 36B/290 served in the 1st Battalion, 13th Regiment and was wounded at Ulundi. He died in Belfast, County Antrim on 4 September 1941.

Tarrant MD, Thomas, Surgeon Major, Army Medical Department was born in Queenstown, County Dublin on 13 November 1830 and served in South Africa from 10 May until 13 November 1879. He was the senior medical officer with Pearson's column circa March 1879 – receiving a mention in despatches. He also held the same position with Wood's column from July to September 1879, as well as being present at Gingindlovu and the relief of Eshowe. Tarrant was PMO of the 1st Division for the second invasion of Zululand and he died at Queenstown on 3 February 1909 – having been awarded the CB (Military), the Crimea War Medal 1854-56, the Indian Mutiny Medal 1856-59 and the South Africa Medal 1878-79. He is buried in Cobh Old Church Cemetery, County Cork; the grave is now unmarked.

Thirkill, John, Lieutenant, 88th (Connaught Rangers) Regiment was the son of The Rev Thomas Thirkill and had been born in Ireland. He died of disease at Herwen on 22 April 1879, aged 28, although some sources quote the age of 27. His headstone carries the following: 'Brave, generous and devoted, he was universally and deservedly popular'. There is a memorial in Ross on Wye Parish Church, Herefordshire.

Todd, William, Private, 36B/107 served in the 1st Battalion, 13th Regiment and was discharged on 1880. He returned to his home in Carrickfergus, County Antrim.

Torry, Gervase Kirton, Lieutenant, 2nd Tower Hamlets Militia volunteered and served with the 80th Regiment. He served throughout the Zulu War and was present at Ulundi – receiving the Zulu War Medal with clasp. On 9 June 1880, he was appointed as a Captain in the 3rd Battalion, Royal Dublin City Militia – The Queen's

Own Royal Regiment. In November 1882, he joined the Reserve of Officers – at which time he was serving in the 4th Battalion, Royal Dublin Fusiliers. In January 1884, he was adjudged to be bankrupt – and at that time, he gave his address as 2 Little Stanhope Street, Mayfair.

Tottenham, Arthur Ely Heathcote, Lieutenant, 91st (Princess Louise's Argyllshire Highlanders) Regiment was present at the Battle of Gingindlovu and died on 9 June 1908. He is buried in Mount Prospect Cemetery, Dublin.

Lieutenant Arthur Ely Heathcote Tottenham, 91st Highlanders.

Townsend MD, Sir Edmund, Surgeon Major, Army Medical Department was born in Cork on 22 April 1845. He served in South Africa from 13 March 1879 (aboard *City of Paris*) to 14 May 1880, as well as in Zululand and against Sekhukhune – receiving a mention in despatches. He served as medical officer with the northern column and, subsequently, Wood's column. Townsend arrived in Ladysmith on 16 April 1879 and was medical officer to 2nd Battalion, 21st Regiment. During his military career, he was awarded the KCB, CMG, Abyssinia 1867-68; the South Africa Medal 1879, the Egyptian Medal with clasp for Tel-el-Kebir, the Indian General Service with clasp for Burma 1885-86, 1897-98; the Ashantee Medal 1895, the South Africa Medal 1899-1902 and the Khedive's Star. He died on 3 January 1917 at Clontymon, County Cork.

Tredennick, James Richard Knox, Major, 57th (West Middlesex) Regiment died on 8 November 1928. He is buried in Mount Jerome Cemetery, Dublin. His family seat was Wood Hill, Ardara in the Barony of Banagh, County Donegal. The Tredennick family – of Cornish extraction from St Brock (near Bodmin) – lost their estates through their adherence to the cause of Charles I. They were established in Ireland during the reign of William III.

Tumilty, Henry, Private 36B/228 served in the 1st Battalion, 13th Regiment and was discharged in 1886; name sometimes rendered as 'Tumelty'.

Twiss MD, George Edward, Civilian Surgeon, Army Medical Department was born at Dublin Castle on 5 November 1856. He served in the operations against Mbelini waMswati and later served with the 1st (King's) Dragoon Guards and the Transvaal Field Force. Twiss joined the AMD on 5 February 1881 – and during his military career, he was awarded the Commander Order of St Michael & St George, the South Africa Medal 1879, the Egyptian Medal 1882-85, the South Africa 1899-1902, 1914-20 War Medal and the Khedive's Star. He died in Southampton, Hampshire on 27 June 1921.

Ussher, Beverley William Reid, Lieutenant was born in Dublin on 4 April 1854 and commissioned as a Lieutenant on 25 November 1871 in the 1st Regiment of the Duke of Lancaster's Own Militia. He resigned his militia commission on 25 October 1875 and enlisted in the ranks of the 18th Hussars, in which he rose to the rank of Sergeant. On 12 June 1878, he was commissioned for a second time – on this occasion becoming a Second Lieutenant in the 80th Regiment. He served with them throughout their operations – initially with Rowlands' and, subsequently, with Wood's column. He was present at the Battle of Ulundi and was awarded the South Africa Medal 1878-79 with clasp. He was promoted to Lieutenant on 12 January 1881 and served in the South Staffordshire Regiment during the Nile campaign of 1884-85 – being present at the Battle of Kirbekan. At the conclusion of that campaign, he was promoted to Captain and exchanged to the 20th Hussars on 23 December 1885. He exchanged once again (this time to the 7th Dragoons) on 16 March 1887 – going on half pay in 1894 and retiring from the army in 1899.

In November 1914, he returned to the General List as a Captain and on 13 January 1915 was promoted to Major in the 17th Battalion of the Durham Light Infantry. He died while in service on 5 February 1917 in Chelsea, London and is buried in South Ealing Cemetery; his grave is marked by a Commonwealth War Graves headstone.

Ussher MB, James Henry, Surgeon, Army Medical Department was born in Ireland on 1 November 1884 and served in South Africa from 19 July 1879 until 22 December 1880. He was awarded the Ashantee Medal 1873-74 and the South Africa Medal without clasp. He died on 16 January 1902 at Dunfanaghy, County Donegal.

Vevers, J.W., Bandsman, No.802, 1st Battalion 13th Regiment is buried in the Military Cemetery, Crinkill, Birr, County Cork.

Wall, John, Private, 36B/414 served in the 1st Battalion, 13th Regiment and was discharged in 1885. His intended place of residence was given as Goldenbridge, Inchicore, Dublin.

Wallace, John, Surgeon Major, Army Medical Department was born near Parsonstown on 6 June 1832. He served in South Africa from 2 April 1879 with General Newdigate's staff and aboard *China*, and was present at Conference Hill on 25 May 1879. Wallace was awarded the Afghanistan Medal 1878-80, the South Africa Medal without clasp, the Egyptian Medal 1884 and the Khedive's Star. He died on 22 December 1892 in Italy.

Ward, Espine, Surgeon Major, Army Medical Department was born in Ireland on 10 June 1843. He served in South Africa from 11 April 1879 as medical officer aboard *Clyde* and then *Tamar* until 29 September. He then served as medical officer with 10 Battery, 7th Brigade, Royal Artillery and was awarded the Ashantee Medal 1873-74 and the South Africa Medal without clasp. He died on 23 August 1881.

Ward, Espine Charles Robert, Surgeon, Army Medical Department was born in Ennis, County Cork on 20 December 1848. He first served in South Africa from 28 July 1879 until 28 November 1882 and then in the First Boer War 1880-81 – being present and wounded at Bronkers Spruit. He died at Castle Connell on 28 November 1909 and is believed to be buried in the family plot at Castle Connell Anglican Church, where there is also a memorial window. During his military career, he was awarded the South Africa Medal without clasp; his son died during the siege of Kut el Amara.

Ward, Patrick, Private, 36B/281 served in the 1st Battalion, 13th Regiment and was discharged in 1886. His intended place of residence was given as 44 Lettuce Hill, Belfast, County Antrim.

Wasson, James served in the 13th Regiment and was discharged in 1886. He returned to his home in Ballymena, County Antrim. His initial is 'W' on the Medal Roll.

Wheeler, George, Private, No.1419 served in the 1st Battalion, 13th Regiment and was discharged in 1887. His home address was given as 5 Ryans Cottages, Goldenbridge, Inchicore, Dublin.

White, David, Private, 36B/1735 served in the 1st Battalion, 13th Regiment and was discharged in 1890. He returned to his home in Enniskillen, County Fermanagh.

White, James Grove, Lieutenant, 57th (West Middlesex) Regiment was present at the Battle of Gingindlovu and is buried in Doneraile Churchyard, County Cork.

Lieutenant James Grove White, 57th (West Middlesex) Regiment.

Willey, Alexander served in the 1st Battalion, 13th Regiment and was discharged in 1880. His home address was given as Dunmurray, County Antrim. He is not listed on the Medal Roll.

Wills, Caleb Shera, Surgeon Major, Army Medical Department was born in Carrick-upon-Shannon on 24 August 1834. He served from 28 December 1879 to 20 February 1880. He was senior medical officer at the base of operations in Durban and on the lines of communication between Durban and the Lower Tugela; he also served as sanitary embarking officer at Durban. Wills was awarded the CB (Military) and the South Africa Medal without clasp. He died on 12 October 1906 and is buried in Lancaster Cemetery, Lancashire, with his coffin being borne by non-commissioned officers from Bowerham Barracks. His wife is buried in Mount Jerome Cemetery, Dublin.

Wilson, John, Corporal, No.433 served in the 1st Battalion, 13th Regiment and was discharged in 1885. His home address was listed as York Street, Belfast.

Wilson, William Frederick, Captain, 90th (Perthshire Volunteers) Light Infantry was present at Khambula and Ulundi – surviving the war. He died on 14 April 1909 and is buried in Deans Grange Cemetery, Dun Laoghaire, Dublin.

Woods MD MCh, Arthur A., Civilian Surgeon, Army Medical Department had attended Queen's University, Belfast, County Antrim circa 1876.[5]

---

5   At the time of writing, the authors had checked various website and newspaper sources, but could not find any reference to Arthur Woods' death.

Bibliography

Ashe, W. & Wyatt-Edgell, E.V., *The Story of the Zulu War* (London, 1880).

Atkinson, C.T., *The South Wales Borderers, 24th Foot 1689-1937* (Cambridge, 1937).

Bancroft, J.W., *Rorke's Drift* (Tunbridge Wells, 1988).

——, *The Zulu War VCs* (Eccles, 1992).

Barthorp, M., *The Zulu War: A Pictorial History* (Poole, 1980).

Baynham Jones, A. and Stevenson, L., *Rorke's Drift by Those Who Were There* (Brighton, 2003).

Bennett, I., *Eyewitness in Zululand* (London, 1989).

Binns, C.T., *The Last Zulu King – The Life and Death of Cetshwayo* (London, 1963).

Butler, W.F., *Sir William Butler, An Autobiography* (London, 1913).

Callwell, C.E. (ed.), *The Memoirs of Major-General Sir Hugh McCalmont K. C. B., C. V. O.* (London, 1924).

Castle, I. and Knight, I., *Fearful Hard Times The Siege and Relief of Eshowe, 1879* (London, 1994).

Chadwick, G.A. and Hobson, E.G. (eds.), *The Zulu War and the Colony of Natal* (Mandini, 1979.)

Child, D. (ed.), *The Zulu War Journal of Colonel Henry Harford, C.B.* (Pietermaritzburg, 1978).

Clammer, D., *The Zulu War*, (London, 1973).

Clarke, S., *Invasion of Zululand 1879* (Houghton, 1979).

——, *Zululand at War 1879 – The Conduct of the Anglo-Zulu War* (Houghton, 1984).

Clements, W.H., *The Glamour and Tragedy of the Zulu War* (London, 1936).

Coghill, P., *Whom the Gods Love* (Halesowen, 1968).

Colenso, F.E. and Durnford, E., *The History of the Zulu War and its Origin* (London, 1880).

Coupland, R., *Zulu Battle Piece* (London, 1948).

D'Arcy, P., *What Happened to a V.C.* (Dundalk, 1973).

Durnford, E. (ed.), *A Soldier's Life and Work in South Africa, 1872 to 1879. A Memoir of the late Colonel A. W. Durnford, Royal Engineers* (London, 1882).

Dutton, R., *Forgotten Heroes – Zulu & Basuto War Including Complete Medal Roll 1877-8-9* (Prenton, 2010).

Edgerton, R.B., *Like Lions They Fought – the Last Zulu War* (London, 1988).

Elliott, W.J., *The Victoria Cross in Zululand and South Africa, How it was Won* (London, 1882).

Emery, F. (ed.), *The Red Soldier: Letters from the Zulu War, 1879* (London, 1977).

French, G., *Lord Chelmsford and the Zulu War* (London, 1939).

Furneaux, R., *The Zulu War: Isandhlwana and Rorke's Drift* (London, 1963).

Glover, M., *Rorke's Drift – A Victorian Epic* (London, 1975).

Gon, P., *The Road to Isandlwana: The Years of an Imperial Battalion* (Johannesburg, 1979).

Grant, J., *British Battles on Land & Sea* (London, 1894 edition).

Harris, R.G., *The Irish Regiments, a Pictorial History 1683-1987* (Tunbridge Wells, 1989).

Hart, H.G., *New Annual Army List... for 1878, 1879 & 1880* (London, 1878, 1879 and 1880).

Holden, W.C., *British Rule in South Africa, Illustrated in the Story of Kama and his Tribe & the War in Zululand* (London, 1879).

Holme, N., *The Noble 24th: Biographical Records of the 24th Regiment in the Zulu War and the South African Campaign 1877-1879* (London, 1999).

Jackson, F.W.D., *Hill of the Sphinx: The Battle of Isandlwana* (London, 2002).

Jones, H., *The Boiling Cauldron: Utrecht District and the Anglo-Zulu War 1879* (Bisley, 2006).

Knight, I. (ed.), *There will be an Awful Row at Home About This* (Shoreham-by-Sea, 1987 revised 2nd edition).

Knight, I., *Brave Men's Blood – The Epic of the Zulu War, 1879* (London, 1990).

——, *Zulu – Isandlwana and Rorke's Drift 22nd-23rd January 1879* (London, 1992).

——, *Nothing Remains but to Fight – The Defence of Rorke's Drift, 1879* (London, 1993).

——, *The National Army Museum Book of the Zulu War* (London, 2003).

——, *Zulu Rising – The Epic Story of iSandlwana* [sic] *and Rorke's Drift* (London, 2010).

Laband, J., *Fight Us in the Open* (Pietermaritzburg, 1985).

——, *The Battle of Ulundi* (Pietermaritzburg, 1988).

——, *Kingdom in Crisis: The Zulu Response to the British Invasion of 1879* (Manchester, 1992).

——, *Rope of Sand* (Jeppestown, 1995).

——, *The A to Z of the Zulu Wars* (Lanham, 2009).

Laband, J. & Matthews, J., *Isandlwana* (Pietermaritzburg, 1992).

Laband, J. & Thompson, P., *Kingdon and Colony at War* (Pietermaritzburg, 1990).

——, *The Illustrated Guide to the Anglo-Zulu War* (Pietermaritzburg, 2000).

Lloyd, A., *The Zulu War* (London, 1973).

Lloyd, W.G., *John Williams, V. C. a Biography* (Pontyclun, 1993).

Lock, R., *Blood on the Painted Mountain: Zulu Victory and Defeat, Hlobane and Kambula* (London, 1995).

——, *Zulu Conquered – The March of the Red Soldiers, 1828-1884* (Barnsley, 2010).

Lock, R. & Quantrill, P., *Zulu Victory: The Epic of Isandlwana and the Cover-up* (London, 2002).

——, *Zulu Vanquished* (London, 2005).

Lucas, T.J., *The Zulus and the British Frontiers* (London, 1879).

Ludlow, W.R., *Zululand and Cetewayo* (London, 1882).

Lugg, H.C., *Historic Natal and Zululand* (Pietermaritzburg, 1949).

Lummis, W.M., *Padre George Smith of Rorke's Drift* (Norwich, 1978).

MacKinnon, J.P. & Shadbolt, S.H., *The South Africa Campaign of 1879* (London, 1880).

McToy, E.D., *A Brief History of the 13th Regiment (P.A.L.I.) in South Africa During the Transvaal and Zulu Difficulties, 1877-8-9* (Devonport, 1880).

Maxwell, L., *The Ashanti Ring – Sir Garnet Wolseley's Campaigns 1870-1882* (London, 1985).

Mitford, B., *Through the Zulu Country* (London, 1883).

Molyneaux, W.C.F., *Campaigning in South Africa and Egypt* (London, 1896).

Montague, W.E., *Campaigning in South Africa, Reminiscences of an Officer in 1879* (London, 1880).

Moodie, D.C.F., *The History of the Battles and Adventures of the British, the Boers and the Zulus in Southern Africa* (Adelaide, 1879).

Morris, D.R., *The Washing of the Spears* (London, 1966).

Norbury, H.F., *The Naval Brigade in South Africa during the Years 1877-78-79* (London, 1880).

Norris-Newman, C.L., *In Zululand with the British throughout the War of 1879* (London, 1880).

Parr, H.H., *A Sketch of the Kafir* [sic] *and Zulu Wars* (London, 1880).

Parry, D.H., *The Death or Glory Boys – The Story of the 17th Lancers* (London, 1899).

Paton, G., Glennie F. and Symons, W.P., *Historical Records of the 24th Regiment* (Devonport, 1892).

Richards, W., *Heroes of our Day or Recent Winners of the Victoria Cross* (London, 1892).

Smith, K., *Local Orders relating to the Anglo-Zulu War of 1879* (Doncaster, 2005).

——, *Selected Documents: A Zulu War Sourcebook* (Doncaster, 2006).

——, *Dead Was Everything – Studies in the Anglo-Zulu War* (Barnsley, 2014).

Smith-Dorrien, H.L., *Memories of Forty-Eight Years' Service* (London, 1925).

Snook, M., *How Can Man Die Better, The Secrets of Isandlwana Revealed* (London, 2005).

——, *Like Wolves on the Fold, The Defence of Rorke's Drift* (London, 2006).

Sole, T., *For God, Queen and Colony* (Honiton, 2011).

Stalker, J., *The Natal Carbineers* (Pietermaritzburg and Durban, 1912).

Stevenson, L., *The Rorke's Drift Doctor James Henry Reynolds, V. C., and the Defence of Rorke's Drift 22nd – 23rd January 1879* (Brighton, 2001).

Vijn, C. (translated and edited by Colenso, J.W.), *Cetshwayo's Dutchman* (London, 1880).

War Office (compiled by Rothwell, J.S.), *Narrative of Field Operations Connected with the Zulu War of 1879* (London, 1881: 1907 reprint).

Whitehouse, H. (ed.), *A Widow-Making War* (Nuneaton, 1995).

Wilmot, A., *History of the Zulu War* (London, 1880).

Wood, (H.) E., *From Midshipman to Field Marshal* (London, 1906).
———, *British Battles on Land and Sea* (London, 1914).
York, E.J., *Rorke's Drift 1879 Anatomy of an Epic Zulu War Siege* (Stroud, 2001).

Suggested websites

www.rorkesdriftvc.com
www.1879zuluwar.com

Index